THE RIGHT WAY TO KNIT

Book 2

Basic Knits

≈≈≈ How to Block And Finish ≈≈≈

by

EVELYN STILES STEWART

Graphics and Art Supervision by Edward G. Tracy

© **Evelyn Stiles Stewart**
Published by

Knit Services, Inc.
281 E. Kelso Rd.
Columbus, Ohio 43202

Printed in the United States of America

1969

TABLE OF CONTENTS

ABBREVIATIONS, SYMBOLS AND DEFINITIONS VI
INTRODUCTION VII
KNITTING VIII
CARDIGAN 1
  Selecting the proper size for a knitted garment 1
    New sizing table for body measurements 1
    Garment must be correct size "around" 2
    Comparing sizes with ready-to-wear garments 2
    Selecting sizes for men's knits 2
    Selecting sizes for babies and children 2
  Amount of yarn needed 3
  Knitting to gauge 3
    Tension 3
    Swatches 3
      Size of swatches 3
      First Check Point — measuring swatch 4
  Reading instructions 4
  Getting ready 5
    Keeping knitting clean 5
  Order of knitting pieces 5
  V-Neck cardigan pattern 5
INSTRUCTIONS FOR KNITTING SIZE 10 V-NECK SWEATER 9
  BACK 9
    Casting on 9
      Is cast-on row counted as first row? 9
      Using Row 1 of pattern as cast-on row 10
      Casting on in pattern 10
    Ribbing 10
      Counting rows of ribbing 10
      Measuring ribbing 10
    Changing needles from one size to another 10
    Second Check Point, measuring 10
      To determine width of piece in inches 11
    Ending with a purl or knit row 11
    Measuring length 11
      To measure flat knitting 11
    Marker 12
    Shaping armholes 12
      Some shapings for sleeve caps 12
      Measuring armhole 13
    Shaping shoulders 13
      Stitch holders 13
      How to bind off to eliminate "jogs" and "steps" when shaping shoulders 13
        Slanted shoulder shaping 14
    Do you have enough yarn to finish garment? 14
  LEFT FRONT OF CARDIGAN 14
    Borders 14
      Slip stitch for turning facing edges 14
      Working two pieces of knitting at one time 14

Instruction for different sizes and all sizes 15
"AT THE SAME TIME" 15
Confusion in reading shoulder shaping instructions for fronts 15
Marking for buttons 16
Reversing shapings 16
  Reversing fronts 16
RIGHT FRONT OF CARDIGAN 16
  Double buttonholes 16
SLEEVES 17
FINISHING 18
  What is finishing? 18
  How do you assemble pieces? 18
  Sewing 19
    What kind of seam? 19
    Some basic equipment for finishing 19
    Where to use basic sewing stitches for seams 19
  Sewing underarm seams 20
    Pinning back to front 20
    Sewing ribbing 20
      Matching ribbing pattern at seams 21
    Back stitch seams 21
      Length of back stitch in knits 21
      How to sew back stitch seam 21
      Tension of sewing yarn 22
      Ending with old yarn 22
      Beginning with new yarn 22
    A "tailoring trick" 22
  Sewing shoulders 23
  Sewing in sleeves 23
    Alternate order for sewing in sleeves 24
  Weaving in ends not in seams 24
    Why short ends? 24
    How many inches to be woven in? 24
  Back of neck border 24
  Grafting 24
    "Kitchener" stitch 25
    Grafting with knitting on needles 25
      Requirements, method and to work 25
      To practice grafting 25
      Basic grafting 25
    Grafting with knitting off needles 26
    Grafting Garter stitch 26
    Grafting ribbings 26
      K 1, P 1 ribbing in Continental method 26
  Sewing facings 27
    Knitted facings on flat pieces 27
      How to make knitted hem facings fit 28
    Hemlines 28
    Sewing hemlines and facings 28
    Knitted facings on circular pieces 28

To weave up a hem 28
Making facings for coats 28
Bias facings 29
  Basic bias strips 29
    Stockinette stitch, shaped to left or right 29
  Bias strip with turning edge 29
    Stockinette stitch, shaped to left or right 29
  Bias strip with straight edges on ends 29
  Bias strip with turning edge and straight edges on ends ... 30
Buttons 30
  Are buttons sewed on before blocking? 30
  Making crocheted buttons 30
    Over plastic rings 30
    Round or ball buttons 30
    Button molds covered with knitted fabric 30
  Sewing on buttons 31
BUTTONHOLES 31
  Horizontal 31
    Bound-off knitted-in basic buttonholes 31
      Single thickness of knitting 31
      Finishing 32
    One-Row buttonhole 32
    Some methods to eliminate loose stitches or "holes" when cast-
      ing on top of buttonholes 33
    Some methods to eliminate loose stitch or "holes" on bind-off
      row 33
    YO buttonholes 34
      One stitch YO buttonhole 34
      Two stitch YO buttonhole 34
  Vertical 34
    On single thickness of knitting 34
  Making buttonholes by hand (not knitted) 35
    "Finger" buttonhole 35
  Cut buttonhole made with back stitch 35
  Machine-made buttonhole 36
    Reinforced with ribbon 36
    Outlined and finished with yarn 36
  Horizontal buttonholes knitted in, bound off and faced with
    ribbon 37
    To finish using ribbon with machine-made buttonholes 37
    To finish with ribbon and hand-worked buttonholes 37
  Double buttonholes 37
    Double facing knitted-in bound-off buttonholes 37
      Finishing 38
    Machine-made buttonholes 39
  Cut buttonholes 39
  Contrast color buttonholes 39
  Knitting bias or bound buttonholes 40
    Finishing 40
ABOUT YARNS 40
  Basic weights of yarns and needle range 40
  Substituting yarns 41
    Yardage method of substituting 41

Substituting multiple strands of yarn 41
Yarn contents 41
  Different content different needles 41
Washing and cleaning of knits 41
BLOCKING 42
  What is blocking? 42
  Should you knit to fit or block to fit? 42
  Who does blocking? 42
  To block pieces by hand 42
    Size of pieces 42
    What do you block on? 42
    Know your yarns before blocking 43
    Preparation for blocking 43
    To do your own blocking 43
    How to block pieces before assembling 43
  How to block knits after assembled 43
RIBBON 44
  Grosgrain 44
    Preparing ribbon 44
    Should garment be blocked before ribbon is applied? 44
    Should edges be crocheted? 44
    Fitting ribbon 44
    Sewing ribbon 45
    As a trim 45
    Use of netting 45
  Handknitting 45
ZIPPERS 46
  Preparation and sewing 46
    In cardigan or jacket sweaters 46
    In dress or sweaters 46
    In skirts 46
COATS 46
  Width (gauge) of coat 47
  Length of coat 47
    To measure for finished length of coat 48
      To determine actual length of pieces to be knitted 48
      To determine the length of armhole plus shoulder shaping
        (set-in sleeves) 48
      To determine how many inches to knit to armhole 48
      To determine the depth of raglan armhole 48
  Knitting and checking gauge on back of coat 48
  Finishing coats 48
LININGS 49
  To line knits 49
    To line coats 49
      Underlining of coats 49
    To line skirts 49
    To line dresses 50
    To line sweaters 50
BORDERS 50
  Making vertical borders 50
    Finishing knitted border and body in one piece 50

Separate borders 51
    Why are borders made separately? 51
    Separate V-neck border for pullover 51
    Sewing separate borders 51
Pick up and knit borders 51
Crochet 51
    On vertical edges 51
        To crochet borders 51
        To crochet front border for buttons 52
        To crochet front border for buttonholes 52
    On horizontal rows 52
        Crocheting around neck 52
        Shaping with crocheting 53
        Decreasing on horizontal rows 53

POCKETS 53
    Kinds of pockets 53
    Basic placement of pockets on cardigan fronts 53
    Sewing knitted pocket lining 53

PICKING UP STITCHES 54
    Pick up and knit method 54
        Where and how many threads to pick up? 54
        Method of picking up stitches with crochet hook 55
    Picking up stitches with knitting needles 55
        In every row on edges 55
    My method of picking up stitches on edges of knitting for borders 55
        Pattern stitches and their multiples 55
        Development and rule for my method 56
            Preparation round 56
            Increase and knitted round 57
            First Pattern stitch round 58
    Miter 58
        Matching pattern stitches on each side of miter 58
        Mitering patterns 58
    Double ribbed border bands for raglan and V-necks (for flat or circular knitting) 58
        Basic double band 58
        Double band with turning edge (hemline) 58
        Double band for V-neck 58
    Round neck pullover 58
    V-neck cardigan border in one piece 59
    Round necked cardigan border, mitered corners 60

COLLARS 60
    Picking up stitches for collars 60
        Sewing 60
    Substituting collar for ribbing 60

ABOUT NEEDLES 60
    Circular needles 60
        Round knitting on circular needles 61
        To eliminate twisting of stitches 61
        Alternate method of beginning circular knits 61
        Tubular ties 62
        Flat knitting with circular needles 62

        Jumper needles 62
        Double-pointed needles 62
            Eliminating lines and loose spaces between double-pointed needles 63

KNITTING ACCESSORIES and MACHINES 63

DECREASES AND INCREASES 64
    Decreases 64
        Every row 64
        In pattern 64
        How to determine first stitch on broken pattern rows 64
    Increases 65
        Broken pattern on circular sleeves 65
        Increasing evenly across row 65

DARTS 65
    How darts are made 65
    Horizontal darts 65
        Gathered underarm darts 66
        Closed underarm darts 66
        Knitted-in open darts 66
    Vertical darts 66
        Increase dart 66
        Double increase dart 66
        Decrease darts 67
            Where to mark for shoulder dart 67
    Machine-stitched darts 67

SKIRTS 67
    Knitted fabric that goes diagonally 67
    Two-piece skirt with all shapings on the side seams 67
        Correct shaping of skirt 67
    Three-piece skirts 67
    Shaping patterns that cannot be decreased in the row 67

CHARTING 68
    Circular skirt 68
        Preparation for skirt 68
        To make chart for skirt 68
        Charting circular skirt Size 10 68
        Charting for hem facings 69
    A sleeve cap 69
    A collar 69

SHORT ROWS 70
    Tightening slip stitch in short rows 70
    Shaping shoulders in short rows 70
        Binding off short rows shoulder shaping 70

CHANGING PATTERNS AND PIECES 70
    To change size 71
        Add or substract stitches in width 71
        Raise or lower needle size 71
            Using different sized needles on the same yarn 71
        Knit to paper pattern 71
            Knitting to sewing patterns 71

Chart your own pattern 72
Changing basic pieces 72
Sleeves too tight 72
Changing armholes and sleeve caps for under and over sizes 72
Cuffs 72
To measure accurately for cuff size 72
Changing shape of sleeve to armhole 72
Changing or altering sleeve caps that are too long 73
To fit and reknit cap of sleeve 73
Adjusting sleeve caps that are too short 73
Changing long sleeves to three-quarter sleeves and vice versa ... 73
Increases spaced by rows 73
How to knit sleeves (not raglan) from top down 74
Set-in sleeves (separate pieces), worked from top down 74
To pick up and knit sleeves from top down 74
To pick up and knit in long sleeves 74
Shaped cap sleeve picked up around armhole and knitted
down in circular knitting 74
Gusset 75
Changing the depth of a V-neck 75
Using back of sweater as guide in making a short V-neck .. 75
Changing from a regular V-neck pattern to a short V-neck .. 76
Raglan shapings 76
Adjusting raglan armholes 76
Too long raglan shaping 76
Too short raglan armholes 76
Edges 76
To make raglan armholes longer 76
To measure raglan pieces already knitted 77
To keep a raglan sweater from "hiking up" in back 77
To make small cap at shoulder on sleeveless shells 77
Casting on at ends of rows 77
If cast-on stitches too tight 77
If cast-on stitches too loose 77
To make opening in back of knit 77
To make shoulders more narrow 77
Length of armholes in shells 78

ALTERATIONS 78
By hand 78
Separating a knitted piece 78
To shorten sweaters, dresses, coats and sleeves 78
Sweaters 78
Ribbing at bottom edge 78
Facing 79
Dresses 79
Skirts 79
Coats 79
Shortening sleeves 80
To graft cuffs on 80
How to make cuffs smaller 80
Knitting on additional length 80
Solving one knitter's problem 80
By machine on hand or ready-to-wear knits 81

Altering garments 81
Making a pullover into a cardigan 81
If garment is too wide under the sleeves and underarms.. 81
If shoulders hang down too long 81
If sleeves are too long 81
If making short sleeves out of long sleeves 81
If sleeves are too long and too wide 81
If entire garment is too large 81
If pullover too tight around neck 81
For garment where neck only fits 81
Machine stitched sweaters 82

COLOR KNITTING 82
Knitting in colors 83
Color applied after piece is worked 83
Bobbin knitting 83
Bobbins 83
Basic rule in changing colors with bobbins 84
Exception when changing colors on diagonal designs 84
Chart 84
Direction of design 84
Working the first two rows of an Argyle color chart 85
Fair Isle knitting 85
Color knitting with stranded yarn 85
Instructions for Fair Isle patterns 86
Repeat sections in a chart 86
Changing colors in Fair Isle 86
Working with yarn in one hand 86
Working with yarns in two hands 86
Changing colors when three or more colors are in a row.. 87
Stranded yarn 87
To what length should a yarn be stranded? 87
When stranding yarn 87
"Catching" stranded yarn when knitting with two
hands 87
How to "catch" stranded yarn on left hand 87
How to "catch" stranded yarn on right hand ... 87
Slip stitch patterns 87
Combination of bobbin and Fair Isle knitting in the same row 88
Christmas stockings 89
Colored stripes 89
Carrying or not carrying yarn along with knitting 89
Intertwining or twisting yarn carried up side seam 90
Sewing and weaving ends of yarn from stripes 90
What color yarn to sew stripes? 90
Changing colors in stripes when ribbing 90
To eliminate mixed purl nubs 90
Weaving ends in ribbing 90

Duplicate stitch (Swiss darning) 90
Embroidering with yarn 91
Knitting with Beads 91
Patterns 92
To All Knitters 100

V

ABBREVIATIONS

KNITTING

beg	beginning	rpt or rep	repeat
cc	contrast color	rnd (s)	round (s)
dec (s)	decrease (s)	skp	slip, knit and pass
dp	double-pointed	sl	slip
in (s)	inch (es)	sl st	slip stitch
inc (s)	increase (s)	st st or ss	Stockinette stitch
incl	inclusive	st (s)	stitch (es)
k	knit	tog	together
mc	main color	wyab	with yarn at back
p	purl	wyif	with yarn in front
pat	pattern	yo or o	yarn over
psso	pass slip stitch over		
p2sso	double decrease as: Slip 2nd and 1st sts knitwise off needle tog., K 1, pass both sl sts over and off K st		

CROCHET

bl	block	sdc	short double crochet (same as half double crochet)
ch	chain		
dbl tr	double triple crochet	sk	skip
dc	double crochet	sl	slip
dec	decrease	sl st	slip stitch
hdc	half double crochet	sp	space
inc	increase	st (s)	stitch (es)
join	join with slip stitch	tr	treble
rnd (s)	round (s)	tr tr	triple treble
sc	single crochet	yo or o	yarn over

SYMBOLS AND DEFINITIONS

*	asterisk or star
* to *	Instructions between *'s are going to be repeated. First, work from * to *. Then continue repeating between *'s as many times as indicated after second *.
**	Double asterisk or stars are used in same manner as single *. These ** to ** are often used to indicated a repeated section within * to *.
† to †	Dagger, used in same manner as *. This is used more often in crocheting.
Blocking	Steaming or pressing knits into shape.
( ) [ ]	Parentheses or brackets are used:

	1. In listing sizes of garments, as: Size 10 (12-14-16)
	2. To indicate sections that are to be repeated a given number of times as: [YO, K 1] 6 times.
"Ending with a knit or purl row"	The row has been worked.
Garment	Any knitted item to be worn.
Gauge	The number of stitches per inch horizontally and the number of rows per inch vertically.
Item	Object being made.
K 1	Knit one stitch.
K 2 tog.	Knit two stitches together.

Knitwise	Work like a knit stitch.
Loop	A stitch on a needle.
Motif	A group of stitches that makes a design or pattern.
Multiple	The number of stitches that are necessary to make a motif or design.
⅋	Marker
Multiple plus a given number of st (s)	The plus number of stitches are necessary to center the motifs or designs or to allow enough stitches to make pattern work.
o	Increase
Piece	Any sized section of knitting, finished or unfinished.
Ply	Strand or thread as knitting worsted is a 4 ply yarn (four threads).
P 1	Purl one stitch.

P 2 tog.	Purl two stitches together
Purlwise	Work like a purl stitch.
Swatch	A test piece or a small knitted sample of the pattern stitch.
Tension	The tightness yarn is held when knitting.
Test Piece	A swatch made with the yarn and needles used in the body section of a garment to learn pattern and check stitch gauge.
Thread	Yarn or materials for knitting.
Turn	Reverse work so needles are in opposite hands, even if this is in the middle of a row.
Work	Continue in established pattern.
Work even	Continue in established pattern without increasing or decreasing.
X or /	Decrease

VI

INTRODUCTION

Several years ago I visited the New York City Public Library looking for literature on the history of knitting. In a small booklet, I was delighted to find the introduction expressing the author's reasons for writing the booklet were the same as mine in writing a basic manual. However, it was a real shock to read at the bottom of the page—"1837"—and to realize that although over 132 years ago knitters were having problems with understanding patterns, instructions, measurements, weights of yarns, etc., we have the same problems yet today.

It is amazing, until the last two years, that more literature was not written to instruct the knitters in explanation of patterns and procedure. It is interesting to see what the different writers feel knitters should know, their viewpoint and approach to knitting.

To help this situation, I finished writing "THE RIGHT WAY TO KNIT — A Manual for Basic Knitting." It has been published and is available at yarn shops, art needle-work departments, book stores, libraries or can be secured directly from Knit Services, Inc.

"BOOK 2" covers knitting of a basic sweater, coat and skirt and the blocking and finishing of knits. If you can knit and finish the items in the Manual and Book 2, you can make beautiful knits from any pattern. The procedure and problems of knitting garments from patterns and anticipating as many of your questions as possible are the basic work of a knitting instructress in a yarn shop and, as an instructress, is what I present here.

For several years I have been quite concerned about the number of people who have stopped knitting for various reasons (mainly because they were unhappy with the "looks" of the finished item) and about the many who continue to knit but do not improve the quality of their work. It is not necessary to make the same mistakes over and over, giving unsatisfactory knits that do not have a "professional look"; are larger, smaller, shorter or longer than pattern should be; do not look like the picture of the pattern; look "home-made" instead of "custom-made"; do not hold their shape; and do not fit the individual.

Because of ambiguous or poorly written instructions, many knitters do not understand what they are to do and many are confused and get intensely irritated with the result they quit knitting and become what I call a "lost knitter". I hope this book will bring some of them back! It is very discouraging for beginners and even for the experienced knitter sometimes to learn the "intent" of some instructions.

BOOK 2 is for knitters who would like to resume knitting successfully, for that great majority of knitters who have no professional instruction available and for those who just love to make beautiful knits.

Since most of the basics in knitting are learned while making a cardigan, our model sweater will be a V-neck cardigan, with knitted-in buttonholes in double facing edges on fronts, set-in sleeves, with ribbing at bottom edges of sweater and cuffs. The pattern is printed in full and then a detailed sentence by sentence explanation follows, exactly as I would instruct a knitter through knitting and finishing a sweater.

After knitting this cardigan, you will find that many of the things you have learned are repeated when making pullovers, sleeveless sweaters, dresses, shells, coats, etc. Additional KNITNOTES that may be helpful are given concerning these different styles of garments.

In teaching the finishing of garments, it is difficult to actually SHOW the knitter how this is done, let alone write and illustrate it. However, I approach the finishing of knits from the viewpoint of the average knitter, not a seamstress, designer or even an expert knitter. If you sew, excellent— you will do fine finishing. If you have never "shortened a skirt" or "sewed on a button", you can still learn to sew together your knits quite satisfactorily. The set-in sleeved cardigan was selected deliberately to teach and prove that sleeves can be sewed in with excellent results and that you do not need to be confined to knitting raglans all the time to eliminate the sewing of seams.

References, information and illustrations of basic knitting techniques and stitches from the Knitting Manual are not repeated in BOOK 2. However, references to the Manual will be indicated as follows: (Manual, page _____).

I wish to thank the knitters and yarn shop owners who replied to my questionnaire. They confirmed my opinion that knitting questions and problems, such as making buttonholes and sewing seams, are basically the same whether in Hawaii, Alaska, Puerto Rico, Canada, Guatemala or any of the mainland states. It has been a real pleasure to make new knitting friends, to learn how many, many knitters were so pleased to have the opportunity of expressing what THEY would like to know about knitting.

The subject of needles, interchangeable charts showing weights of yarn, gauges and yardage, and the technique of basic crocheting are all adequately covered in other publications. Since BOOK 2 is not a pattern book but really an advanced knitting manual, the numerous requests for particular patterns and sizes will be forwarded to yarn designers and editors for their information as to what knitters want in patterns.

It has been difficult in BOOK 2 to make a choice of what and how much to write about a particular subject. If a direct statement was made, I instantly thought of one or more exceptions—so please accept the overuse of words like "usually" and "sometimes", as being necessary. The limitation of space allows a general, basic presentation of procedure, problems and answers.

In BOOK 2 you are shown how to alter patterns to fit the individual where a reasonable and workable adjustment is possible. Fitting problems that require major or extreme changes in patterns need to be designed, which is a complete subject in itself. For those who wish to design knits "from scratch", there are several excellent books now available at book stores and libraries with this information. These publications are of great merit and necessary to knitters who wish to build their own library and widen their knitting knowledge.

As a word of caution to knitters, BOOK 2 contains what I have learned, what I do and how I instruct knitting. If you are getting fine results with your knitting which you have not done exactly in the same manner as I do, I see no reason for you to change your method. I believe in correcting, changing or seeking a new way of doing something when there is a problem that needs correcting or an easier or better way can be developed. Experiment! Select what is useful to you! Think for yourself!

For the new knitter and those who have used the Knitting Manual,

probably all the information will be useful. Instructions, patterns and details are more difficult and complicated in BOOK 2. CAREFUL READING, SOMETIMES SEVERAL TIMES, AND DRAWING A DIAGRAM ALONG WITH KNITTING A SAMPLE MAY BE NECESSARY TO UNDERSTAND THE SMALL DETAILED DIFFERENCES, as in working buttonholes. For the more experienced knitter, I will be very happy if several of these ideas are new and useful. But regardless of how much or how little information you use, get out your yarn and needles. Relax and enjoy making a beautiful knit.

Sincerely

Evelyn Stiles Stewart

KNITTING

When you make a knitted item, you are doing three things: Making, shaping and sizing knitted fabric, all at the same time.

To secure a pattern, instructions or directions for this knitted fabric, there are three approaches:

First, you can work to a specific pattern, usually designed and prepared by the company selling the yarn.

Or second, you can design your own patterns. This is quite a challenge and should be attempted when willing to work "trial and error" method and to reknit pieces when necessary. Usually you will make two models, one to work design and the second to correct it.

Since most knitters do not have the ability, desire or time to spend on designing and since there are thousands of fashionable easy-to-understand patterns of unlimited styles, it is usually a waste of time for most of us to attempt designing.

Or third, you can strike a happy medium and work from a pattern, adjusting it to fit figure requirements.

CARDIGAN

We are going to knit or talk you through knitting a V-neck buttoned cardigan with double facings on the front borders. The complete pattern is written on pages 5 - 9.

Consecutive sections from these instructions will be printed like this type, followed by a sentence by sentence explanation.

For the experienced knitter, much of this explanation may seem too detailed and too simple to need explaining. Please remember there is always a first learning time for everyone and it is always easy to do something after you know how.

Most knitters are constantly looking for ideas to improve their knitting and new knitters need to understand why things are done in a certain manner. I recently had a beginner ask me why you had to weave in ends of yarn. Couldn't you just cut them off? Yes you could. But it just hadn't occurred to me that anyone would want to leave unsightly knots and ends unfastened, unwoven or not worked in.

To do the finest quality of knitting and finishing and to make the work as beautiful as possible, knitters learn with explanation and demonstration. On each succeeding knit, strive for a more perfect garment. There is always the challenge to constantly improve. But what a great feeling and pleasure it is to make a beautiful knit!

Beginners enthusiastically approach knitting with a new, fresh outlook, as a really exciting adventure. Many times in the excitement of learning, trying and creating, they discover new ideas, new patterns and even mistakes that can be incorporated in future designs.

Of course, mistakes are made, not only by beginners through lack of knowledge, but through incorrect advice from others. As an old proverb goes, "Forewarned is forearmed." So I'll try to forearm you so you may by-pass many of the usual trial and error mistakes that knitters make.

SELECTING THE PROPER SIZE FOR A KNITTED GARMENT

IMPORTANT KNITNOTE: The yarn and fabric industry have adopted the "New Sizing" for body measurements which corresponds to the sizes for ready-to-wear garments.

NEW SIZING TABLE FOR BODY MEASUREMENTS (in inches)

MISSES

Size	Bust	Waist	Hip
6	30½	22	32½
8	31½	23	33½
10	32½	24	34½
12	34	25½	36
14	36	27	38
16	38	29	40
18	40	31	42

MEN

Size	Bust	Waist
34	34	30
36	36	32
38	38	34
40	40	36
42	42	38
44	44	40
46	46	42
48	48	44

GIRLS

Size	Bust	Waist	Hip
6	24	22	26
8	27	23½	28
10	28½	24½	30
12	30	25½	32
14	32	26½	34

BOYS

Size	Bust	Waist	Hip
6	24	22	25
8	26	23	27
10	28	24	29
12	30	25½	31
14	32	27	33
16	34	29	35½

WOMEN

Size	Bust	Waist	Hip
38	42	34	44
40	44	36	46
42	46	38	48
44	48	40½	50
46	50	43	52
48	52	45½	54
50	54	48	56

JUNIORS

Size	Bust	Waist	Hip
5	30	21½	32
7	31	22½	33
9	32	23½	34
11	33½	24½	35½
13	35	26	37
15	37	28	39

TEENS

Size	Bust	Waist	Hip
5-6	28	22	31
7-8	29	23	32
9-10	30½	24	33½
11-12	32	25	35
13-14	33½	26	36½
15-16	35	27	38

INFANTS & TODDLERS

Size	Bust	Waist
6 mos.	19	19
1	20	19½
2	21	20½
3	22	20½
4	23	21

There will be some confusion as to pattern sizes unless you are aware of the NEW SIZING figures. The yarn industry is continuing to base their patterns on body measurements plus a basic 2″ for the blocked measurements or plus any number of inches necessary for the design of the garment.

There is actually no difference in the size or proportion of the patterns—just that what was formerly called a Size 12 will now be called a Size 10, a Size 14 a 12, Size 16 a 14, and Size 18 a 16. It is really immaterial what size the pattern is called. It is important ONLY that the garment fit!

ALWAYS CHECK THE BODY OR BLOCKED MEASUREMENTS IN ALL PATTERNS TO BE SURE YOU HAVE SELECTED THE CORRECT SIZE. This will eliminate the problem of whether the pattern is based on the old or new sizing.

Body or blocked measurements will be listed, or should be, at the beginning of a single pattern or on separate instruction page in pattern books.

Misses' body measurements are based on the bust measurement. If you do not wish knits to pull tight across the bust, take your outside measurements. This has nothing to do with bra size! This measurement may surprise you a little. You might have a 36″ bust measurement and wear a size 10 dress but remember your sweater must comfortably cover 36″ plus at least 2″ more for ease in fit. If you are a 36″ bust, you will need a size 14, which will be at least a *finished* 38″.

CARDIGAN SWEATER	SIZES			
	10	12	14	16
BODY MEASUREMENTS	32-½″	34″	36″	38″
BLOCKED MEASUREMENTS (minimum)	34-½″	36″	38″	40″

The above table shows the minimum blocked measurement. For example, with a bust measurement of 32-½″ for a size 10, size would be a finished or blocked measurement of at least 34-½″, sometimes 35″, with some European patterns as large as 37″ and very bulky coats and sweaters 40″ to 41″—all for a size 10. The difference in widths occurs because of additional stitches necessary to design that particular style.

GARMENT MUST BE CORRECT SIZE "AROUND"

Since each knitter's taste in fit and fashion is different, it is well to learn the actual finished measurement of your pattern before beginning.

The best and easiest way to find this width is to take the number of stitches on the back at the underarm just before starting armhole shaping and divide that number by the stitch gauge. Result is inches in width.

EXAMPLE: 100 (sts) divided by 5 (gauge of sts per 1″) = 20″ (width)

On a pullover, where front and back are the same width, you would multiply this width by two and therefore should have a finished bust measurement of 40″. On a cardigan you would have a finished 41″, 42″ or 43″, depending on the width of the fronts, which are frequently wider because of possible extra stitches in the fronts, plus the width of one front border (the other being overlapped.)

The gauge of the stitches per inch is the most important factor for

correct width. Do not worry about the number of rows per inch. Do not worry about the length of the garment for this can be measured by inches and easily be adjusted in the body and sleeve length. If the garment does not fit "around", the length will be of no importance.

An exception to this is when a section is done by rows, as for raglan sleeves, where adjustment may be necessary. See page 76.

COMPARING SIZES WITH READY-TO-WEAR GARMENTS

Many persons purchase very loose fitting ready-to-wear sweaters. For example, a young person who wears a 10 to 12 dress buys a size 40 sweater and yet it may not look too large on her. Under no circumstances would this person, who has a probable bust measurement of 30″ to 34″, make a hand knit size 18 sweater, which would be a finished 42″.

It is sometimes helpful to measure the width under the armholes of one of your own sweaters of similar style to determine width you wish.

FOR SWEATERS: Select same size as blouse. For an easy fitting sweater, select one size larger than your blouse size.

FOR SHELLS: Select same size as blouse.

FOR DRESSES: Pick same size as your regular dress size.

FOR COATS: Select the dress size, or one size smaller, depending on the finished measurements of coat and the style.

SELECTING SIZES FOR MEN'S KNITS

FOR SWEATERS: Use the same size as his sport or suit coat. Men's knit patterns are designed today to be at least 2″ larger than the chest measurement and a Size 38 would be a finished 40″ sweater although the new sizing indicates a Size 38 would be finished 38″.

To measure for size, measuring tape should be straight around chest, under the arms at armpit, across the heaviest part of the back.

FOR VESTS: Fit should be snug, so should be actual chest measurement, as 38″ chest, 38″ finished vest.

SELECTING SIZES FOR BABIES AND CHILDREN

Children's sweaters should be at least one size larger than their shirt or dress size. If a boy's shirt is size 4, make a size 6 sweater; a girl's dress size 8, make a size 10 sweater. Adjustments in length can always be made for taller or shorter children. Often the length of body and sleeves is made longer and cuffs turned back which will usually give an extra year's wear. A raglan sweater, rather than one with set-in sleeves, will also give at least one extra year's wear.

Unless you wish a very small outfit "to bring the baby home in", which looks like doll clothes, make Size 1 for the baby. If there is a difference in patterns from different companies, Size 1 on a basic baby sweater should measure 10″ across the back and 11″ across the back for a Size 2. If baby is of average size or larger and at least four months old, start on Size 2. If making gifts, make Size 1 or 2.

All of these measurements, of course, assume you are knitting to proper gauge for the instructions.

Although this may seem very confusing to the new or not so experienced knitter, many knits that don't fit occur from selecting the wrong size pattern. Checking bust or chest measurements in the pattern before beginning is a must. I always do this.

Now, make your final decision and select the size sweater you are going to make.

AMOUNT OF YARN NEEDED

After selection of proper size, you will find listed at the beginning of the instructions the amount of yarn needed for the different sizes. Following are manners of listing material requirements:

Example 1:	Size	10	12	14	16
Knitting Worsted 4 oz.		5	5	6	6

Example 2: Directions are for Size 10.
Changes for 12-14-16 are in parentheses
Knitting Worsted 4 oz. - 5 (5-6-6)

Purchase enough yarn (Fig. 1) of one dye lot to complete entire garment and one pair each No. 5 and No. 8 needles.

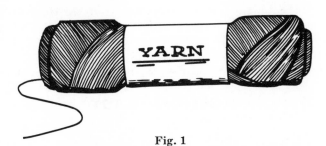

Fig. 1

KNITTING TO GAUGE

Gauge is the number of stitches per inch horizontally and rows per inch vertically knitted on a specific size needle on a specific yarn for a pattern.

The information from the stitch gauge of how many stitches there are per inch, allows the designer to write instructions for knitted pieces with the proper number of stitches to obtain correct size and fit.

Knitting is made very easy for you but IT IS YOUR RESPONSIBILITY TO KNIT TO GAUGE SO THE SWEATER WILL FIT WHEN FINISHED. YOU ARE REQUIRED TO WORK SO MANY STITCHES IN SO MANY INCHES AND THIS CAN BE ONLY BE DONE BY SELECTING THE PROPER SIZE NEEDLES TO GET THE CORRECT

GAUGE FOR YOUR INDIVIDUAL KNITTING. THIS IS ESTABLISHING YOUR GAUGE FOR YOUR MATERIAL.

I would suggest that you keep a record of the gauge you get with specific pattern stitches, yarns and needles for your future reference.

TENSION

Tension is the tightness with which the yarn is held and fed to the needles while knitting. For adjusting tension, see Manual pages 21-22.

SWATCHES (Fig. 2)

What is a swatch or test piece? A swatch is a small sample of your knitting, with the yarn to be used in sweater, in the pattern stitch of the body of the sweater, on the needles used for the body of the sweater, to determine if you knit to gauge pattern calls for to assure proper size after being knitted.

SIZE OF SWATCHES

Make a 3″ swatch with fine, sport and knitting worsted yarns. Make a 4″ swatch with bulky and gigantic yarns. When stitch gauges have ½ stitches like 9 sts = 2″ or 4-½ sts = 1″, it is advisable to make a 4″ swatch so you will have an even number and no half stitches to measure.

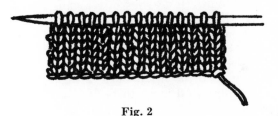

Fig. 2

FIRST CHECK POINT - MEASURING SWATCH

Example of preparing swatch:
"Knitting Worsted yarn
No. 8 needles
Pattern: Stockinette stitch
Gauge: 5 sts = 1″, 6 rows = 1″

Cast on 15 sts for a 3″ swatch. Work in pattern of Stockinette stitch with size needles called for on body of the garment (No. 8) in the pattern of the body of the garment (Stockinette stitch) and work until piece is 3″ square. Then laying the piece flat, measure across the width of the swatch one-half the way up from bottom edge."

If piece measures exactly 3″, you have the correct size needle to make your sweater the size you have selected. Should your swatch measure wider than 3″, select needles one size smaller and continue working until swatch does measure 3″ across. If your swatch is too narrow, select a size larger needle and work until proper gauge is obtained.

The needle size giving the correct gauge is used for the body of your sweater. If pattern calls for No. 8 for body and No. 6 for ribbing, keep the needle size adjustments in proportion. If a smaller needle is needed, use No. 7 and No. 5, or if a larger needle is needed, use No. 9 and No. 7. I have found that it is necessary sometimes to raise or lower needles as much as two sizes. More than this, indicates incorrect tension. Correct your tension.

After making a few knits, you will find whether your natural tension is average or on the loose or the tight side. LOOSE OR TIGHT KNITTING DOES NOT MEAN THE STITCHES ON THE NEEDLE ARE TIGHT OR LOOSE, although this can be a factor, BUT WHETHER YOU ARE KNITTING WITH A TENSION THAT MAKES THE GARMENT COMES OUT TOO LARGE OR TOO SMALL.

It requires a little patience to learn the size needles to make your sweater fit. Each person's knitting is highly individual. Therefore, after a little experience, you will learn how to adjust your needles or correct your knitting tension before or while making a swatch. A great percentage of people knit the same all the time but may still make numerous needle adjustments to get gauge.

If you have any doubts as to the correct gauge, measure frequently. Usually by the time you have knitted half-way up the back, your gauge and tension are pretty much set. However, new knitters may not work evenly until the back and sleeves have been done and usually they are worked too loose, which makes these pieces wider. I have seen some sweaters where the back was 4″ wider than the fronts on a cardigan. Few people rip and knit these again. We finish and block them as nicely as possible and chalk it up to experience.

If this has happened to you, don't let it discourage you. This happens all the time on first sweaters. Learn from your mistakes and do better on the next one. My piano teacher had a great old saying, "A mistake seen is half corrected."

For fancy stitches and lace patterns make a large swatch, like 6″ square, to allow accurate measurement. These swatches are difficult to measure and frequently the gauge to determine size needle is based on Stockinette stitch. I have often wondered, along with many other knitters, why this couldn't be done more often. After correct needle is secured by the designer for fancy or lace patterns, a swatch in Stockinette stitch on that needle would be much easier to check for gauge.

Sometimes, heathers, such as charcoal, made of the same kind and same brand of yarn, seems to be a little thinner. These should be handled exactly as any other color but if in doubt as to gauge, make your swatch.

Since few people work at exactly the same tension, don't let anyone else work on your knitting. The stitches will look different and the size will be changed.

A note of caution: Don't allow yourself to continue knitting when you KNOW you are not knitting to gauge. Don't "con" yourself into thinking that just a little bit of difference in gauge won't matter. You'll be sadly mistaken! If you KNOW your gauge is only 4-1/2 sts to 1″ instead of the needed gauge of 5 sts to 1″, here's what happens to size.

EXAMPLE: Size 16 sweater with Gauge of 5 sts = 1″
Back contains 100 sts which measures 20″ wide.
Size 16 sweater with Gauge of 4-1/2 sts = 1″
Back contains 100 sts which measures 22-1/2″ wide
or 5″ TOO BIG AROUND SWEATER

READING INSTRUCTIONS

In reading cardigan pattern, you will find the basic instructions for all sizes are listed at left side of page and number of stitches in the columns for each size are at the right. This saves space, printing costs and unnecessary reading when several sizes are written at one time. This is an example of a basic or classic sweater pattern.

There are several ways to assure using the correct column of number of stitches: (1) Rewrite the numbers for your size in the blank spaces in the basic instructions (with pencil); (2) rule a line on each side of numbers to be used; or, (3) circle the numbers.

GETTING READY

In learning to knit this cardigan sweater, we will use the Size 10 pattern as a model. If you wish to make a different size, just substitute the correct number of stitches for your size as we work through the instructions.

Gather all materials and equipment in one place. If yarn is not already in pull skeins or balls, prepare it for knitting (Manual, page 7).

Some other equipment which you will need but will not find listed on patterns is:

1 good non-stretch tape measure
1 pair scissors
1 blunt end yarn needle for sewing
1 needle and thread, for sewing buttons if yarn is not used
1 crochet hook to pick up dropped stitches
2 stitch holders

KEEP KNITTING CLEAN

Always keep your yarn on top of a linen or turkish towel, plastic bag or in some kind of protection from contact with your clothes. Most soiling of knitting comes from rubbing against clothing across the stomach.

Hands should be clean each time you knit. I have seen some knitting that was terribly soiled and the knitter just couldn't understand why yarn wouldn't wash out clean and look brand new.

Be sure in washing your hands that no soap remains on the hands, especially those persons who have a tendency to perspire freely. I have seen nylon and wool three-ply yarn marked with oil, soap and soil, which either came from too much soap or the individual's skin. No amount of washing or dry cleaning ever took this out. It was disappointing to this fastidious knitter, after many hours of fine and good knitting, to have a garment she could not wear. It was also very disappointing to lose such a good knitter through no fault of the yarn shop but lack of care and knowledge on the part of the knitter.

ORDER OF KNITTING PIECES

First, we will make the back of the sweater, then two fronts, and then two sleeves.

For beginners, I usually recommend they make the back and two sleeves before the front, so their best and most experienced knitting

will be done on the fronts, which are the most important since they show the most. Also each sleeve, as for a man's sweater, has as much knitting in it as a back and some knitters like to get them out of the way before working the fronts.

Fig. 3

V-NECK CARDIGAN PATTERN (Fig. 3)

The following pattern is the complete and uninterrupted instructions for the model cardigan, written in a manner you will find in knitting pattern books. Following the pattern will be a sentence by sentence detailed explanation of some of the instructions I would give you, if working with you in person.

V-NECK CARDIGAN

SIZES (New)		10	12	14	16
BLOCKED MEASUREMENTS:	Back	17"	18½"	19½"	21"
	Front	11"	11½"	12"	13"
	Buttoned	35½"	38½"	39½"	43½"

MATERIALS: 4-5-5-6 SKEINS KNITTING WORSTED (4 oz.)
1 PAIR EACH NO. 5 AND NO. 8 KNITTING NEEDLES
5 BUTTONS ⅝"
GAUGE: 5 sts = 1", 6 rows = 1"
PATTERN STITCH: Stockinette

	SIZES (new)			
	10	12	14	16
BACK:				
With No. 5 needles, cast on _____ sts	86	92	98	104
Work in pattern of K 1, P 1 ribbing for _____ rows	14	14	18	18
Change to No. 8 needles and work in Stockinette stitch (K 1 row, P 1 row) until piece measures _____ ins.	14"	14"	14½"	15"
from beginning, ending with a P row. Place marker one-fourth across row for armhole measurement.				

	10	12	14	16

SHAPING ARMHOLES:

Bind off ____ sts at beginning of next 2 rows.

	10	12	14	16
Bind off ____ sts at	5	5	6	6

Dec. 1 st each end of needle every other

	10	12	14	16
row ____ times	5	6	6	7
Work even on ____ sts until armhole	66	70	74	78
measures ____ ins. from marker	7½"	7¾"	8"	8¼"

ending with a P row.

SHAPING SHOULDERS:

	10	12	14	16
Bind off ____ sts.	10	10	11	11

at the beginning of the next 2 rows.

	10	12	14	16
Bind off ____ sts at beginning of	10	11	11	12

next 2 rows.

	10	12	14	16
Bind off remaining ____ sts	26	28	30	32

LEFT FRONT:

	10	12	14	16
With No. 5 needles, cast on ____ sts	55	58	61	64

FOR SIZES 10 AND 14 ONLY:

Row 1: *K 1, P 1 repeat between *'s up to last 14 sts, ending with K 1, (border) P 1, K 6, Sl 1, K 6.

Row 2: P 13, K 1 (border), *P 1, K 1, repeat between *'s across row, ending with P 1.

	10	12	14	16
Repeat last 2 rows ____ times MORE, ending	6	6	8	8
with a P row (____ rows)	14	14	18	18

FOR SIZES 12 AND 16 ONLY:

Row 1: *P 1, K 1, repeat between *'s up to last 14 sts, (border) P 1, K 6, Sl 1, K 6.

Row 2: P 13, K 1 (border), *P 1, K 1, repeat between *'s across row.

	10	12	14	16
Repeat last 2 rows ____ times MORE,	6	6	8	8
ending with a P row (____ rows)	14	14	18	18

FOR ALL SIZES:

Change to No. 8 needles and work in pattern as follows:

Row 1: K to last 14 sts, (border) P 1, K 6, Sl 1, K 6.

Row 2: P 13, K 1 (border), P across row.

Keeping border pattern as established, repeat these 2 rows until piece measures

	10	12	14	16
____, ending with a P row	14"	14"	14½"	15"

	10	12	14	16

SHAPE ARMHOLE:

	10	12	14	16
At armhole edge, bind off ____ sts	5	5	6	6
one time and dec. 1 st every other row ____ times	5	6	6	7

and AT THE SAME TIME, work decreases of
neck shaping as follows: Work to last
16 sts, K 2 tog., P 1, K 6, Sl 1, K 6.
Work in established pattern, decreasing at armhole edge until
decreases are finished and AT THE SAME TIME CONTINUING
TO DECREASE AT NECK EDGE, inside border,

	10	12	14	16
every 4th row until ____ decreases have been made	11	11	13	14
Work even until armhole measures ____ ins., ...	7½"	7¾"	8"	8¼"

ending with a P row at armhole.

SHAPE SHOULDERS:

	10	12	14	16
Bind off ____ sts one time	10	11	11	11

Work 1 row.

	10	12	14	16
Bind off ____ sts one time, ending with a K row	10	11	11	12

NECK BORDER:
Row 1 (wrong side): P 14.
Row 2: K 7, Sl 1, K 6.

	10	12	14	16
Repeat these 2 rows for ____ ins.	2½"	2¾"	3"	3"

Put stitches on stitch holder.
Cut yarn leaving 10" end.

MARKING FOR BUTTONS AND BUTTONHOLES:
Mark bottom button even with center of
ribbing and top button at the first
neck decrease, with balance of buttons
evenly spaced between.

RIGHT FRONT:

	10	12	14	16
With No. 5 needles, cast on ____ sts.	55	58	61	64

FOR SIZES 10 AND 14 ONLY:
Row 1: K 6, Sl 1, K 6, P 1 (border),
*K 1, P 1, repeat between *'s across row, ending with K 1.
Row 2: P 1, *K 1, P 1, repeat between *'s
up to last 14 sts, (border) K 1, P 13.
Repeat last 2 rows one time MORE ending

	10	12	14	16
on the right side with ____ rows	4	4	4	4

FOR SIZES 12 AND 16 ONLY:
Row 1: K 6, Sl 1, K 6, P 1 (border),
*K 1, P 1, repeat between *'s across row.
Row 2: *K 1, P 1, repeat between *'s
across to last 14 sts., (border), K 1, P 13.
Repeat last 2 rows one time MORE, ending

	10	12	14	16
on wrong side with ____ rows	4	4	4	4

	10	12	14	16

FOR ALL SIZES:
BUTTONHOLES (DOUBLE)
BIND OFF ROW: K 2 sts, bind off next 2 sts,
K 2, Sl 1, K 2 sts, bind off next 2 sts,
K 2 (two sts have been bound off in
the center of each K 6-section of border),
P 1, work across row.
CAST-ON ROW: Work across row casting on
2 sts over bound-off sts of previous row.
Repeat these two rows for double buttonholes **each time**
you reach row opposite markers on left front.
REPEAT Rows 1 and 2 (ribbing and border)

	10	12	14	16
until _____ rows have been worked	14	14	18	18

ending with a P row at border edge.

RIGHT FRONT CONTINUED:
Change to No. 8 needles and work as follows:
Row 1: K 6, Sl 1, K 6, P 1, K across row.
Row 2: P to last 14 sts, K 1, P 13.
Repeat these 2 rows, making buttonholes
opposite markers on left front, working

	10	12	14	16
until piece measures _____ ins., ending	14″	14″	14½″	15″

with a K row.

SHAPE ARMHOLE:

	10	12	14	16
Bind off _____ sts	5	5	6	6

one time.
Next row: Work decreases of neck shaping as follows:
K 6, Sl 1, K 6, P 1 (border), K 2 tog.,
work across to last 2 sts, K 2 tog. (armhole decrease).
Work in established pattern decreasing every other row

	10	12	14	16
at armhole edge until _____ decreases are finished	5	6	6	7

and AT THE SAME TIME continuing to decrease
at neck edge inside border, every 4th

	10	12	14	16
row until _____ decreases have been made	11	11	13	14
Work even until armhole measures _____ ins.,	7½″	7¾″	8″	8¼″

ending with a K row at armhole.

SHAPE SHOULDER:

	10	12	14	16
Bind off _____ sts	10	11	11	11

Work 1 row.

	10	12	14	16
Bind off _____ sts, ending with a P row	10	11	11	12

NECK BORDER:
Row 1: K 6, Sl 1, K 7.
Row 2: P 14.

	10	12	14	16
Repeat these 2 rows until piece measures _____ ins.	2½″	2¾″	3″	3″

Place stitches on stitch holder, leaving
a 10″ end.

SLEEVES:	10	12	14	16
With No. 5 needles, cast on ____ sts	40	42	44	46
Work in K 1, P 1 ribbing for ____ rows	14	14	14	14
Change to No. 8 needles and working in Stockinette stitch, increase 6 sts evenly across first knit row (Method No. 3, Manual, page 42).				
Increase 1 st each end of needle every ____ ins.	2″	2″	2″	2″
____ times	5	5	5	5
Work even on ____ sts	56	58	60	62
until piece measure ____ ins. or desired length to armhole.	16½″	16¾″	17″	17″
ARMHOLE SHAPING:				
Bind off ____ sts at the beginning of the next 2 rows.	5	5	6	6
Dec. 1 st each end of needle every other row until piece measures ____ ins from the first bound off row.	4½″	4½″	4¾″	5″
Bind off 2 sts at the beginning of the next ____ rows. Bind off remaining sts.	4	4	4	4

FINISHING:

Sew underarm, shoulder and sleeve seams. Set in and sew sleeves. Fit ends of neck border together at back of neck and join with Kitchener Stitch. Sew border to back of neck. Fold front facings and neck border to inside and sew to knit stitch around fronts and across back of neck. Finish buttonholes. Sew on Buttons. Block.

INSTRUCTIONS FOR KNITTING SIZE 10 V-NECK CARDIGAN

BACK (Fig. 4)

CASTING ON

"BACK: With No. 5 needles, cast on 86 sts."

You may use any method of casting on you wish. Various methods are listed in the Manual and although they all have their uses, I prefer Method No. 3 Knitwise or In Pattern (Manual, pages 51-52).

Always leave an end of yarn about 12″ long after casting on. This will give you enough yarn to sew up through ribbing on sides of sweater without having to attach a new piece of yarn and will eliminate extra knots, thicknesses and ends to weave in.

IS CAST-ON ROW COUNTED AS THE FIRST ROW?

In basic patterns, the cast-on loops do not count as a row.

When casting on Knitwise and working an even number of rows of ribbing, outside bottom edge will be a purl edge (rough) and working an

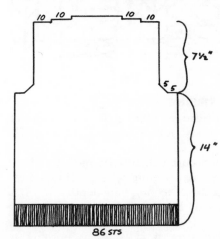

Fig. 4

uneven number of rows of ribbing, outside bottom edge will be a knit edge (smooth). This model sweater is worked with an even number of rows of ribbing, making a purl edge on the outside of all pieces.

Sometimes it is advisable to cast on Purlwise (Manual page 51) to set up a flat edge for patterns to be started immediately after the cast-on row, as for fancy, lace and Stockinette patterns, ribbings and cables with twists beginning on the first or third rows.

USING ROW #1 OF PATTERN AS CAST-ON ROW

There are some instances, as for flat knitting (Stockinette), where the cast-on row is also Row 1 of pattern.

EXAMPLE 1:   Row 1: Cast on knitwise. Row 2: Purl.
EXAMPLE 2:   Row 1: Cast on purlwise. Row 2: Knit.

Both of these examples establish flat knitting. Remember, if you work two rows in succession of either knits or purls, you will have a ridge at the bottom of the piece, which is incorrect and undesirable for flat knitting. You particularly do not want this to occur when knitting hems and facings.

CASTING ON IN PATTERN

Many times after a sweater is finished we notice that the back and one front has the same kind of stitch on the bottom edge and the other front has the opposite stitch, which spoils the looks of the garment.

To eliminate the problem of having to match the bottom outside edges with the same kind of stitch, cast on the stitches of Row 1 In Pattern, omitting the printed instructions for cast-on row.

RIBBING

"Work in pattern of K 1, P 1 ribbing for 14 rows."

For casting on In Pattern for this model cardigan, you would cast on Row 1 of ribbing pattern using 86 sts and work 13 more rows in ribbing.

COUNTING ROWS OF RIBBING

It is easier to count the nub of purls or one side of a knit stitch, rather than the center of a stitch (Fig. 5)

Ordinarily we do not count the stitches on the needle as a row. However, the stitches on the needle (Row 14) have been worked in ribbing and therefore, would count as a row of pattern in the garment.

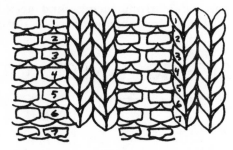

Fig. 5

MEASURING RIBBING

If ribbing is measured by inches instead of rows, it is well to stretch it sideways to the width it will fit the body, for in wearing, ribbing will spread and therefore shorten in length.

As an example, on the top of socks, a cuff will usually measure about ½″ more when knitted than when worn. If you wish a finished 3″ ribbed cuff, it may be necessary to knit 3-¼″ to 3-½″ in depth.

Whether ribbing is worked by rows or by inches, sometimes you are unable to end the section exactly as instructed and also have the correct depth. A row more or less than pattern calls for is nothing to worry about. It is not as important that you have the correct depth as

it is important the ribbing sections have the same number of rows to be sewed together, as a back and front. A row counter is most helpful to do this accurately.

EXCEPTION: Where a knitter has two ribbed edges to be sewed together with the same number of rows and for various reasons or errors they do not measure the same depth in inches, work additional rows on the one piece to make pieces match. This will eliminate undesirable gathering and puckering when seams are sewed.

CHANGING NEEDLES FROM ONE SIZE TO ANOTHER

Some knitters slip the stitches one by one to new size needle only to find needle point at wrong end to work. Use second new needle and slip stitches back across row to end of yarn.

Other knitters think "to change size of needles" you actually pull the stitches off a needle and then pick up these loose stitches again with another size. Do not do this! It is not only dangerous and difficult, but unnecessary.

To change from small needles (used on ribbing), to large needles (used on body of sweater), drop your free No. 5 needle, pick up one of the No. 8 needles and work across the row. Now, drop the second No. 5 needle, and with second No. 8 needle, work next row. Now you have completed changing from small to large needles. Set aside the No. 5 needles until needed again. Follow the same procedure for changing from large to small needles or making any change in size of needles.

"Change to No. 8 needles and work in Stockinette stitch (K 1 row, P 1 row) until piece measures 14″ from beginning, ending with P row."

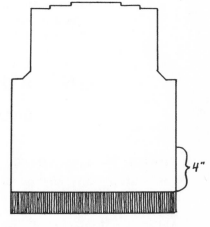

Fig. 6

SECOND CHECK POINT FOR MEASURING (Fig. 6)

When 4″ to 5″ has been knitted in pattern of the body of the sweater above the ribbing, border or hemline, work across to center of row. Smooth knitting flat across both needles in manner material will lay after blocking. Pull out corners of bottom edges until square and pin.

TO DETERMINE WIDTH OF PIECE IN INCHES

The number of stitches on the needle divided by stitch gauge equals the number of inches in width, as: 86 (sts) divided by (5 sts per 1") = 17" (width of back). If garment is 18" or 1" too wide, use one size smaller needle or if 16" or 1" too narrow, change to one size larger. On basic yarns, like sport, knitting worsted and 3-ply yarn, one size needle change will usually make 1" difference in width on the back or front of a sweater. If more than 1" too large or small, correct your tension before continuing (Manual, page 21-22).

If you do change needles one size larger or smaller, start at the beginning of the row and work carefully. You can change needles at this place on the back without marking the yarn or having to start the piece again. A change of more than one size in needles may necessitate unravelling to the top of ribbing to begin again or perhaps the whole piece started again, particularly if ribbing is too wide or too loose.

THIS IS THE PLACE IN KNITTING THAT WILL TELL YOU IF THE SWEATER IS GOING TO BE THE CORRECT SIZE WHEN FINISHED.

The pattern stitch and kind of yarn along with the individual's knitting are all factors in how a yarn will work and to what gauge. Many knitters are fortunate to knit to the basic gauge but will also have to adjust needle size on some pattern stitches and yarns. Hundreds of other knitters have learned or are constantly being taught, like we are learning here, not only how to knit to gauge but to recognize by measuring when you are NOT knitting to gauge.

If you have had the experience of knitting too large or too small sweaters, it is better to learn this a few inches after beginning and correct the situation, than to knit an entire sweater that will not fit.

Also do not be alarmed on your first sweater if your stitches are not exactly the same size on the beginning back piece and balance of sweater. After knitting up about four ounces of knitting worsted, your knitting should be pretty much set and remain the same in evenness, tension and texture for the rest of the cardigan.

ENDING WITH A PURL OR KNIT ROW

WHEN YOU END WITH A PURL ROW, THE PURL ROW HAS BEEN WORKED AND IS A FINISHED PURL ROW.

WHEN YOU END WITH A KNIT ROW, THE KNIT ROW HAS BEEN WORKED AND IS A FINISHED KNIT ROW.

In this instance, you end with a purl row, so when you turn piece and begin to shape armhole, you will be able to begin to bind-off on the knit side, which is the right side of the sweater.

Be neat and consistent in ending and beginning new sections of your knitting. This will make finishing easier, minimize errors and enable you to have the knit pieces match in size.

MEASURING LENGTH

Before beginning shaping of armhole, be sure back measures correctly in length. All measuring is done from bottom of piece unless the pattern says, "measure from the top of ribbing," "measure from first bound-off row at armhole", "measure from the hemline", etc. Measuring pieces with knitted hems or facings is always done from the hemline or turning edge, since they would not be included in the finished length of the piece.

MEASURING IS ONE OF THE MOST IMPORTANT AND SEEMS TO BE ONE OF THE MOST DIFFICULT THINGS FOR KNITTERS TO DO CORRECTLY. Use a good grade, non-stretch tape measure. Some tape measures, like cloth and plastic, have a tendency to slip and stretch and you may get three different measurements three different times. More exact measuring can be done with a good quality tape measure, the fiberglas one on the market today being excellent.

TO MEASURE FLAT KNITTING

Knitted pieces must be flat to be measured. Since many are wider than the length of one knitting needle, they are more easily measured

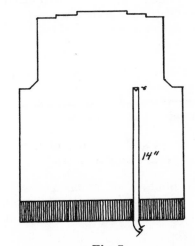

and sometimes only possible to measure correctly, when spread flat across the two needles. To divide stitches on two needles, you may either work across to the center of row or slip half the stitches onto the other needle.

Spread knitting until it lays flat across the two needles as it would be after blocking. Do not stretch. Do not bunch together. Pull out ribbing to make corners square and pin.

Fig. 7

Place tape measure at the 14" mark (or whatever length desired) along the bottom edge of ribbing. Lay the tape measure flat toward the needle and when it is "up to the needle", length is correct. Never include the knitting needles in the measurement. (Fig. 7)

MARKER
Fig. 8

"Place marker one-fourth across row for armhole measurement."

Place a piece of white cotton thread in a stitch about one-fourth across the row as a measuring point for checking armhole depth later. Other markers can be used, but yarns and plastic and metal markers (Fig. 8) often mark the yarn at this particular spot because they are too heavy or thick. Do not use colored thread or yarns since the color dye has been known to rub off. Some knitters like to knit the white mercerized thread along with the yarn until about one-fourth the way across the row.

Knitting thread along with yarn for three or four stitches at regular intervals at the edge of piece is used to keep track of every so many rows or every inch, instead of using safety pins or markers.

SHAPING ARMHOLES

Most armholes are shaped by using both binding off (flat) and decreasing (slanted). Sleeve shapings are usually set-in, full-fashioned, raglan, saddle or ladder, or drop shoulder. Often the decreases are made to show as pattern stitches which trim or decorate, as on full-fashioned raglan sleeves. (Fig. 9G)

On this model cardigan, we are going to use a basic armhole shaping for a set-in sleeve. Now, knitters, don't groan! You need to learn how to do a good job of fitting and sewing sleeves. Also it is so foolish to limit yourself to one kind of sleeve just to get out of sewing seams.

"SHAPING ARMHOLES: Bind off 5 sts at beginning of next 2 rows. Dec. 1 each end of needle every other row 5 times."

This basic armhole will be shaped by binding off 1″ on a straight line and decreasing 1 st every other row on a slant until a certain depth is reached. The top of sleeve cap is shaped in four rows and remaining stitches bound off. (Fig. 9C)

Often the question is asked, "When binding off stitches, is there any particular reason for the instructions stating, bind off as to knit or bind off as to purl?" Yes. We wish to keep seams as flat and thin as possible, particularly under the arm and keeping knits or purls in pattern will help this.

12

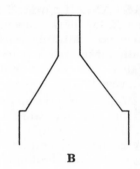

A

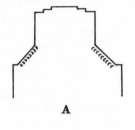

B

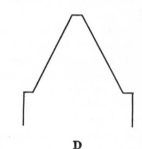

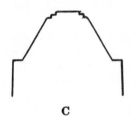

C

D

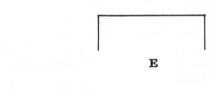

E

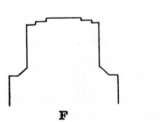

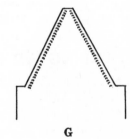

F

G

Fig. 9

"Work even on 66 sts until armhole measures 7-½″ from marker, ending with a P row."

TO WORK EVEN MEANS: WORK IN PATTERN AS ESTABLISHED WITHOUT INCREASING OR DECREASING.

MEASURING ARMHOLE

THIS IS THE MOST IMPORTANT MEASUREMENT IN THE ENTIRE SWEATER. THE KNITTED PIECE MUST HAVE A LONG ENOUGH AND LARGE ENOUGH ARMHOLE TO ALLOW AN EXACT FIT OF THE SLEEVE CAP.

You never measure at edge or the curve (armseye) because edges stretch and roll under.

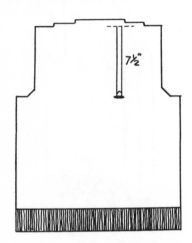

Fig. 10

Place tape measure at the marker you have already placed in the first bound-off row for armhole and measure "up to the needle" (Fig. 10). If the length from the marker is exactly 7-1/2", armhole is correct length. On this back you will finish on the purl side, with an even number of rows, so you may begin shoulder shaping on the knit or right side of garment.

SHAPING SHOULDERS

"SHAPING SHOULDERS: Bind off 10 sts at the beginning of the next 2 rows. Bind off 10 sts at the beginning of the next 2 rows. Bind off remaining 26 sts."

TO WORK: Beginning on the knit row, bind off 10 sts (knitwise) and knit across row. Turn. Bind off 10 sts (purlwise) and purl across row. These last two rows are repeated one time MORE or until 10 sts have been bound off 4 times (two times on each shoulder). Then bind off remaining 26 sts for back of neck.

Why don't the instructions just say to bind off 10 sts four times? Note that the number of stitches to be bound off is different for different sizes. For Size 10 it just happens that both the first and second shapings on the shoulder are the same number of stitches but to cover instructions to be used for all sizes, they must be written in this manner.

WHEN BINDING OFF STITCHES, ALWAYS KEEP THE PATTERN STITCH, AS ON THE KNIT SIDE, BIND OFF KNITWISE AND ON PURL SIDE, BIND OFF PURLWISE.

On some pattern stitches, if you do not bind off in pattern, you will not get the correct results. In binding off Seed stitch, if you bind off

what shows, your last two rows will end up as two rows of ribbing and destroy the continuity of the pattern and if you bind off in knit or purl stitch, it will still interrupt the pattern. If ribbing is not bound off in pattern, a horizontal, tight ridge occurs which is contrary to the wanted result of an elastic in-and-out edge.

STITCH HOLDERS

Fig. 11

Stitch holders (Fig. 11), which look like over-sized safety pins, are blunt-end pins of various sizes used to hold stitches that you wish to put aside, called "out of work", until needed later. When sweaters are to have neck ribbing worked later, like pullovers, the remaining stitches on back of neck are put on a stitch holder.

Sometimes when we are ready to knit the stitches off holders, the open end of the holder is facing the wrong way. Slip the stitches first to a free needle and then knit stitches from needle.

For other pieces which are complete and are to be sewed, bind off the remaining stitches as done for this back.

There are a few times when back neck seam needs to be reinforced. If back of neck stitches have been put on a stitch holder and you are making a sailor collar where front border continues up to shoulders and the stitches across back of neck are picked up and worked as one piece for collar, often the sweater will stretch wide, lose its shape and allow shoulder to drop down.

This can be fixed by (1) fitting and sewing on seam binding or ribbon on wrong side for reinforcement across shoulders and back of neck; or (2) the back of the neck stitches can be bound off instead of put on holder and then necessary stitches picked up for making of sailor collar. This last method is the most satisfactory for lasting results.

HOW TO BIND OFF TO ELIMINATE "JOGS" OR "STEPS" WHEN SHAPING SHOULDERS

You will note with this regular shaping of shoulders (Fig. 10), you have the appearance of jogs or steps. When sewing garment, of course, all this unevenness will have to be put in the seam and sewed deep enough on the shoulder that no holes show. These jogs can be eliminated by using the slanted shoulder shaping or shaping shoulders with short rows.

SLANTED SHOULDER SHAPING (Fig. 12)

To eliminate these excess stitches and thicknesses, some knitters slip the first stitch of each bound-off group. This will help some but will not take all of the jog out of the shaping.

TO ELIMINATE BOTTOM CORNER OF JOG, DECREASE 1 ST AT END OF THE ROW JUST BEFORE TURNING TO BEGIN BIND-OFF ON NEXT ROW.

TO ELIMINATE TOP CORNER OF JOG, SLIP 1 ST AT BEGINNING OF BIND-OFF.

ALL SLIP STITCHES ARE DONE PURLWISE. THE SLIP STITCH IS CONSIDERED AND WORKED OFF AS A REGULAR STITCH IN BINDING OFF.

Fig. 12

Shoulder shaping instructions say to bind off 10 sts at the beginning of the next 4 rows for this Size 10 cardigan.

TO WORK SLANTED SHOULDER SHAPING:

Row 1: Bind off 10 sts knitwise and knit across row. Turn.

Row 2: Bind off 10 sts purlwise and purl across to last 2 sts, P 2 tog. Turn. (This takes off the bottom corner of the jog.)

Row 3: Sl 1 st and bind off 9 sts knitwise. (This takes off the top corner of jog.) (The reason we bind off one less stitch than instructions call for, as binding off 9 sts instead of 10 sts is because we have used one stitch of the shaping BEFORE we turned the row.) K across to last 2 sts, K 2 tog. Turn.

Row 4: Sl 1, bind off 9 sts purlwise, purl across to last 2 sts, P 2 tog. Turn.

Row 5: Sl 1, bind off remaining sts at back of neck.

YOU WILL NOT FIND THIS SHAPING WRITTEN OUT IN PATTERNS AND WILL HAVE TO INCORPORATE IT YOURSELF. To work this shaping, three or more stitches are necessary in one bind-off.

To shape shoulders with short rows, see page 70.

DO YOU HAVE ENOUGH YARN TO FINISH SWEATER?

About this time some knitters begin to doubt if they have purchased enough yarn to finish their sweater.

For a rough estimate of how much yarn is going to be used in a long-sleeved sweater, multiply by four the amount of yarn that has been knitted into the back. One long sleeve has about the same amount of yarn as a back. Even though it may look smaller, the sleeve is more narrow but usually longer than a back.

If you have problems with dye lots, etc., see Manual page 8.

LEFT FRONT OF CARDIGAN (Fig. 13)

BORDERS

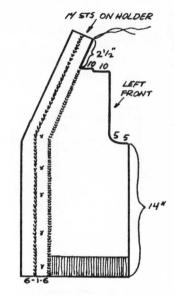

Fig. 13

On this cardigan, we are going to knit along with the sweater, the front border and its facing which when folded in half, turned under and sewed, makes a double thickness on the edge or what is called "a double facing."

Note that one purl stitch is worked between border and the body of the sweater. This not only gives an accent or a defining line between the border and the body of the sweater but on the wrong side, conveniently furnishes a straight line on which to sew edges of facing.

SLIP STITCH FOR TURNING FACING EDGES

Why slip stitch for turning edges? If you will inspect the back of border, you will see the slip stitch is worked only every other row. This makes this section thinner and therefore it will fold thin, flat and straight for a good edge and will block well. Without this slip stitch, edges "puff out" and have just the opposite results.

We will make the left front of cardigan first to allow the marking and even spacing for buttons. Buttonholes will be made opposite these markings on corresponding rows of right front.

For men's and boy's cardigan sweaters, make the right front first, since buttonholes are worked on the left front.

WORKING TWO PIECES OF KNITTING AT ONE TIME (Fig. 14)

If no buttonholes are needed, you can use two separate balls of yarn and knit both fronts at the same time. This can also be done with two sleeves, two mittens, etc. BE SURE THAT PARTS OF BOTH PIECES OF KNITTING ARE ON THE SAME NEEDLE IF YOU PUT WORK DOWN BEFORE FINISHING A ROW ACROSS BOTH PIECES. If they get separated, it would be very difficult to determine which piece to start on.

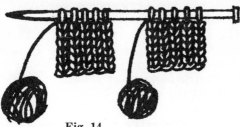

Fig. 14

"LEFT FRONT:
With No. 5 needles, cast on 55 sts.
FOR SIZES 10 AND 14 ONLY:
Row 1: *K 1, P 1, repeat between *'s up to last 14 sts,
ending with K 1, (border) P 1, K 6, Sl 1, K 6.
Row 2: P 13, K 1 (border), *P 1, K 1, repeat between
*'s across row, ending with P 1.
Repeat last 2 rows 6 times MORE, ending with
a P row (14 rows)."

Cast on knitwise or In Pattern so bottom edge will match bottom edge of back. For those casting on In Pattern, use Row 1 of pattern omitting the first sentence for casting on 55 sts.

INSTRUCTIONS FOR DIFFERENT SIZES AND ALL SIZES

You will note that in the number of stitches to be cast on in the four different sizes, there are even and uneven numbers of stitches. Therefore, it is necessary to write instructions for the even number of stitches separately from the uneven number, so the purl stitch and borders result in the proper continuity with the ribbing.

When these sections are finished, the words "FOR ALL SIZES" indicates the return to one set of instructions.

Since ribbing section ends on wrong side, you begin pattern for body of sweater on the right side, as follows:

"FOR ALL SIZES:
Change to No. 8 needles and work in pattern as follows:
Row 1: K to last 14 sts (border), P 1, K 6, Sl 1, K6.
Row 2: P 13, K 1 (border), P across row.
Keeping border pattern as established, repeat these 2 rows
until piece measures 14", ending with a P row."

Body section is worked in this two-row pattern until it measures 14" or same as back, ending on the wrong side at underarm.

"SHAPING ARMHOLE:
At armhole edge, bind off 5 sts, one time and dec. 1 st every
other row 5 times and AT THE SAME TIME, work decreases
of neck shaping as follows:
Work to last 16 sts, K 2 tog., P 1, K 6, Sl 1, K 6."

Work in established pattern, decreasing at armhole edge until decreases are finished and AT THE SAME TIME continuing to decrease at neck edge, inside border, every 4th row until 11 decreases have been made. Work even until armhole measures 7-½", ending with a P row at armhole."

I will write out instructions for each row explaining these directions until the armhole decreases have all been completed and then you will find it easy, without a row by row explanation, to continue neck decreases every 4th row until all have been worked.

Please note when every other row, or in this case the even-numbered rows, are worked the same, instructions are written ONE TIME ONLY as per Row 2.

TO SHAPE NECK AND ARMHOLE OF LEFT FRONT.
Row 1: Bind off 5 sts. Knit across row to last 16 sts, K 2 tog.
(1st neck dec.), P 1, K 6, Sl 1, K 6.
Row 2 and all even numbered rows: P 13, K 1, P across row.
Row 3: K 2 tog. (1st armhole dec.) K across row to last 16 sts, P 1,
K 6, Sl 1, K 6.
Row 5: K 2 tog. (2nd armhole dec.) K across row to last 16 sts, K 2
tog., (2nd neck dec.), P 1, K 6, Sl 1, K 6.
Row 7: K 2 tog. (3rd armhole dec.) K across row to last 16 sts, P 1
K 6, Sl 1, K 6.
Row 9: K 2 tog. (4th armhole dec.), K across row to last 16 sts, K 2
tog. (3rd neck dec.), P 1, K 6, Sl 1, K 6.
Row 11: K 2 tog. (5th armhole dec.), K across row to last 16 sts, P 1,
K 6, Sl 1, K 6.

Since armhole decreases have been finished, continue in established pattern, making neck decreases every 4th row, which in this instance are Rows 13, 17, 21, etc., until all decreases have been made. Work even until armhole measures 7-½", ending with a P row at the armhole edge.

"AT THE SAME TIME"

Always be aware that whenever you see "AT THE SAME TIME", which is always printed in caps or italics, you are going to be working TWO different shapings at the same time, always retaining your pattern stitch.

"SHAPE SHOULDERS: Bind off 10 sts one time. Work 1 row.
Bind off 10 sts one time, ending with a K row."

CONFUSION IN READING SHOULDER SHAPING INSTRUCTIONS FOR FRONTS

Many knitters become very discouraged in reading instructions because so much is unexplained, not specific, or not written for easy understanding. Following are some of the confusing instructions on shaping shoulders for fronts.

"Bind off like back", "Bind off like side of back", "Bind off like left side of back", "Bind off to match corresponding side of back"—on all of these, you do not bind off on BOTH sides of the front as for a back, only at ONE armhole side. You use only the shaping like ONE-HALF of a back, which would be the same as the left shoulder shaping or the right shoulder shaping.

You cannot halve the instructions and use one-half of the sentence, which is where knitters make their mistake, since this would still be binding off on both sides of the piece.

You must select, as you read the instructions, those portions which have to do with the matching shapings for the front. A left front shoulder must match the left back shoulder and a right front shoulder must match a right back shoulder.

It is best to think of how this sweater fits you when worn. An easy way to use the knitted back is to fold it in half vertically. Turned one way, the right shoulder shaping shows. Turned the other way, the left shoulder shaping shows. In this manner you can easily check and determine that shoulder shapings on the front are being started at the correct edge, are bound off from one edge only and have the same kind and number of stitches bound off as the matching shoulder of the back.

After finishing shoulder shapings, you will still have 14 sts on needle. Continue working on border as follows:

"NECK BORDER:
Row 1 (wrong side): P 14.
Row 2: K 7, Sl 1, K 6.
Repeat these 2 rows for 2-½".
Put stitches on stitch holder.
Cut yarn leaving 10" end."

This left front border will meet at middle of back of neck with right front border and be woven together with the Kitchener stitch, folded and border and facing sewed flat across back neck edge.

MARKING FOR BUTTONS

"MARKING FOR BUTTONS: Mark bottom button even with center of ribbing and top button at the first neck decrease, with balance of buttons evenly spaced between."

See Fig. 13 and please refer to page 14 for measuring, spacing and marking of buttons.

One of the handiest tools I have is a buttonhole spacer which folds in and out like a baby's gate. It is made of metal and will measure eight buttonholes to any measurement up to 3-½" apart.

REVERSING SHAPINGS

Reversing shaping is like setting a table with plate, silverware and glassware—one setting for a right-handed person and one setting for a left-handed person.

YOU DON'T CHANGE THE ITEMS, JUST THEIR POSITION.

When reversing shaping, you don't work stitches backward, up-side-down, nor inside out, but just move them to the other piece in the opposite order.

REVERSING FRONTS

Looking at outside of sweater, as in Fig. 3:

RIGHT FRONT	LEFT FRONT
Underarm binds off at beginning of row on purl side. Border instructions are at the beginning of the row.	Underarm binds off at beginning of row on knit side. Border instructions are at the end of the row.

RIGHT FRONT (Fig. 15)

"RIGHT FRONT:
With No. 5 needles, cast on 55 sts.
FOR SIZES 10 AND 14 ONLY:
Row 1: K 6, Sl 1, K 6, P 1 (border), *K 1, P 1, repeat between *'s across row ending with K 1.
Row 2: P 1, *K 1, P 1, repeat between *'s up to last 14 stitches, (border) K 1, P 13.
Repeat last 2 rows one time MORE ending on the right side with 4 rows."

DOUBLE BUTTONHOLES

Double buttonhole means that a buttonhole is made in each K 6-section of the border, so when folded, it can be placed over a button through both pieces of knitting.

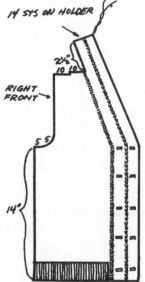

"FOR ALL SIZES: BUTTONHOLES (DOUBLE)
BIND OFF ROW: K 2 sts, bind off next 2 sts, K 2, Sl 1, K 2 sts, bind off next 2 sts, K 2 (Two center sts have been bound off in the center of each K 6-section of border.), P 1, work across row.

Fig. 15

CAST-ON ROW: Work across row casting on 2 sts over bound-off sts of previous row.
Repeat these two rows for double buttonholes each time you reach row opposite markers on left front.
Repeat Rows 1 and 2 (ribbing and border) until 14 rows have been worked, ending with a P row at border edge."

Be sure you have the same number of rows of ribbing on both right and left fronts.

"Change to No. 8 needles and work as follows:
Row 1: K 6, Sl 1, K 6, P 1, K across row.
Row 2: P to last 14 sts, K 1, P 13.
Repeat these 2 rows, making buttonholes opposite markers on left front, working until piece measures 14", ending with a K row.

"SHAPE ARMHOLES:
Bind off 5 sts one time."

Since we must shape armhole as well as bind off at the beginning of the row, these 5 sts will have to be bound off on the purl side at the beginning of the row. This reverses the shaping.

Note that decreases for armhole and neck shaping will begin on the next row and will be worked on the knit or right side of sweater.

"NEXT ROW: Work decreases of neck shaping as follows:
K 6, Sl 1, K 6, P 1 (border), K 2 tog., work across to last 2 sts, K 2 tog. (armhole decrease).
Work in established pattern decreasing every other row at armhole edge until 5 decreases are finished and AT THE SAME TIME continuing to decrease at neck edge inside border, every 4th row until 11 decreases have been made.
Work even until armhole measures 7-½", ending with a KNIT row at armhole.

"SHAPE SHOULDER:
Bind off 10 sts. Work 1 row. Bind off 10 sts, ending with a P row.
NECK BORDER:
Row 1: K 6, Sl 1, K 7.
Row 2: P 14.

Repeat these 2 rows until piece measures 2-½".
Place stitches on stitch holder, leaving a 10" end.

SLEEVES (Fig. 16)

"SLEEVES:
With No. 5 needles, cast on 40 sts.

Work in K 1, P 1 ribbing for 14 rows.

Change to No. 8 needles and working in Stockinette stitch, increase 6 sts evenly across first knit row (Method No. 3-Manual page 42). Increase 1 st each end of needle every 2" 5 times."

The increases for the underarm of sleeve are made using Method No. 3 between the second and third stitches from each end of increase row (Fig. 17). This allows straight edges for sewing seams and the opportunity for much neater finishing. I use this always on Stockinette stitch and in pattern stitches that will allow the increases to be worked without interrupting pattern.

"Work even on 56 sts until piece measures 16-½" or desired length to armhole.

ARMHOLE SHAPING:
Bind off 5 sts at the beginning of the next 2 rows.
Dec. 1 st each end of needle every other row until piece measures 4-½" from the first bound-off row. Bind off 2 sts at the beginning of the next 4 rows. Bind off remaining sts."

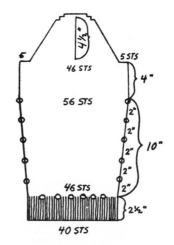

Fig. 16

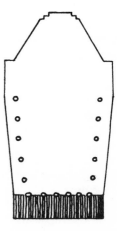

Fig. 17

FINISHING

"Sew underarm, shoulder and sleeve seams.

Set in and sew sleeves.

Fit ends of neck border together at back of neck and join with Kitchener stitch.

Sew border to back of neck.

Fold front facings and neck border to inside and sew to knit stitch around fronts and across back of neck.

Finish buttonholes. Sew on buttons. Block."

WHAT IS FINISHING?

It is the sewing, stitching, weaving, crocheting, or assembling of the pieces; tying and weaving in of ends; knitting of pieces like neckband and borders; crocheting edges, finishing buttonholes, sewing on ribbon and buttons, making hand-made or machine buttonholes; blocking or steaming garment into shape—or anything that needs to be done to put the garment together completely, ready for use or wear.

Finishing, the most important part of making knits, is what makes the knit look good, or as we usually say, "gives it the professional look." Our aim always is for the professional custom-made look, which is a knit created of good design and excellent workmanship, out of appropriate materials.

The inside of a finished knit should look as good as the outside. Of course, it will not be as smooth along the seams but should be good in appearance and very neat. We have had several sweaters that finished so well they could have been worn wrong side out.

Knitting can be uneven, which often happens with beginners, it can have mistakes and can be simply not very good work, but, if finished and blocked correctly the garment will look very nice, be satisfactory and a pleasure to use.

Quite the opposite can happen with the very best of knitting if pieces are put together poorly. Inadequate and poor finishing is the reason many knitters are not satisfied with the "looks" of their knitted garments when ready to wear.

If a knit is finished and blocked properly, a very nice to a very fine looking garment can be accomplished, the quality of the finishing depending on the skill of the finisher. Problems with finishing usually occur because (1) finisher does not know or do basic sewing, (2) does not have the knowledge of how to go about finishing or (3) has not had enough experience nor time to constantly try to improve.

You do not need to be a seamstress or even be able to "sew on a button", but just able to push a needle through the knitted fabric, plus the willingness and determination to work as evenly and neatly as possible. Anyone can do finishing who is willing to learn and to try. This has been proven many, many times with all ages and abilities of people.

Since there are numerous ways of finishing garments, the model cardigan will be used as an example of basic finishing as I do it and teach it. Other methods, their merits and usage will also be shown and discussed because there is a time and place to use all these ideas and you will have this knowledge to use when needed.

On your first knit you can do a very good job of finishing but it is only reasonable to expect you will do much better after knitting and finishing several garments. As in any of the arts or handicrafts, only through work and experience does creating and quality progress.

Fine finishing has been a so-called professional trade secret for many years but since we are a do-it-yourself people now, there is no reason why those who wish to should not learn or be able to improve their finishing.

I have found from my own personal experience that a shop will not suffer loss of business by teaching finishing. In fact, if it has the reputation for excellent work, it is almost impossible to keep up with the work to be done for the many knitters who just don't or won't do finishing and are very happy to pay for these services.

Knitters who do their own finishing prefer to do so because they take great pride in their work or wish to "do it ALL by myself". Others do it to save the cost which allows further purchases of yarn. Finishing is considered a necessary evil and rarely do you find a person who really likes to do it. There's no doubt it's much more fun just to knit.

It is the right and privilege of a shop to reserve finishing services and free instruction to merchandise purchased ONLY from their business. The really responsible shop will always try to supply all the services needed and if not available, direct you to where the needed services might be or are available.

HOW DO YOU ASSEMBLE PIECES?

(1) We can assemble pieces by hand with yarn and needle by sewing and weaving.

On rare occasions, I have used double cotton thread on linens, cottons and ribbon knits. Colorless nylon thread, either the light or dark shade, can be used where many different colored pieces need to be sewed and using yarn of one or different colors does not work. Beware of eye strain from trying to see these nylon stitches—which you can't.

Many garments today are worked in a combination of seamless knitting, like raglans knitted from the top down, with perhaps an underarm seam, a collar or front bands still to be sewed.

Obviously, if garment is knitted entirely without seams, no assembling is necessary but additional finishing is usually needed to complete garment.

(2) We can sew knits by machine with thread. I use this method for alterations only.

(3) We can assemble by crocheting pieces together using a slip stitch.

There are always very strong pro and con opinions from knitters about sewing vs. crocheting pieces together. The only time I crochet pieces together is when a yarn will not sew and a substitute yarn is not satisfactory or available.

I sew pieces together for the best all-round results and have proven my point many times particularly when finishing identical boys' sweaters, one sewed with yarn and one crocheted together with slip stitch. The crocheted sweater lost at least one year's wear because of the lack of natural elasticity of seams caused by the slip stitch, which in itself is a rigid stitch, used mainly for connecting. Even with great care the seams were thicker, partly because you could not get as close to the edge to avoid leaving holes or loose stitches and also because crocheting itself is three to four threads thick and knitting and hand sewing is only two threads thick.

A slip stitch is very easy and quick to do and lays flat but is difficult to get just the right tension to hold pieces together, not show holes and still have some "give" in the seams.

You never do single crochet over the edges of the seams. It is most unsatisfactory. I can think of no instance to use this or where it would be acceptable.

(4) We can knit pieces together.

There are few finishers who do this. Mainly this is used in a manner of shaping and binding off shoulders together as on page 70.

This method also would be easy to do on straight edges but is qualified by the ability of the finsher to pick up stitches well and to ascertain the number of stitches for a correct length seam, not too short or too long.

Shaped edges, such as armholes, should be sewed in.

I think this method difficult and not worth the effort to avoid sewing or crocheting seams.

Remembering that every garment is different and has different problems in assembling, you will with experience, decide which methods are suitable for particular sections of the garment; which seams you will use and where; which seams are best for the wear and tear of the garment, for the support of the garment, and last but not least, for the beauty of the garment.

SEWING
WHAT KIND OF SEAM?

After you learn a few basic sewing stitches and rules, if you don't already know them, you will say, "How do I know which way to sew a seam and where?"

BASICALLY, WE OVERCAST RIBBING AND BACK STITCH THE BALANCE OF THE SEAMS.

This applies to most garments. Otherwise, I use any of the other methods to see what works and looks good. Every once in a while even the best seam does not quite satisfy us. But let's accept it. We are only human, this is a hand-made creation and should have the human touch.

As you finish the cardigan sweater, you will quickly see how easy it is to sew pieces together and to do it correctly so it will "look good".

Many dress and novelty yarns are difficult to sew because of their textures. Often the use of a plastic yarn needle will allow you to sew with a rough or nubby yarn when a metal needle will not work. Otherwise, it may be best to join these pieces with a slip stitch, using the same kind of yarn if possible or a smooth yarn in a matching color and of sufficient weight to make a correct seam.

Finishing finally comes down to the place where it is really a matter of judgment where and what kind of seam to use. I do basic sewing of seams unless there is some reason, as seams would be too thick, flat seams are needed, materials will not sew together well, etc.

SOME BASIC EQUIPMENT FOR FINISHING

1 regular metal blunt end sewing needle (for fine through knitting worsted yarn)
1 large metal blunt end sewing needle (for bulky, gigantic and jet knitting)
1 plastic sewing needle (for dress and novelty yarns)
1 pair sharp, pointed scissors
1 non-stretch tape measure
Pins, straight rustproof, T-pins or card pins
Sewing machine for altering, plus zig-zag attachment for making buttonholes
Plastic rings for buttons
Crochet hooks
Optional —
Plastic T-pins (as for hair rollers) for gigantic or jet knitting
1 buttonhole spacer

WHERE TO USE BASIC SEWING STITCHES FOR SEAM
OVERCAST OR WHIP STITCH: (Flat seam)
1. Ribbing, Seed and Garter stitch patterns (can be sewed on right or wrong side)
2. Borders of ribbing, Seed stitch and Garter stitch
3. Hems and facings
4. Afghans
5. Some underarm seams depending on pattern
6. Collars
7. Dresses at waist line

BACK STITCH:
1. Underarm, shoulder and sleeve seams
2. On ribbing, Seed and Garter stitch patterns, only if heavy, reinforced seams are needed using one-half or one stitch in seam
3. Sock and stocking seams
4. Some afghans, depending on pattern stitch
5. Any place you want a flat, elastic seam

SEWING FROM RIGHT SIDE OF GARMENT:

(Flat, rigid; needs careful work)
1. For strong shoulder seams
2. Bands on fronts of cardigans
3. Double facings or borders across back of neck on garments
4. Seams where uneven or excess materials are to go to wrong side

WEAVING ON RIGHT SIDE OF GARMENT:

(Flat; watch tension; tendency to spread if too loose, to pucker if too tight)
1. Seams with even edges
2. Kitchener stitch
3. Bottom and top edges of double facings
4. Leg seams of socks and stockings
5. Underarm seams where little pulling occurs
6. Seams on jet knitting, under "bumps"

RUNNING STITCH:

(Rarely used; small stitches sewed once up and once down each seam; hard to control; has tendency to "skid")
1. Straight side seams.

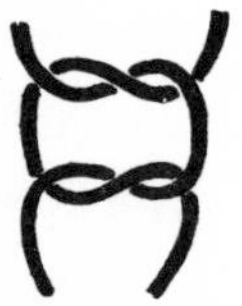

SEWING UNDERARM SEAMS

"Sew underarm . . . seams."

It is best to follow the order for assembling pieces as listed with each pattern.

Fig. 18

Before pinning and sewing piece, take ends of yarn which have been joined on the sides, tighten to fit edge and tie in square knot (two loops only) (Fig. 18). Ends will be woven into seams after sewed.

If you wish to try on sweater before assembling, baste pieces together with sewing thread. Never try to sew knits together with bastings in seams. Pin pieces together and remove all bastings. This will allow stitches to be free and easy to pick up when sewing.

If you do not have professional blocking available for your completely finished garment and are going to do the blocking yourself, it is advisable to block each piece separately to proper size before assembling. See page 42 for blocking.

For Left Handers: Turn or adjust the piece of knitting so your sewing will **END** at the same places as instructed for right handers.

PINNING BACK TO FRONTS

On a table, take the back and lay right side up. Take fronts and place on top of back with right sides down, being sure that front neck shapings are at the center of garment.

We will sew together the underarm seams beginning at bottom edge and working to armhole. Pinning in order as numbered in Fig. 19 and with pins pointing toward armhole, pin together back and left front at first bound-off stitches of underarm; match stitches of first purl rows at top of ribbing; smooth out rolled edges until flat and pin together at center. Pin remaining sections at even intervals and at bottom edge of ribbing.

Turn sweater and pin other side seam of right front and back together.

Six to eight pins usually are sufficient for each side seam. Recently I have found the T-pins and card pins hold and stay in medium to heavy yarns better than regular straight pins. For jet knitting, large plastic T-pins work well.

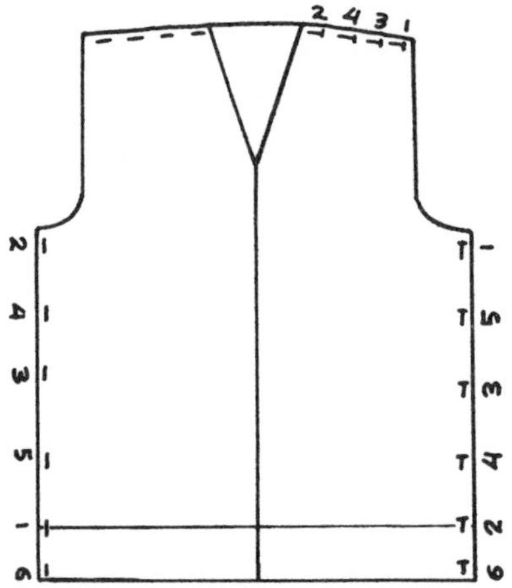

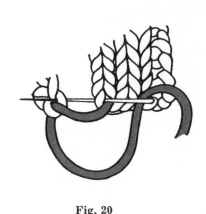

Fig. 19

Fig. 20

SEWING RIBBING

Using end of yarn which was left when you first began casting on, thread into blunt end steel or plastic sewing needle. If there is no end of yarn at the beginning at bottom of ribbing, use a new piece, leaving a 5" end to be woven in later.

WE DO NOT MAKE KNOTS IN SEWING WITH YARN.

Working from wrong side of sweater, insert needle in piece **OPPOSITE** where thread is attached, into the very corner thread and pull yarn through. Repeat, putting needle through the very corner threads of **BOTH** pieces and pull yarn through. This will make a straight line at the bottom edge eliminating a jog or pucker at seam (Fig. 20).

To sew the ribbing, we will overcast or whip stitch the edges together, from back to front of work facing you, through the tight little nub which is at the end of every other row of ribbing (Fig. 21). Between the nubs, the alternate rows end with a straight, loose thread. Since we want a good strong joining, do not go into these loose threads but into the nubs which will give a firm, closed, flat seam.

However, if you have miscounted and have more rows of ribbing in one piece than the other, you may need to go into rows between the nubs to ease in the extra knitting to come out even at top of ribbing.

When sewing ribbing is finished, put needle straight through and under top threads of seam to back of work in preparation for back stitch on body seam of sweater.

Fig. 21

MATCHING RIBBING PATTERN AT SEAMS

In arranging these stitches, if there must be a choice of casting on fewer or more stitches than pattern requires, cast on fewer stitches and increase to required number for pattern on last row of ribbing or first row of body pattern.

Knit stitches lend themselves to both woven and back stitch finishing but the correct number of purl stitches on the edges make a better back stitch seam.

FOR K 1, P 1 PATTERN: The easiest arrangement is to have knit stitch on the outside of each seam edge to be matched and sew using one-half of a stitch from each seam.

OR, FOR K 2, P 2 PATTERN: Have two knits on each seam edge, using one stitch from each side in seams. Sewing one stitch from each side gives a strong seam and is particularly useful for hard wearing quality as for men and boys' sweaters.

BACK STITCH SEAMS

Fig. 22

BACK STITCH SEAM

FRONT

BACK

START HERE

Fig. 23

How do you make a back stitch? To make a back stitch you take a long stitch and then go back half the length of the stitch to begin the

next long stitch. (Fig. 23) Repeat this for length of seam. Back of seam will have continuous, overlapping, long stitches and front will have continuous, short, consecutive stitches. (Fig. 22)

KNITNOTE: YARN NEVER GOES OVER *TOP* OF A BACK STITCH SEAM.

The back stitch is the stitch most used for fine finishing. The interlocking nature of the stitches makes it excellent for knits because it will hold the garment firmly and not allow seam to spread apart; looks as if it had been machine stitched; is elastic, or a little "bouncy", which allows for good fitting and long wear; lays flat regardless of amount or unevenness of excess material left in seam; and can be used for all weights of yarn from the finest to the bulkiest.

LENGTH OF BACK STITCH IN KNITS

Although this will vary with different weights of yarn and gauge, from fine to knitting worsted yarns, the long stitch of back stitch will be the length of two rows or two stitches. On bulkies or novelty yarns perhaps the long stitch would only sew nicely the length of one stitch, the new long stitch beginning back one-half stitch each time. There is no definite rule on this but stitches must be close enough together and tight enough to give a firm yet elastic seam.

HOW TO SEW BACK STITCH SEAM

RULE :

FOR EVEN (STRAIGHT) EDGES ON SEAMS, SEW BACK STITCH WITH TWO MOTIONS.

FOR UNEVEN (SHAPED) EDGES ON SEAMS, SEW BACK STITCH WITH ONE MOTION.

This stitch is worked with two motions (from back to front and front to back) on even edges to guarantee that sewing will not use more than one stitch in depth of seam, resulting in a straight, uninterrupted line in knitting on outside.

For uneven or shaped edges, one motion is used, as for sewing in sleeves, to allow uneven or excess material to go to wrong side.

TO WORK (Fig. 24): *YARN IS NOW AT BACK OF WORK. Skip one row.

FIRST MOTION: Bring needle from back of work under both loops of one stitch in next row, and through opposite stitch (both loops) on front piece (Fig. 25). Pull yarn through with one motion until it "hits bottom".

SECOND MOTION: Insert needle from front into row just skipped and through opposite stitch on back piece (Fig. 26). Repeat from * always picking up one complete stitch on each side.

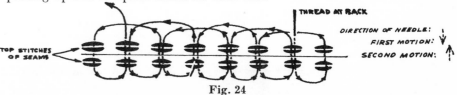

TOP STITCHES OF SEAMS

THREAD AT BACK

DIRECTION OF NEEDLE:
FIRST MOTION:
SECOND MOTION:

Fig. 24

As you sew, remove pins from under your hand before sewing, always easing and rolling edges together. Do not allow edges to roll back into a wide seam. Keep working edges up between fingers so that the two edges lay almost flat on top. They will meet and can be sewed evenly when they are held together between the first and third fingers with the second finger smoothing the stitches.

Do not try to pick up both sides of the seam at the same time but pick up a stitch on each side one at a time because it is so easy to get too far down into the piece of knitting, making a crooked seam and losing the outside vertical line of the finished seam.

As you work, inspect the seam often on the outside to be sure you are always sewing in the same rows on even edges.

The back stitch seam can be undone but is a little difficult and takes patience. To undo, spread seam apart a little. With eye end of needle, pull the SECOND thread in the seam first to get end of yarn.

There will be times when there are more rows of knitting in one piece than the other. You will not be able to sew row for row but ease in the excess rows and sew as evenly as possible.

This manner of sewing is very regular and neat and really simple to do. It's certainly much more difficult to write about than to do.

Fig. 25   **Fig. 26**

TENSION OF SEWING YARN

You will pull yarn through to be firm, not tight, and the elasticity of the yarn will allow for "give" in the seam. Seam should not be "hard".

Do not pull up yarn and then tuck and tuck or pull and pull several times as for embroidering. Once is enough! Sew all stitches with one motion, with the same tension and all stitches will be even and neat.

It is a good habit to check your work frequently to eliminate spending time and labor in making corrections. Be patient.

ENDING WITH OLD YARN

Ends of yarn are woven back into the seam it sewed and all ends are woven into back stitch seams in the same manner.

When you reach the end of a seam, bring needle up through center and out top of seam. YARN NEVER GOES OVER TOP OF A BACK STITCH SEAM.

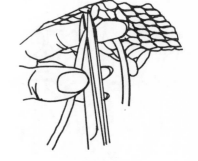

Fig. 27   **Fig. 28**

Turn work, insert needle in the hard core or center of seam and making small in-and-out motions, fasten for about 1" (Fig. 27). Pull up end of yarn tightly. Cut yarn slantwise (Fig. 28). Pull the seam on each side of fastening and end will disappear. If this is done correctly, there will never be any "popping out" of ends.

BEGINNING WITH NEW YARN

Should you not have enough yarn to finish the entire seam, when a 5" end of yarn remains, fasten off as above. To begin with new piece of yarn, insert needle from front to back where last stitch ended, leaving a 5" end and continue sewing.

A "TAILORING TRICK"

When sewing underarm seams and going from ribbing sewed with an overcast stitch into a back stitch seam on the body, often a dip or indentation is made immediately above the ribbing because two full stitches have been used for the back stitch seam. This destroys the smoothness and continuity of the lines along the seam. To eliminate this dipping-in on seam and not change the number of stitches used in the body of the garment, there is a "tailoring trick" which you can incorporate in your patterns.

To do this, we will subtract from the cast-on stitches, one stitch from each side of back ribbing (substract 2 sts) and one stitch from each seam side of front ribbing (subtract 1 st only from each front piece). These substracted stitches will be cast on last row of ribbing to provide the stitches necessary to make a back stitch seam.

TO WORK:

Knit in ribbing pattern up to the last row. Cast on (Method No. 1) the number of stitches subtracted as: On back, cast on 1 st at each end of needle and on fronts, cast on one stitch at side seam to be sewed.

These stitches cast on will provide one stitch on each seam edge necessary to make back stitch seam and replace those subtracted at the beginning of the ribbing.

SEWING SHOULDERS

"Sew . . . shoulder seams . . . ."

With right sides of garment together, pin shoulder seams. If shoulder shaping has been done correctly, you will be able to match bound-off stitches stitch for stitch.

KNITNOTE: WHEN YOU HAVE UNEVEN EDGES, BACK STITCH WILL BE WORKED IN ONE MOTION (Fig. 23).

KNITNOTE: AFTER SEWING, CAST-OFF STITCHES SHOULD *NEVER* SHOW ON RIGHT SIDE AT SHOULDER SEAMS.

Most garments need strength of a good seam on the shoulders. Although many knitters may be reluctant to use the stitches necessary for a good seam, it must be done and a deep enough seam taken that no bound-off stitches show on outside of sweater. Bound-off stitches showing on the outside is very unprofessional and the mark of an amateur.

Treat the edges of the knitted pieces as fabric and sew in a straight diagonal line deep enough from edges to avoid any holes or bound-off stitches (Fig. 29). After sewing, any rough, uneven or thick edges of this seam will lay flat, block easily and not be noticeable in appearance or wearing.

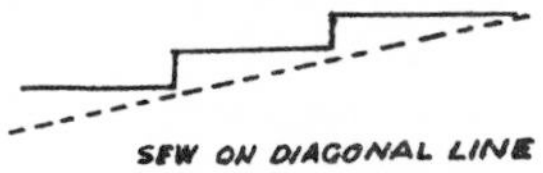

Fig. 29   SEW ON DIAGONAL LINE

Learning some of the fine points of binding off shoulders will help eliminate a number of these irregular edges such as jogs at the top of shoulders (page 14).

SEWING IN SLEEVES

"Sew underarm . . . and sleeve seams. Set in and sew sleeves."

Sew sleeve underarm seams, overcasting ribbing and using back stitch in one motion on uneven edges.

To sew in a sleeve, insert sleeve inside garment with right sides together. As in Fig. 30, take center top of sleeve cap, match and pin to center top of shoulder (A). Match and pin underarm seam with underarm of sweater (B). Pin the last bound-off stitches of sleeve cap flat and straight along top edges of shoulder (C). You will have 2" to 4" of straight edges here.

At the armpit, fit and pin the curve of the arm (D). Fit in the balance of bound-off stitches of sleeve cap (E) and beginning to pin at center first, ease in balance of edges (F).

If sleeve cap is incorrect in size, reknit to fit or see changing patterns and pieces page 73.

If sleeves are knitted with any kind of pattern that has definite vertical lines like lace or ribbing, be sure that these lines are placed in the armhole so when worn the pattern lines lay straight. The tendency is for the lines to curve toward top of shoulder and give a gathered look which spoils the appearance and indicates poor finishing. If in any doubt as to how it will look, baste sleeves in place and try on sweater. This is one of the few times I baste knits.

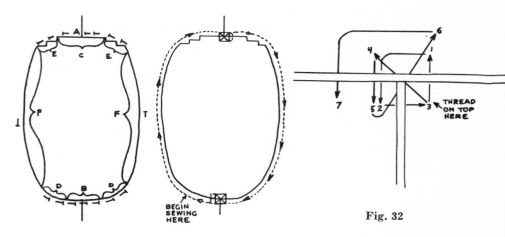

Fig. 30   **Fig. 31**   **Fig. 32**

Sew in sleeves from the **BODY SIDE OF THE GARMENT**, even if this is contrary to general instructions for sewing fabric where the sleeves are usually sewed from the fullness of the sleeve side. This allows you to see stitches better, to sew and to keep the straight vertical line of knitting along the armhole edge.

As in Fig 31, I begin and end sewing at curve of arm (D) since this will keep endings away from the already thick underarm seams.

Since we never go over the top of a back stitch seam, we have to go through the other seams as we come to them as at shoulder and underarm. If sewed only with one back stitch, these seams have a tendency to roll or fall open at shoulder edges where naturally there is pulling from the arms and shoulders.

To eliminate this I go around the thickness of this seam like making sides to a little box and then an X. To sew, follow number sequence in Fig. 32, always going under the edges of seams. At (7), continue in back stitch. When finished you will have a perfect right angle seam that will stay put. Work through the seams at underarm in the same fashion.

ALTERNATE ORDER OF SEWING IN SLEEVES

Some sweaters set in sleeve cap before sewing underarm seams. I like this particularly on drop shoulder patterns because cap seems to go in and fit better.

Finishing instructions would read: Sew shoulder seams. Set in and sew sleeve cap. Sew underarm and sleeve seams in a continuous line.

WEAVING IN ENDS NOT IN SEAMS

I have had many sweaters brought in that had only ½" to 1" ends. Many knitters did not know or realize that all ends are woven in or that it would be the desirable thing to do to make a well-finished garment. Other knitters knew ends were to be woven in but wanted to know where and how.

If ends of yarn are too short to thread into a yarn needle, use a crochet hook and pull in and out of seams as best you can. This is difficult to do and I am usually unhappy with the results because yarns split, ends may "pop out" and often it is doubtful if the results are worth your time and trouble. Perhaps it is better under some circumstances not to try to weave these at all, as long as ends are tied securely and do not show on the outside of garment.

WHY SHORT ENDS?

Unless knitter is trying to save yarn, it is difficult to understand why anyone would cut off short ends, particularly since, with rare exception, there is always yarn left over. This is another example of not realizing the need here, not thinking ahead to the finishing or perhaps the knitter is being a little too thrifty. Be a little more generous with the amount of yarn and it will allow you easier work and a much finer finished garment.

HOW MANY INCHES OF YARN SHOULD BE WOVEN IN?

If you have sufficient yarn to work with, 1" to 2" of ends woven in is sufficient to hold.

To weave in ends: Tie yarns in a square knot to fit knitting. Let ends of yarn fall to show you which way end wants to go. Thread yarn into blunt end needle and weave ends in the same direction as the adjacent stitches are made or if at color changes, keep same colors together.

In Garter stitch, I duplicate the in and out lines under the nubs.

In ribbing, work same as page 90.

In Stockinette, on wrong side, weave under the stitches in the same row as joining, going under nubs from one side to the other BUT IN EVERY OTHER STITCH. Using every stitch makes a thick place and

sometimes shows on the outside. Pull up and cut thread on slant to finish. Check outside frequently to see that yarn ends do not show and do not pull stitches out of shape.

To weave pattern stitches, weave along with knitted threads and in tight stitches whenever possible. Some knitters split the different ply and catch lightly these ends through the top of the yarn on the wrong side.

Use as many of these ideas in a garment as necessary for the smoothest, tightest and least noticeable weaving of ends.

BACK OF NECK BORDERS

"Fit ends of neck border together at back of neck and join with Kitchener stitch."

Fit neck borders along neck edge of back. If these are too long, unravel from either border or both, allowing for one row to fill in for joining and being sure that joining will be in the center back. If pieces are too short, knit on more rows until borders fit and meet in the center of back.

Frequently the grafting here can be done so well that no joining line shows. But if it does look a little different from the rest of the stitches, it should be centered to be the least noticeable.

GRAFTING

Grafting is the joining horizontally of two pieces of knitting by weaving with a tapestry or yarn needle and yarn, resulting in one continuous piece in pattern, with no seam. Grafting row will not show if done correctly (Fig. 33)

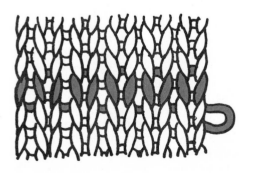

A   Fig. 33   B

"KITCHENER" STITCH

The most common grafting, usually called the "Kitchener" stitch, is used on Stockinette, for joining toes of socks, closing tops of mittens, joining bands, facings, shoulder seams, baby sweaters, etc.

GRAFTING WITH KNITTING ON NEEDLES

REQUIREMENTS :
1. Stitches must not be bound off.
2. Stitches of each piece are put on a separate needle for easy handling.
3. Each piece is worked with the same number of stitches on each needle.
4. Each piece is worked in the same pattern stitch.
5. The same kind of stitches, knits or purls, must be opposite each other on the needles.
6. Pieces are worked on right side of garment, wrong sides held together.
7. Points of needles must be in same direction and parallel.

METHOD :
1. Use blunt end tapestry or yarn needle.
2. Weave with same yarn as used in knitting.
3. Grafting is worked horizontally on right side of pieces, beginning at the right hand edges.

TO WORK :
1. Length of grafting yarn should be at least 4 times the width of piece.
2. If yarn end on one of the pieces is long enough to do the grafting and is attached at the right end of piece, thread this in needle. Otherwise, join new grafting yarn at right end of FRONT needle (Fig. 33B).
3. Note in grafting that yarn goes through each stitch two times in the weaving back and forth, excepting first and last stitch on same rows as shown in illustrations.
4. Note the basic grafting stitch is worked through two loops on each needle the first one being dropped off. This is repeated, alternating first front and back needles, until all stitches are worked.
5. Keep grafting yarn UNDER tips of needles as you weave and pull up yarn to match stitches of knitting.

Grafting is a very important part of finishing since it is usually done on parts of the garment that show the most. It is often one of the last things you work on a garment, so don't get in a big hurry and do poor work. After all the time, energy and money you have invested, learn to do your grafting well and your neat work will pay off with a fine garment you'll be proud of and enjoy wearing.

TO PRACTICE GRAFTING

Make a 4" swatch and work in Stockinette stitch, with a Main Color for about 2", ending on the wrong side. On right side, work one row in a Contrast Color, leaving ends free, not tied to Main Color. Work balance of swatch in Main Color. Bind off.

Using top of yarn needle or crochet hook, remove the Contrast Color row carefully, stitch by stitch. Place loops of Main Color on separate needles and graft as per following instructions.

TO BEGIN GRAFTING STOCKINETTE :

FRONT NEEDLE: Insert tapestry needle through first loop like a P stitch (Fig. 35). Leave ON needle.

BACK NEEDLE: Insert tapestry needle through first loop like a K stitch (Fig. 37). Leave ON needle.

BASIC GRAFTING

*FRONT NEEDLE: Insert tapestry needle through first loop as if a K stitch (Fig. 34). Slip first loop OFF end of needle.
Insert tapestry needle through first loop as if a P stitch (Fig. 35). Leave loop ON needle. Pull up stitches to match knitting.
BACK NEEDLE: Insert tapestry needle through first loop as if a P stitch (Fig. 36). Slip first loop OFF end of needle.

Fig. 34

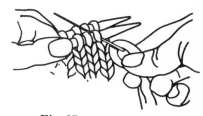

Fig. 35

Insert tapestry needle through first loop as if a K stitch (Fig. 37). Leave loop ON needle.

Fig. 36

Fig. 37

Pull up stitch to match knitting. Repeat from * until all stitches are worked off needles.

GRAFTING WITH KNITTING OFF NEEDLES

When the loops are large enough and of a material, like wool, that will not allow the stitches to unravel easily, grafting can be done from the following illustrations. After checking the GRAFTING REQUIREMENTS, place pieces flat and drop loops off ends of needles as needed to work (Fig. 38).

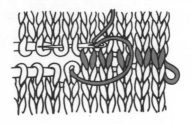 

Fig. 38   Fig. 39

GRAFTING GARTER STITCH (Fig. 39)

The grafting of Garter stitch and ribbings is not impossible but difficult. These grafting are not often used. However, when needed, particular care should be taken to keep loops flat and orderly. Be exact with the beginning grafting so knits will fall over knits and purls over purls. It is easy to get off pattern by one-half stitch. In most instances this would not be important but on ribbings the pattern stitch would be interrupted and therefore incorrect.

Tapestry needle is always held horizontally for the knit stitches and vertically for the purl stitches.

GRAFTING RIBBINGS (Figs. 40 and 41)

If using ribbed bands on a cardigan where bands are to be grafted at the back of neck, be sure that K 1, P 1 uses a multiple of 2 + 1 and the K 2, P 2 ribbing uses a multiple of 4 + 2. Using the knit stitch on the outside edges of the borders gives a finished edge and will allow you to match stitches when bands meet for grafting.

Fig. 40   Fig. 41

Since K 1, P 1 is particularly difficult to graft, the following illustrations show an easy method. Although this is not a "true" graft in comparison with the others, it is easy and quite satisfactory.

26

K 1, P 1 RIBBING-GRAFTING CONTINENTAL METHOD

You will need four needles the same size as used when knitting the pieces. A set of double-pointed needles is very good for this.

As in Fig. 42, slip knit stitches (every other one of ribbing) of one piece on needle A.

Turn piece and slip remaining stitches on needle B.

Arrange other piece on two separate needles, C and D.

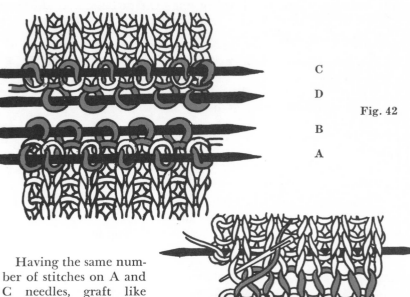

Fig. 42

Having the same number of stitches on A and C needles, graft like Stockinette stitch (Fig. 43).

Turn pieces over and graft remaining stitches on needles B and D together (Fig. 44).

Fig. 43

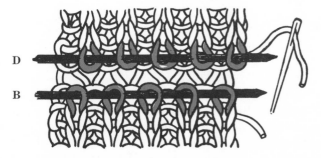

Fig. 44

SEWING FACINGS

"Sew border to back of neck.
Fold front facings and neck border to inside and sew to knit stitch around fronts and across back of neck."

I find a back stitch seam here is too thick so I weave it on the outside. The basic weaving stitch is as in Fig. 45, which can be woven from bottom to top or top to bottom of seam.

In this instance where the lines of the two pieces go in different directions, pick up two threads with each stitch, using one stitch on back and one row on facing (Fig. 46).

Fig. 46

Fig. 45

Yarn must be pulled up tight enough not to allow seam to spread but do not pull tighter than necessary since this is a rigid seam.

Next, turn under facing on slip stitch edge and pin along the knit stitch which outlines the border.

This is a place where you will need to decide how heavy and how much to sew into a seam on this particular knit. If a strong, tight seam is needed, sew through the nub on the edge of facing and all of the knit stitch every second row.

For double facing here, we do not need a heavy seam for strength but only a light, thin seam to keep facing flat and in place. When sewing this facing, overcast every second row and pick up the long, loose thread on edge of facing and only one-half stitch of the outline knit stitch that is closest to the border (Fig. 48).

To sew, begin at the bottom of the fronts and sew to shoulder seams. Fold neck facing over top of seam already sewed across neck and overcast lightly and smoothly.

Fasten ends of double facing together by going in and out, from one piece to another, through the bottom edge stitches.

"Finish buttonholes. Sew on buttons. Block."

See page 37 for double buttonholes, page 31 to sew on buttons and page 42 to block.

KNITTING FACINGS ON FLAT PIECES

Facings can be made with knitted pieces, netting, fabrics, etc. but in this particular instance we are going to talk about knitted facings on flat pieces.

A facing is a piece of knitting worked at the same time and is made as a part of the garment or separately for attaching later. Facings are usually turned under and attached to the underside of an edge.

The purposes of facings are: To make a finished edge, to reinforce a section of a piece, to hold piece in shape and to tailor or give a neat finished appearance to a fine garment.

There are three results with facings:

(1) Those sections faced have an obvious thickness and interrupt the outward smoothness and to some degree the size of the piece. These have probably been knitted with the same size needles for both facing and body piece. (Average results)

(2) Those sections faced are reinforced but the facings do not interfere with the outside appearance of the knitting. These have been made in a manner that the facing is SMALLER than its matching section on outside edge of piece. (Excellent results)

(3) Those sections that have been designed so poorly that facings bulge, ruffle and edges spread when finished. (Unsatisfactory results)

The thick and obvious seam line as in (1) is well liked, acts as a trim or accent and is often used in Europe.

Most American women prefer (2) with a smooth uninterrupted look and indicate a very strong dislike for bulging and ruffly faced edges, as in (3). How many, many times I have heard, "I can't wear this! What is wrong? I followed the instructions exactly." Although many times knitters are guilty of not following instructions correctly, in these instances, they probably did. Many times this is not the knitter's fault but the result of poor designing. With the present lack of written instructions for proper technique of making good fitting facings and no indication of changing the manner of writing these instructions in patterns, we lose a few more knitters or the knitters learn to adjust pattern instruction themselves.

Many knitters who dress smartly and carefully and take pride in their appearance, are very disappointed when they can not wear their knitted garments after being finished. This kind of garment not only looks sad but it is a sorry experience after all the time, money and loving labor spent—but don't give up!

HOW TO MAKE KNITTED HEM FACINGS FIT

Check your pattern to see if hem facings are worked with smaller needles or if fewer stitches are used than the body piece. If neither of these are done, adjust your pattern using either of the following methods:

METHOD NO. 1 HEM FACINGS: If the same number of stitches and the same size needle are used in the hem facings as on the body of piece, basically use a pair of needles TWO sizes smaller for the hem facing and hemline. Sometimes only one size smaller is needed on fine knitting.

CASTING ON ROW: Use one of the larger needles for casting-on row. Then use the pair of smaller needles to work hem facing and hemline or turning edge. This assures the cast-on row will not be too tight and after being sewed to body of garment does not make a puckered seam. Change to larger needles and continue in pattern.

METHOD NO. 2 FACINGS: Use needles the same size as for body but cast on 20% LESS stitches than pattern calls for. Work to within one row of hemline and increase (the 20% of stitches) evenly across row to the original number to be cast on, using Method No. 3 increase. Work turning edge of hemline and continue.

This sounds like a lot of stitches out of hem facing but it works fine, gives excellent results and, after hem facing is sewed, will leave little or no marks on the outside of piece. This method will also keep the piece the correct size with no unsightly bulges or flaring. I have finished garments knitted in this manner on which you would not know there were hem facings.

HEMLINES

Many times knitters do not read instructions correctly and will get facings reversed resulting in a reverse Stockinette facing and a Stockinette garment piece. This is very difficult to keep firmly in shape, to sew flat and to keep the hemline edge from rolling. You will never have any trouble working Stockinette stitch facing, turning hem and continuing in Stockinette stitch for body if you will remember:

TO MAKE TURNING EDGE, BEGINNING ON RIGHT SIDE OF STOCKINETTE STITCH, WORK THREE KNIT ROWS IN SUCCESSION, resuming pattern by P 1 row, K 1 row, etc.—OR BEGINNING ON WRONG SIDE, PURL THREE ROWS IN SUCCESSION, resuming pattern by K 1 row, P 1 row, etc. The center row of the three knit or three purl rows is the hemline row.

In working the hemline, some patterns say to knit into the back of each stitch (Fig. 47) on this row (twisting the stitch) which makes a tighter, firmer edge. However, if you work the METHOD No. 2 FACINGS above, work turning edge on row with a regular knit or purl stitch.

SEWING HEMLINES AND FACINGS

Since the facing reinforces the edges, tight, heavy seams are not needed. Using yarn, sew with overcast stitch, picking up top thread on edge of facing and one thread on body, sewing in EVERY OTHER STITCH (Fig. 48). Our aim here is to fasten only tight enough to hold and loose enough not to disturb the outside of piece.

Fig. 47

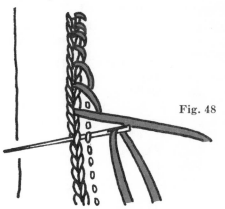

Fig. 48

In turning up facings for hemlines at bottom of skirt, jacket, cuffs, be very careful that you keep the lines of knitting going vertically. If you have bound off a little tight or you get the facing on crooked, even when the garment is finished, it will pull a little to the side and look twisted or puckered. Be sure that your facing is exactly square and keep the lines of the knitting even.

KNITTED FACINGS ON CIRCULAR PIECES

Stockinette stitch circular skirt with facing and turned hemline is knitted around and around for depth of facing. For hemline or turning edge, work one round of purl stitch. Resume knitting around and around.

TO WEAVE UP A HEM

Work until twice the depth of hem.

To weave up hem, fold bottom edge up with wrong sides together. *Insert needle through next stitch and its corresponding stitch in cast-on round and knit these two together. Repeat from * until all stitches of cast-on round are woven up.

MAKING FACINGS FOR COATS

We often make facings where none have been called for in the pattern. Separate facings can be made with the same weight yarn and worked on several sizes larger needles to make the facings thinner or made from lighter weight yarn for the same purpose.

Watch that buttonholes are knitted same distance apart and match corresponding buttonholes on body of garment.

These facings are difficult to join on the edges to lay flat, look well and hold their shape. A back stitch seam does not work here. Sometimes you can weave the edges together as with mohair. Usually I single crochet this kind of joining to keep edges from sagging, holding edges in shape to give good support to fronts of garment.

BIAS FACINGS

Bias facings, sometimes called bias strips or bands, are of knitted fabric, usually sewed to face edges that are shaped as neck and sleeve edges and for binding buttonholes.

After knitting, if there is any doubt as to the correct length, place stitches on a holder and do not make final bind-off until fitted and proper length determined.

BASIC BIAS STRIPS

1. BASIC STOCKINETTE STITCH (SHAPED TO LEFT) (Fig. 49)

"Cast on 8 sts purlwise.

Row 1: K 2 tog., K to last st, inc. 1 st in last st (knitting in front and back of stitch).

Row 2: Purl

Repeat these 2 rows until length desired.

Bind off."

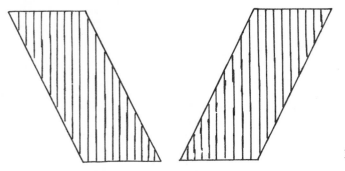

Fig. 49   Fig. 50

2. BASIC STOCKINETTE STITCH (SHAPED TO RIGHT) (Fig. 50)

"Cast on 8 sts purlwise.

Row 1: Inc. 1 st in first st, K to last 2 sts, K 2 tog.

Row 2: Purl.

Repeat these two rows until length desired.

Bind off."

3. BASIC STOCKINETTE STITCH (SHAPED TO LEFT, WITH SMOOTHER EDGES)

"Cast on 8 sts purlwise.

Row 1: K 2 tog (as K 2 tog leaning to left, Manual page 47), K across to last st, inc 1 st before last stitch (Method No. 2, pick up purl nub below and in back of next stitch and place on left needle and K) and K 1.

Row 2: Purl.

Repeat these 2 rows for pattern."

BIAS STRIP WITH TURNING EDGE

STOCKINETTE STITCH BIAS STRIP (SHAPED TO LEFT) (Fig. 51)

"Cast on 7 sts purlwise.

Row 1: K 2 tog., K 1, Make a Left Twist (skip the next stitch and leave on needle, at back of piece knit in BACK of second stitch, knit the skipped st, pull both sts off left needle), K 1, inc. 1 st in last st.

Row 2: Purl.

Repeat these 2 rows for pattern.

Bind off."

STOCKINETTE STITCH BIAS STRIP (SHAPED TO RIGHT) (Fig. 52)

"Cast on 7 sts purlwise.

Row 1: Inc. 1 st in first st, K 1, make right twist (skip next stitch leaving it on needle, from front of work K in the FRONT of second st, K st skipped, pull both sts off left needle), K 1, K 2 tog.

Row 2: Purl. Repeat these 2 rows for pattern. Bind off."

I would probably use this left-shaped bias because the nub left by increase done by knitting in front and back of stitch is less noticeable on the end of the row than at the beginning as for the shaped-to-right bias.

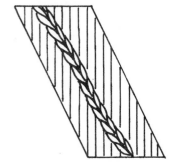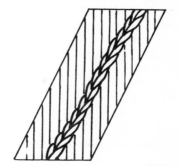

Fig. 51   Fig. 52

BIAS STRIP WITH STRAIGHT EDGES ON ENDS

STOCKINETTE STITCH BIAS (Fig. 53)

"Cast on 3 sts purlwise.

Row 1: Inc. 1 st in the first st. K to last st, inc. in the last st.

Row 2: Purl.

Repeat Rows 1 and 2 until 7 sts are on needle or width desired. Work like basic bias pattern (Fig. 50) until length desired, ending with a P row.

Decrease Row 1:   K 2 tog., work to last 2 sts, K 2 tog.

Decrease Row 2: Purl.

Repeat these two decrease rows until 3 sts remain. Bind off."

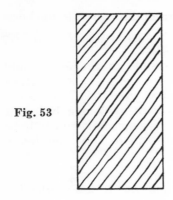

Fig. 53

Fig. 54

BIAS STRIP WITH TURNING EDGE AND STRAIGHT EDGES ON ENDS (Fig. 54)

Work the same as BIAS STRIP WITH STRAIGHT EDGES ON ENDS until number of stitches for width are on needle. Begin working a turning edge at center of bias strip, using a left twist for turning edge as previously instructed. Then work decrease rows until 3 sts remain. Bind off. There will be small areas at beginning and end where there is no turning row. These stitches can be put on by hand after sewing to stimulate the turning edge if needed.

BUTTONS

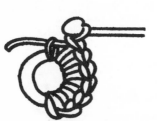

Fig. 55

Fig. 56

ARE BUTTONS SEWED ON BEFORE BLOCKING?

All buttons are sewed on before blocking except wooden, leather or any material that would be spoiled by water or steam. In case buttonholes are not exactly in the correct place, check placement of buttons to see if they match buttonholes before sewing.

MAKING CROCHETED BUTTONS

OVER PLASTIC RINGS (Fig. 55)

Use a crochet hook that picks up yarn well. Leave a 6″ end of yarn at beginning and an 8″ end at end of crocheting.

Using knitting worsted and ⅝″ or 1″ plastic ring, work 20 to 24 sc in center of ring. If this many sc looks thin and only covers about half the ring, yarn should be doubled.

Thread the 8″ end of yarn in needle and pick up outside edge of every other sc around. Carefully pull up and gather all stitches together into center of ring. Run needle through yarn to opposite side from beginning end and tie ends into a square knot at center.

Gathering every stitch around is too much and too difficult. Be careful you do not pull yarn too tight for it will sometimes break and button will have to be made again.

These stitches can be pulled together to the under side of button, leaving a space in the center of button for trims of French knots, fancy stitches, or button centers, or stitches can be gathered together on the top side, which will decorate and fill in the center of ring.

FLAT CROCHETED BUTTON ON 1″ PLASTIC RING (Fig. 116) DIRECTIONS:

Round 1: Using knitted worsted, work 18 sc into center of ring. Join with sl st.

Round 2: 1 sc in each sc around. Cut yarn, leaving 12″ end.

Push button flat and sew center together at back by gathering or weaving back and forth. Trim if desired.

ROUND OR BALL BUTTONS (Fig. 116)

There are many variations in making these. They can be worked to cover small molds for flat rounded buttons or stuffed to make ball buttons. DIRECTIONS FOR BALL BUTTONS ARE:

With crochet hook and working firmly, ch 3. Sl st in 1st ch.

Working IN BACK LOOP ONLY, inc. every stitch around until 12 sts. DECREASE ROUND: Work 2 sc tog. 6 times. Cut yarn leaving 8″ end.

Using a piece of same yarn and color, wrap around tip of index finger about 8 times. Stuff this into center of button. Theard yarn end into needle. Pick up outside edge of 6 sts. Pull up to close button and fasten off. Use end of yarn to sew button on knits.

BUTTON MOLDS COVERED WITH KNITTED FABRIC

If you wish to cover molds yourself, they can be purchased in notion departments or many fabric stores offer this service.

To knit material for covered button molds, it is usually worked in Stockinette stitch and should be knitted a little tighter than the basic stitch gauge because material is pulled very tight and spread in the work of covering molds. This should be of fine yarn, like 3-ply, or split heavier yarn to make knitting as thin as possible.

Work a generous size piece of Stockinette stitch with your yarn. This is easier to handle than strips or small pieces of knitting.

SEWING ON BUTTONS

1. REGULAR BUTTONS SEWED WITH THREAD

Use thread doubled and make a knot in end. Begin on right side of garment. Insert needle down through and up again and bring needle between the two strands and under the knot in thread (Fig. 56). This will lock in the knot and you will not lose buttons.

Sew two or three times through buttons and knitting, ending on the right side of garment but UNDER THE BUTTON. Wrap thread around two of three times under button and pull thread through this thickness once. Cut thread.

2. REGULAR BUTTONS SEWED WITH YARN

Use yarn to sew all buttons whenever possible to get needle and yarn through buttonhole.

A. Work as (1) above using single strand of yarn.

B. If sewing through two thicknesses with yarn as double facing or ribbon-faced edge, begin on wrong side and sew through knit and buttons two times ending on wrong side. Tie ends into square knot and weave ends between the two thicknesses of material.

3. SEWING CROCHETED BUTTONS

A. If there are no ends on crocheted buttons to sew with, use regular sewing thread.

B. If sewing with yarn on double facing, sew like 2B above.

BUTTONHOLES

If you wish a buttoned garment, buttonholes are either knitted in by hand, machine stitched or crocheted in edges after knitting.

Some questions you might ask yourself are:

Do the edges need reinforcing—with a double facing, ribbon, crocheting, or none at all?

Is this garment for everyday use that machine-made buttonholes would be more practical, stronger and give more lasting wear?

Is this garment a very light and fragile knit for dress-up occasions and does it require the complete custom-made look with hand finishing of a very fine seamstress?

Are you going to button this sweater in wearing?

Are you going to use crocheted buttons, fabric-covered buttons or any chunky-sized button that would require larger buttonholes?

Are your buttonholes always too large? Are they too large because they weren't finished?

Can you knit on a double facing where the pattern does not call for this and eliminate ribbon? Can you have machine buttonholes made in double facings?

Are you going to have horizontal or vertical buttonholes?

Is there a way to eliminate "loose places" when making bound-off knitted-in buttonholes?

I have yet to meet a person who was satisfied with their knitted-in buttonholes. This does not mean that you shouldn't knit them in but try several of the following ideas for working buttonholes. Use the one, or any combination of methods, that will make your garment look its very best and will fit the usage of the garment.

If you are a person who never buttons a sweater, often you can sew on buttons and omit buttonholes and few people will notice.

I make buttonholes a little less wide than the button and seldom make them as large as the pattern calls for since they will be larger and stretch after finishing and wearing.

In facing with ribbon, the cutting and hand finishing of ribbon is difficult and I will not personally take the time and effort to work ribbon by hand. Therefore, I knit no buttonholes in the piece, but sew by machine. I particularly recommend this for a beginner's first sweater.

HORIZONTAL
BOUND-OFF KNITTED-IN BASIC BUTTONHOLES
SINGLE THICKNESS OF KNITTING

On Stockinette stitch or any pattern that is fairly flat or where the pattern lays horizontally, this shape is best (Fig. 57). A vertical buttonhole here of average or larger size would have a tendency to spread and double up on the border edge. I have seen this kind of unattractive buttonhole and border that just would not lay flat with normal wear.

This buttonhole is made on two successive rows of knitting beginning shaping of buttonholes on the right side of garment. On the first row you bind off a specified number of stitches and on the next row cast on loops in the same number that were bound off in the previous row. These cast-on stitches are usually made with a single loop (Method No. 1 Purlwise) (Fig. 58). An extra heavy and rigid cast-on can be done by using Method No. 2 (Fig. 59).

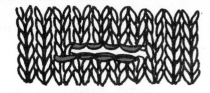

Fig. 57

Fig. 58

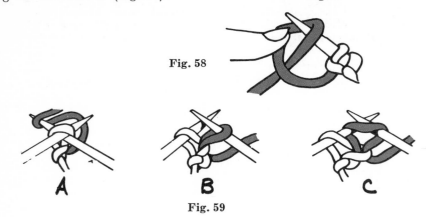

Fig. 59

FINISHING

It has always been my policy (and successful too) NOT to do anything more to knitting than is necessary. For example, some knitters make a running stitch around and close to the edge of buttonholes before finishing. Use your own judgment as to when this is necessary.

Using yarn needle and yarn the same as the knitting, (1) overcast each stitch bound off, one stitch in end, each stitch cast on and one stitch in end. Tie into square knot and weave in ends (Fig. 60).

Or, (2) using yarn needle and yarn same as knitting, either full ply or split, buttonhole stitch around buttonhole (Figs. 61 and 62).

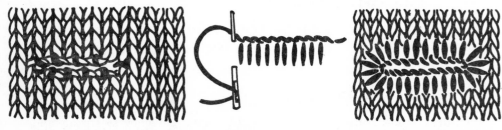

Fig. 60   Fig. 61   Fig. 62

Or, (3) crochet around buttonhole with either a slip stitch or single crochet, whichever works the best. This will fill in buttonholes and make thicker edges.

Except as a very last resort, I do not use regular sewing thread on the hand finishing of knits. Personally I do not like the shrinkage or cutting quality of thread, nor the shine of the thread which will usually show against the yarn. This is made necessary sometimes because of novelty yarns that are too heavy or will not split or if matching colors and satisfactory yarns are not available for sewing.

A ONE ROW BUTTONHOLE (Fig. 63)

This is an excellent buttonhole that does not require additional finishing unless desired. It is fine on Stockinette, ribbing and Seed stitch borders.

If ribbon is to be used as facing, finish as for other horizontal knitted-in buttonholes.

Although this looks a little complicated, it just needs to be tried a couple of times to learn how it works.

Fig. 63

EXAMPLE: Three stitch buttonhole.

KNITNOTE: WHEN BINDING OFF, ALWAYS USE THE FIRST TWO LOOPS ON RIGHT HAND NEEDLE.

ALL STITCHES ARE SLIPPED PURLWISE.

DIRECTIONS : Work to spot for buttonhole :
RIGHT SIDE : Slip 1 st and bring yarn to front of work.
Slip 1 st. Bind off 1 st. (Ignore yarn on front).
Slip 1 st. Bind off 1 st.
Slip 1 st. Bind off 1 st (3 sts bound off).
Slip first stitch on right needle to left needle.
Turn work.

WRONG SIDE : Bring yarn between needles to purl side.
Make top of buttonhole as follows:
Purl into the first stitch on left needle and slip the new purl stitch back from right needle to the left.
Repeat this 3 times MORE until 4 sts (one more stitch than was bound off) have been made.
Turn work.

RIGHT SIDE : Slip first st from left needle to right needle and bind off 1 st (the extra stitch).
Slip first st on right needle back to left needle and knit each stitch across row.

SOME METHODS TO ELIMINATE LOOSE STITCHES OR "HOLES" WHEN CASTING ON TOP OF BUTTONHOLES

1. Cast on one more stitch than specified (Fig. 64). On next row, knit to within one stitch of this extra stitch and work together next stitch (which is usually the loose one) and extra cast-on stitch (Fig. 65).

Fig. 64

Fig. 65

2. Or, increase one stitch in last stitch BEFORE CASTING ON, casting on one LESS number of stitches than specified (Fig. 66). Make increases as follows: Garter stitch, knit in front and back of stitch; Stockinette stitch, purl in second nub under loop of next stitch and put stitch on needle.

Fig. 66

Fig. 67

Fig. 68

3. Or, work to spot for casting on over buttonhole. (Fig. 67). Turn work. Cast on specified number of stitches using Method No. 2 (Fig. 59). Turn work again and finish row.

On the next row, work up to the cast-on stitches of previous row. Insert right needle from the front under threads of first stitch bound off and through last stitch cast on and knit these together (Fig. 68). Knit across row.

In medium to fine yarns, try picking up the front loop only. On bulkies I find you need the whole stitch.

SOME METHODS TO ELIMINATE LOOSE STITCHES OR HOLES ON BIND OFF ROW

1. Work up to spot for buttonhole. Bind off all except one stitch, slip last stitch from right to left needle and K 2 tog. (Fig. 69). This is good for bulkies.

Fig. 69

2. Or, bind off 1 st less than number indicated in your pattern. For example, if pattern says to bind off 4 sts, bind off only 3, and work as follows:

Pull up first loop on right hand needle until large enough to pass ball of yarn through it. Drop loop off needle. Pull up yarn to fit knitting, making a knot (Fig. 70).

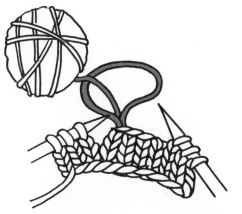

Fig. 70

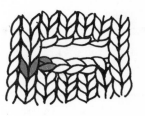

Fig. 71

Continue in pattern and on next row cast on over buttonhole the same number of stitches as pattern stated to be bound off for buttonholes (Fig. 71). This method is often used on bulkies but does leave a rather nubby, hard knot.

YARN OVER BUTTONHOLES

These are worked in single thickness of knitting and result is a round buttonhole. This is good for baby garments and borders where edges will lay flat and need no reinforcing. Ribbon facing is difficult to finish for this shape and is not satisfactory to use for this buttonhole.

ONE-STITCH YO BUTTONHOLE

Work up to place for buttonhole, YO, K 2 tog. (Fig. 72). On the next row, YO is worked as a regular stitch. Overcast edges (Fig. 73), if desired.

| Fig. 72 | Fig. 73 | Fig. 74 |

TWO-STITCH YO BUTTONHOLE (Fig. 74)

Work in Stockinette stitch up to within two stitches of spot for buttonhole.

K 2 tog., YO two times, decrease the next 2 sts by slipping each of the next two stitches knitwise, inserting left needle from the back through the center of both stitches, K 2 tog. (This is a K 2 tog decrease, leaning to left-Manual P 47). On next row, purl the first YO and purl in the BACK of the second YO. If this row is knitted, knit in the front of first YO and in back of second YO.

If added strength is needed and it will not interrupt the style of the garment, overcast edges, which will make more circular buttonholes.

VERTICAL

ON A SINGLE THICKNESS OF KNITTING

These buttonholes are not particularly good for knits, unless small ones for tiny cardigan buttons, on Garter stitch, or for pieces like pocket flaps, since they have a tendency to spread, roll and fold under. In fact, I have never knitted in vertical buttonholes on hand knits because they usually need reinforcing and create a problem in finishing. On Stockinette

stitch, ribbon facing when split vertically is almost impossible to handle by hand and if worked by machine on the ribbon only, then attached over buttonholes, the ribbon does not seem to hold up as well as when stitched horizontally.

Placement of buttonhole should be 3 or 4 stitches from the edge and if the garment has a definite border edge, in the center of the border. A good border edge for this buttonhole is ribbing, since a horizontal bind off in ribbing would give a rough edge, will not lay flat and does not allow for good finishing.

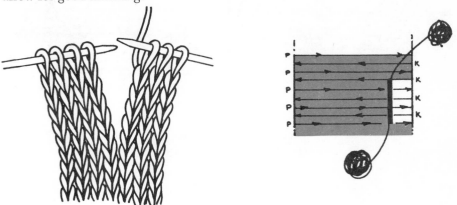

| Fig. 75 | Fig. 76 |

In making a vertical buttonhole, work towards the border edge to spot for buttonhole. Here knitting will be "divided" into two sections (Fig. 75). Continue to use the large ball of yarn for body section and pick up an extra ball of yarn or about one yard of yarn and work in pattern across balance of row. Although you can work each section separately, I think it less confusing to work each section across each row in pattern, like knitting two sleeves at the same time with two balls of yarn, until buttonhole opening is depth desired, ending with extra yarn at top of buttonhole (Fig. 76).

Pick up the large ball of yarn and resume knitting all stitches with this.

A basic number of rows in vertical buttonhole would be eight rows for fine yarn, six for sport and four for medium weights. Joining and ending of ends of yarn for the border section at the buttonhole will allow you to reinforce the buttonhole and conveniently leaves no ends to be woven in at outside border edge.

I seldom approve of slip stitches on edges to be sewed or finished since it does not allow fine finishing. But if buttonhole is worked in Stockinette stitch and is long enough, tighter edges can be made by slipping each knit stitch KNITWISE (Fig. 77) each time you BEGIN an edge on the buttonhole, which will make a slip stitch every other row on both sides. If row begins with a purl stitch, slip PURLWISE in

BACK of stitch (Fig. 78) every other row. This will not only slip stitches but also twist them, making buttonhole edges a little tighter and more firm.

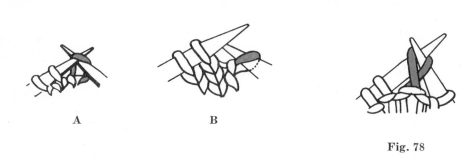

A   B

Fig. 77

Fig. 78

If desired, reinforce bottom and top to opening by overcasting two or three times the same spot for strength as you would in a machine-made buttonhole. Weave in yarn ends on side edges (Fig. 79).

If buttonhole is deep enough, edges will be less likely to roll if two stitches of Garter Stitch are worked every row on each side of buttonhole (Fig. 80). This will interrupt stockinette stitch pattern and should only be used when suitable for the style of the garment.

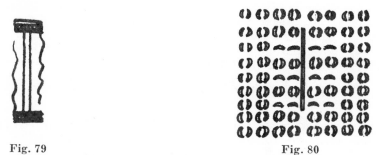

Fig. 79

Fig. 80

MAKING BUTTONHOLES BY HAND (NOT KNITTED IN)

"FINGER" BUTTONHOLE

On loose bulkies and some mohairs, separate yarn with finger at spot for buttonhole and overcast around hole with yarn. This is especially good and less noticeable in a ribbing border. Not the most beautiful buttonhole by any means but satisfactory.

CUT BUTTONHOLE MADE WITH BACKSTITCH

On garments such as heavy, thick coats which cannot be outlined or buttonholed on the machine, make buttonhole horizontally by hand.

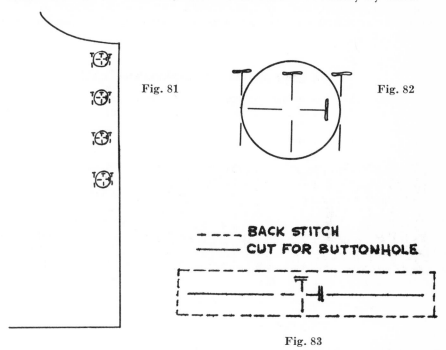

Fig. 81

Fig. 82

BACK STITCH

CUT FOR BUTTONHOLE

Fig. 83

As an example, a coat has been sewed, blocked, lined and reinforced on the front edges with interlining. Space, mark and center for buttonholes (Fig. 81). Use four pins for each button, placing one vertically to mark center of the border and one horizontally to mark row. Place button on center mark and third and fourth pins at each side of button. (Fig. 82)

Use a strong sewing thread, double it and sew in back stitch (Fig. 23). Stitches should be close together and will usually work neatly and evenly over each stitch or each one-half stitch of yarn, depending on its bulk. Sew across width, one or two vertical stitches at end, across other side and one or two vertical stitches on other end, leaving only enough space between sewed rows to cut between stitches (Fig. 83).

Now, cut between this outline of stitches, using sharp scissors. With yarn, buttonhole stitch around, working stitches no closer together than necessary to cover edges nicely.

Be sure that buttonhole is put in straight. If rows of knitting are exactly straight, or we might say "level", you can follow the rows and sew horizontally.

35

However, numerous times I have seen edges that were puckered, slanted and uneven. In these instances, I would probably baste around outside the buttonhole area to hold the materials in place. Make buttonhole "level", even if it interrupts the knitting pattern.

This is a little scary to do the first time. I worked it out in this manner because at times there has been no other satisfactory way to do it.

MACHINE MADE BUTTONHOLES
REINFORCED WITH RIBBON

You often hear the statement, "It just doesn't look hand knit with machine-made buttonholes. If you are going to do it by hand, it ALL should be done by hand." That was my feeling for many years but I have found it much more satisfactory to have machine-made buttonholes stitched in a lovely garment than a lovely garment ruined with badly hand-made buttonholes.

Beginners have so much to learn at first and are usually frightened just of the idea of making buttonholes—so I suggest on the first garment that buttonholes be made by machine. Many knitters prefer the neat appearance of machine-made buttonholes and many just will not knit in buttonholes which makes machine stitching necessary.

If you would like the convenience of making two fronts of a garment at the same time, omit the buttonholes and have them made by machine.

Again even a machine-made buttonhole takes some skill. In fact, I worked these for two years before I felt I had control over most situations. If you don't do them yourself, upon inquiry, you will find persons who do these commercially. There is nothing wrong with asking if they have had experience in making buttonholes in knits and to ask to see a sample of their work. I have had knitters who insisted on seeing some of my work before they would leave their garments for buttonholes. If you are not sure of the quality of work to be done, ask that buttonholes not be cut. The stitches can be pulled out if necessary and buttonholes made again.

DO NOT USE A BUTTONHOLER BUT A ZIG-ZAG ATTACHMENT. See page 39. Stitching can be done on yarn side or ribbon side of garment. For the past several years, I have been making these on the ribbon side only (except on double facings), for it gives me more control of material and does not split or shred the yarn (Fig. 84). Also the stitching shows less on the yarn side.

Fig. 84

Should you wish to have the stitching heavier or show more on the yarn side, first stitch on ribbon side taking care to not make stitches too close together nor too many stitches at the ends on the ribbon side. DO

NOT CUT BUTTONHOLE. Turn over piece and stitch the second time on the yarn side. This double stitching is good for boys' and men's sweaters.

With few exceptions, I make these buttonholes vertically. Many times I find the width does not allow me to make a wide enough buttonhole for most garments. However, if you have sufficient width of ribbon to work horizontally, this makes a quite satisfactory buttonhole.

The pattern stitch on borders will also be a factor in deciding direction of buttonhole. If I have enough width in ribbon, horizontal buttonholes work well in Garter, Seed and Stockinette stitch patterns. Vertical direction would be good for Stockinette, Seed, ribbings, etc. ALWAYS GO WITH THE YARN. NEVER FIGHT IT.

OUTLINED BUTTONHOLES BY MACHINE STITCH AND FINISHED WITH YARN

Outline buttonhole with machine stitching—once around for fine yarns and perhaps two times for heavier. Cut buttonhole and working on the right side, buttonhole stitch edges with matching yarn sewing by hand (Fig. 85).

Some of the best finishing I have ever seen was done this way on a 3-ply all wool matching sweater and skirt outfit. It was very lovely and neat.

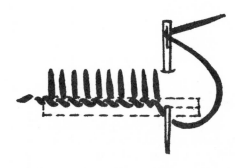

Fig. 85

On heavier yarns, keep rows of machine stitching as close together as possible, still allowing room to cut and in working buttonhole stitch, no closer together than needed to cover edges. Guard against a too heavy or too hard a buttonhole.

This is an excellent way to do buttonholes in mohair coats providing you can get the material in the machine to make outline. If not, see page 35 for working by hand.

HORIZONTAL BUTTONHOLES KNITTED IN, BOUND OFF, FACED WITH RIBBON

Before you knit in horizontal buttonholes on a single thickness, read the following:

So many knitters do not check to see how buttonholes are made or going to be finished and blindly follow instructions and knit them in, not realizing that they will have to be reinforced, usually with ribbon. Yarn edges will also have to be finished as well as the ribbon finished by hand or machine stitched.

To cut ribbon and hand sew ribbon to yarn buttonholes is probably the most difficult finishing in all knitting and rarely done well. While instructing in art needlework at a large department store, I saw one model garment from a yarn company that had hand-worked buttonholes made beautifully. The only other person I have known that could do this kind of buttonhole RIGHT was my mother, who was an expert and professional seamstress. If you are expert with the needle and thread, finish by hand. Otherwise, prepare horizonal machine stitched buttonholes in the ribbon for reinforcing this knitted-in buttonhole.

Always work buttonhole borders first. The opposite border edge for buttons will be finished last so you may match perfectly the length of the ribbon edges.

Unfortunately, another quite common problem occurs when buttonholes are wider than the usual 1" width ribbon used. Ribbon itself is sometimes difficult to get and that over 1" in width gets very scarce and has the disadvantage of usually being too wide and thus not to the liking of the individual.

In this instance, three possible alternatives are: First, using fabric facing, which is difficult to handle and sew on; second reinforce with netting, which is particularly good for thin, fragile, luxury garments; and third, knit on double facings, as on page 50.

TO FINISH, USING RIBBON WITH MACHINE-MADE BUTTONHOLES

See page 44 to measure, fit and pin ribbon to border edge. Mark, with pins placement for buttonholes. Remove ribbon and stitch buttonholes by machine. Pin on ribbon and sew by hand and, if desired, catch together ribbon and yarn edges with sewing thread. Sometimes I have finished the yarn buttonholes before catching together. Sometimes they work better without finishing before catching. Frequently yarn and ribbon sections are finished separately and not joined. Do what looks best.

TO FINISH WITH RIBBON AND HANDWORKED BUTTONHOLES

Measure, pin and sew ribbon to border. Split ribbon over buttonholes, turn under edges and overcast with sewing thread to yarn edges.

DOUBLE BUTTONHOLES
DOUBLE FACING KNITTED-IN BOUND-OFF BUTTONHOLES

A double facing is a border and facing worked on the front edges of a garment at the same time as working front pieces. (Fig. 86). Facing folds back to reinforce the border.

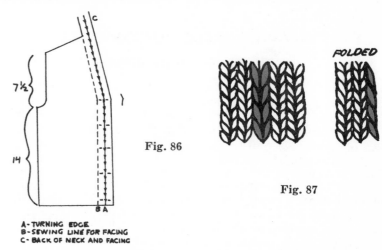

Fig. 86

Fig. 87

A- TURNING EDGE
B- SEWING LINE FOR FACING
C- BACK OF NECK AND FACING

A double facing with knitted-in buttonholes is by far the best method for making buttonholes. The borders are more elastic. There is no problem securing or matching ribbon or sewing it on correctly. There is no shrinkage of facing materials. These buttonholes are the most elastic and can be neatly finished.

For a good-looking tailored garment, use a slip stitch as a turning edge. This allows flat folding and is much easier to sew neatly and correctly (Fig. 87).

Double buttonholes, one on the front of border and one to match in the facing, are made at regular intervals on the edge of one front— women's on the right front and men's on the left front.

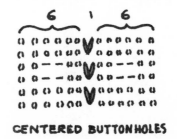

CENTERED BUTTONHOLES

Fig. 88

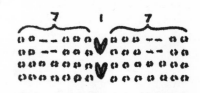

OFF-CENTER BUTTONHOLES

Fig. 89

Decide how many stitches you are going to bind off for buttonholes, center buttonhole (Fig. 88) or decide where they will be placed in border. If buttonhole does not hit the center of the front border, move it in one stitch toward BODY of garment to allow more stitches on front edge for strength (Fig. 89). Be sure that the facing buttonhole is made in right spot to coincide with front buttonhole. An easy way to check this is to have the same number of stitches on each side of the slip stitch after casting off row is done. Always have two or three stitches on OUTSIDE edge of buttonholes, even if buttonholes have to be made smaller.

Often, knitters bind off the wrong stitches in making buttonholes because they do not understand which stitches are to begin the bind-off or that you always have one stitch remaining on needle when bind-off is finished.

The basic method for these instructions, frequently misunderstood, are: "K 2, bind off next 2 sts, K 2, Sl 1, K 2, bind off next 2 sts, K 2."

In this case, since after binding off you have already one knit stitch on the needle, the inexperienced knitter usually will knit TWO more stitches instead of ONE, which makes a total of THREE knits which, of course, is incorrect and will not work out correctly for border.

KNITNOTE: ALWAYS REMEMBER THAT AFTER BINDING OFF, THE NEXT STITCH HAS BEEN WORKED AND IS ON THE RIGHT HAND NEEDLE.

A very specific method of writing these instructions is: "K 2 sts, bind off next 2 sts, work until 2 sts are on needle from last bind-off, Sl 1, K 2, bind off next 2 sts, work until 2 sts are on needle from last bind-off..."

FINISHING DOUBLE BUTTONHOLES

The following is a perfect example of my aim in writing this book: To present numerous methods of working out problems to make your knitting better.

Therefore, I do not say there is only one way to finish double facing buttonholes. Use whatever method you wish that makes them look good and hold together well. However, for those who do not know how to finish or those not satisfied with their previous results, several methods are listed below. Although I work the method under (1), try the various methods and use the one you like best.

Turn facing under along slip stitch edge, matching double buttonholes.

(1) Overcast one stitch in each bound-off stitch, one stitch in end, one stitch in each cast-on stitch, one stitch in end. Pull up ends to size buttonhole desired. Tie in square knot. Thread yarn end into needle and weave ends between layers of facing. Pull up ends a little and cut on slant. Pull border a little and ends will disappear (Fig. 90).

THE SECRET OF THIS FINISHING IS TO USE ONLY THE *OUTSIDE* HALF OF STITCH ON FRONT AND *OUTSIDE* HALF OF STITCH ON FACING (Fig. 91). You will work overcast stitch sewing from back to front. You will not be able to do this well in one motion.

First pick up one outside loop on back facing, put needle through buttonhole space to the front and pick up corresponding outside half of stitch on front. Repeat these two motions around buttonhole as instructed above.

Fig. 91

Fig. 90

Take your time. Work stitch for stitch and pull up to fit. Threads between these stitches will fall or can be pushed down into facing. Don't be upset if you don't do good work on the first few buttonholes you make. Practice on a sample if necessary. If these buttonholes do not look nice after practice and experience, try to be very careful and neat when binding off and casting on for buttonholes. IT IS DIFFICULT TO DO GOOD WORK ON ANY BUTTONHOLES IF THEY ARE BADLY KNITTED.

(2) Buttonhole stitch can be used through both thicknesses but usually this makes a very hard thick edge. I only use this on some coats or for very heavy outdoor wear.

(3) Buttonhole stitch with yarn can be used on front only and facing overcast to buttonhole stitch with yarn or thread.

(4) A crocheted slip stitch can be worked around buttonhole and facing overcast to front piece. This slip stitch will definitely outline the buttonhole and must be done close to edge because the slip stitch just LAYS on the edge and will not necessarily cover it. Be sure slip stitch is done with required tension for it will not stretch.

(5) A single crochet could be used if buttonhole is large enough to permit the single crochet stitch or loose enough to need added strength and thickness.

(6) As a last resort, a double thickness of sewing thread can be used here, remembering the shine of the thread usually makes the buttonhole more obvious.

MACHINE-MADE BUTTONHOLES IN DOUBLE FACING

Some knitters refuse to knit in buttonholes even on double facings, which is the perfect spot, making it necessary to stitch them on the sewing machine.

Use zig-zag attachment for this, since you can control both width and density of stitching. With a buttonholer attachment you have absolutely no control over the stitching once it begins. I have never used a buttonhole attachment since I saw one sweater where the yarn was so badly chewed up from the use of the attachment that the sweater front was completely ruined.

This work on double facing is difficult to do because first, yarn buttonholes always must be reinforced before machine stitching. NEVER DO MACHINE BUTTONHOLES THROUGH YARN ONLY, EITHER SINGLE OR DOUBLE THICKNESS.

Second, it is difficult to keep the vertical lines of the knitting straight since the yarn is soft and has a tendency to skid, spread or split. In this instance, I do the stitching on the OUTSIDE of garment to control the vertical line and allow the best work to show.

Make vertical buttonholes.

In order to stitch these buttonholes, facing must be loose to allow insertion of reinforcing material. If already sewed, loosen facing edge.

Place a piece of light weight organdy or similar fabric under entire

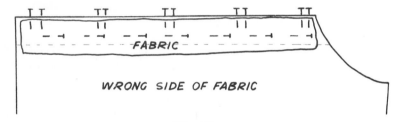

Fig. 92

border. Grosgrain ribbon is usually too thick and heavy. Be sure this is in one piece for easy handling. Place material inside facing and pin facing along lines that will be overcast later, allowing border to lay flat as if finished (Fig. 92). Turn to right side and place pins for vertical buttonholes and machine stitch. Remove all pins. Being very careful not to cut yarn, cut out reinforcing fabric to within 1/2″ from around buttonholes. Sew down facing edges and cut buttonholes.

CUT BUTTONHOLES

These buttonholes are not made until garment is finished. This allows an exact spacing of buttonholes, counting by rows. Mark where each buttonhole is to be and the width of buttonhole. Using small stitches, double machine stitch the size and shape of buttonhole and cut between stitches and buttonhole stitch edges with yarn.

CONTRAST COLOR BUTTONHOLES

These get their name from the manner in which they are knitted in.

Beginning on right side of garment, work to the spot for buttonhole. With a short piece of contrasting colored yarn, work the number of stitches required for buttonhole. Slip these contrast colored stitches

Fig. 93

back on left hand needle. With original yarn, knit across these contrast colored stitches and balance of row (Fig. 93). Continue in pattern.

Don't pull contrast colored yarn out of all stitches before finishing. It is easier to work if you remove the contrast colored yarn from one stitch at a time, as needed when sewing. Finish with yarn and overcast as in Figs. 94 and 95.

These buttonholes can also be finished with crochet. Without removing contrast colored yarn, work around buttonhole with yarn in slip stitch or single crochet. Be sure they are worked in the proper tension to make correct size buttonholes since slip stitch will not stretch. Remove colored yarn.

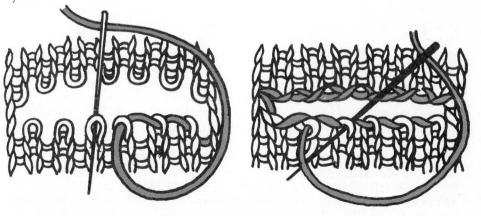

Fig. 94   **Fig. 95**

KNITTED BIAS OR BOUND BUTTONHOLES

This particular manner of finishing buttonholes would be used only where the extra thickness of a bias strip would be satisfactory for the garment, where heavy garments use large buttons and where the fabric lining of coat must be cut to make buttonhole (Fig. 96). Should the inside of the coat not have a yarn facing, yarn finishing does not cover raw edges of fabric satisfactorily. The bias or bound buttonholes, which would cover both pieces, are excellent here.

If yarn used in garment makes too thick a bias strip, try splitting the yarn, using a finer matching yarn or a suitable contrast yarn. The number of stitches needed for width will depend upon the weight of the yarn. Any width bias strip can be made. For pattern instructions for bias facings, see page 29.

FINISHING

On applying bias strip to buttonhole, I would probably put the joining at the center bottom of buttonhole where it would be less noticeable, although you may place it at the top center or at the corner away

Fig. 96

from the border edge. Should one side of a bias strip be less wide than the other, place the more narrow on the inside of garment.

If length of strip is exactly right, I sometimes find it easier to weave ends together as flat and neatly as possible before sewing to outside edge of buttonhole. Sew with yarn or thread. Turn garment to wrong side and sew other half with yarn or thread, depending upon inside material.

ABOUT YARNS

BASIC WEIGHTS OF YARNS AND NEEDLE RANGE

If the size needle to be used for a yarn is not stated, the following table will be helpful in selecting a beginning needle to make a swatch to secure gauge.

WEIGHT OF YARN	SIZE NEEDLES	GAUGE (Stitches per inch)
3 ply yarns	1, 2, 3	9, 8, 7
Sport	4, 5, 6	6-1/2, 6, 5-1/2
Knitting worsted	7, 8, 9, 10	5-1/2, 5, 4-1/2, 4
Bulky	10, 10-1/2, 11	4, 3-1/2, 3
Gigantic	13, 15	3, 2-1/2
Jet (3 strands knitting worsted or its equivalent)	17, 18, 19	2
(4 strands knitting worsted or its equivalent)	35	1-1/2
(6 to 7 strands knitting worsted or its equivalent)	50	1

After some experience in knitting, you will be able to come close to selecting the correct weight classification of a yarn by checking its thickness and elasticity.

Many yarns are not named under the specific weights above but all will fall into these divisions and corresponding gauges. When you can pick up a yarn and say, "This will knit to 4-1/2 sts per inch, probably on a No. 9 needle", you have made a good start in learning to substitute yarns.

The weight classifications of yarns are much easier to learn than selecting the size needle for correct gauge on a specific yarn. The final decision on needle size is always determined by making a swatch.

For a garment to fit, proper gauge must be obtained.

I am always amazed at persons who must knit on a specific size needle, as a No. 10. They really don't care if the yarn is the right weight, if the garment fits or not—just that they knit on this one size only.

Often knitters misunderstand the need and do not wish to change sizes of needles to get gauge because they think it will take longer, look different and make more knitting.

KNITNOTE: IT REALLY DOESN'T MATTER WHAT SIZE THE NEEDLES ARE NUMBERED. For example if 5 sts = 1" is the gauge for a particular yarn, YOU WILL NOT KNIT ANY MORE STITCHES WHEN YOU OBTAIN THIS GAUGE, WHETHER USING A 6, 7, OR 8 OR ANY SIZE NEEDLE YOUR INDIVIDUAL KNITTING REQUIRES.

SUBSTITUTING YARNS

YOU MUST HAVE A SUBSTITUTE YARN THAT WILL KNIT TO THE SAME GAUGE AS THE PATTERN INDICATES.

There are several ways to learn this:

1. From yarn charts of individual companies or a chart listing all major yarn companies' yarns, available from a needlework magazine.

2. By purchasing a small quantity of the yarn to be substituted and making a swatch to determine gauge.

3. From a long experience in the yarn business which knitters and unfortunately many sales personnel do not have.

4. By teaching yourself to inspect a yarn, read the label and estimate its possible gauge on Stockinette stitch. You will have a choice of about three sizes of needles to obtain gauge.

YARDAGE METHOD OF SUBSTITUTING

YOU MUST KNOW AMOUNT OF YARDAGE OF THE ORIGINAL YARN AND THE AMOUNT OF YARDAGE IN THE SUBSTITUTING YARN.

ALTHOUGH AN ESTIMATE OF THE NUMBER OF BALLS OR SKEINS OF A PARTICULAR YARN FOR A BASIC GARMENT IS USUALLY KNOWN, WHEN SUBSTITUTING, THE NUMBER OF OUNCES OR GRAMS IS IMMATERIAL IF YOU DON'T HAVE ENOUGH YARDS OF YARN TO KNIT GARMENT.

Yarns are sold by weight and the yardage on a 2 oz. skein can be anywhere from 32 to 280 yards. NO ONE CAN GUARANTEE AN EXACT SUBSTITUTION OR AMOUNT OF YARDAGE FOR SUBSTITUTION, but I have never had a knitter run out of yarn with the yardage method of substituting.

SUBSTITUTING MULTIPLE STRANDS OF YARN

Combinations of two or more weights of yarn are often used to substitute one weight of another yarn.

A definite size of needle and gauge can not be specified because of the different kinds and brands of yarns but I use the following table as a guide, along with making the necessary swatch, to secure the thickness of yarn and gauge I wish.

COMBINATIONS	RESULTS
2 strands 3 ply yarn	1 sport
2 strand sport	1 knitting worsted
2 knitting worsted	1 bulky
3 knitting worsted	1 gigantic
1 bulky and 1 knitting worsted	1 gigantic
2 gigantic	1 medium jet
3 bulky	1 medium jet
5 or 6 knitting worsted	1 jet
Or any combination to make same weight as 6 knitting worsted	1 jet

YARN CONTENTS

For contents of yarn, read label (see Manual, page 8) which gives you all the information you need to decide if this is the yarn you want, how it will be handled and how it will be maintained.

DIFFERENT CONTENT DIFFERENT NEEDLES

Unless you are a tight knitter, one size smaller needle is usually used when knitting synthetics. To be sure, make a swatch.

In jet knitting it has been my experience to use one size smaller needle or where the sizes of needles would jump from a 50 which is too large to a 35 which would be too small, select one size smaller garment and use the larger needle. Most of the complaints from the sizes of jet patterns have been because they turned out too big.

Be sure tension gives yarn a good "bounce" to hold shape and make your jet swatch 6" square. Read special instructions that come with your jet patterns.

WASHING AND CLEANING OF KNITS

Should knits be washed or dry cleaned? What about lined garments?

Knits can be washed so long as they do not have grease spots in them. Washing will not take grease out and moth dearly love this. If there is any doubt that the soil is grease, have knits dry cleaned. If you wish to block knits yourself, specify "cleaning only." Otherwise, cleaner will do blocking. After two or three years of dry cleaning, many knits do not look "bright". Then wash them.

Lined garments must be dry cleaned for they cannot be hand-washed and hand-blocked effectively.

How do you handle the synthetics, orlons and acrylics? Most of the questions today concern the blocking and maintenance of synthetics. The easiest and best way to handle these is to wash and dry them by machine. They should resume their original shape as knitted. However, if blocked heavily, they may not return to original shape. If removed from dryer just before completely dry, some shaping can be done and drying finished on top of dryer. Some additional blocking after drying can be done if desired.

Why do 50/50 yarns stretch so? The half nylon and half wool yarns have been pretty much replaced with the synthetics and acrylics. When you block half-and-half, be sure yarn is ENTIRELY dry before it is picked up. It will stretch terribly if not dry and will hold shape very well if completely dry. This is one combination of yarn that can be very much out of shape and when wet, worked back to size.

Fisherman and mohair yarns are washed and handled like wool. If you wish to fluff up the mohair, place it in a dryer on cold air for a few minutes or hang outdoors when a good breeze is blowing.

Angora is washed as follows: All washing and rinsing is done in tepid water. Wash in pure soap flakes and rinse three times. Remove excess moisture. Lay out to shape. Before completely dry, pick up two or three times and shake well to fluff up.

Machine washable wool yarns are excellent and can be maintained as advertised. My experience with these seems to indicate these yarns are a little thinner than the same weights in wool and we use needles one size smaller to get gauge.

Mixing wool and synthetic content can be done to use up yarns but I don't believe I would do this as a regular practice.

In jet knitting, there may be all kinds of content and you can mix as many kinds and colors of yarn as you wish but you must remember if any of the material is not machine washable it will have to be washed by hand or dry cleaned.

What do you tell the dry cleaners about your knits? Check to be sure your cleaner "measures" your knits before and after dry cleaning. Take yarn label with you or tell him yarn content or anything unusual about the handling of this yarn and if there should be any change in size when blocking. If not, inform him that garment is exactly right as is and be specific about the measurements.

The dry cleaner will wish to give you good service but if garment does not retain shape and gets too big or too long, it often is not the cleaner's fault, but that the knitting has not been done with enough tension to hold shape. It is wise to select a cleaner that works with hand knits and pay a higher fee, if necessary, to get special handling.

When having knitted coats cleaned, remember they are soft and heavy and may not retain their initial shape and drop in length. Coats may have to be shortened because of the loosening of the stitches during cleaning. We have coats that have been shortened three times, partly because of the change in fashion and partly from the cleaning.

BLOCKING

WHAT IS BLOCKING?

It is the use of water, hot (steam) or cold, to shape yarns or materials necessary to make knitted fabric.

SHOULD YOU KNIT TO FIT OR BLOCK TO FIT?

By all means knit to fit and all the garment will need is a little steaming. However, if garment must be either too small or too large, it is better to be a little small and it can be blocked out. You cannot successfully block in a too large garment.

WHO DOES THE BLOCKING?

Blocking of the completed garment can be done by professional knitters or at dry cleaning establishments or, if you wish to do blocking yourself, pieces should be blocked separately by hand before assembling. After assembling, seams are lightly steamed flat to complete the finishing of garment.

TO BLOCK PIECES BY HAND

SIZE OF PIECES

If your instructions do not tell you the exact measurements of the pieces, figure the measurements by taking the number of stitches at any place on piece and dividing by stitch gauge for inches in width. Your pattern will tell you length in inches.

WHAT DO YOU BLOCK ON?

Any flat piece of material can be used that is large enough, moisture will not damage and will not stain knitting. I often place a piece of clean cloth, like a sheet, between knitting and blocking board.

I have used pieces of wallboard or cardboard carton for hand blocking. The carton pieces are very good since they are easy to stick pins into and are disposable. The ironing board is excellent for small pieces. Special blocking canvas cloths are available and are conveniently marked with lines and squares for easy measuring and shaping.

KNOW YOUR YARNS BEFORE BLOCKING

To learn about yarns, their content and care, read page 41.

Fisherman, mohair and wool yarns are all handled and blocked in the same manner.

Angora is seldom blocked.

Vinyon is a content. If yarn contains more than 10% vinyon, beware in blocking that garment may shrink.

I used a lovely bulky yarn that contained vinyon and written instructions said, "Does not need blocking." It should have said, "Do not block." In the process of blocking (with steam), it was quite a shock to see the sweater shrink before my eyes—about two sizes smaller.

Whenever instructions say, "Does not need blocking.", I interpret this as, you can block if you wish to, but it isn't necessary. I prefer all my knits blocked, including souffles, orlons, etc. However, if I did not have the equipment available for blocking, I would lightly steam seams only on the wrong side. NEVER rest hot iron on these materials. I think of treating them like fine rayon fabric that can so easily be marked and ruined with heat.

PREPARATION FOR BLOCKING

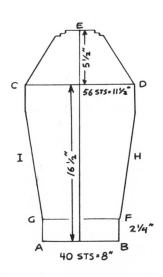

Fig. 97

Fig. 98

All pieces are pinned to shape before blocking (Fig. 98).

Pins should be close enough together and placed parallel with the edges of the piece to eliminate dips or scallops along the edge (Fig. 97).

If knitting is soiled, wash, using one of the detergents specifically for wool or pure soap flakes. If you think washing will not take out all the soil or spots, have the garment dry cleaned.

TO DO YOUR OWN BLOCKING

Pieces should be laid right side down if an iron is to be used in the blocking.

Always remember that if yarn is wet or even damp, it will drop and stretch out of shape from its own weight and should not be lifted up until it is entirely dry.

Whether or not you block the ribbing on a sweater depends on the style of the garment and the preference of the person who is going wear it.

HOW TO BLOCK PIECES BEFORE ASSEMBLING

Blocking can be done in several different ways. Some are:

1. Use a dry cloth and steam iron.

2. Or, a wet cloth, well rung out, and dry iron.

3. Or, spray with water mist. I use this method for hand blocking, using pieces of carton for a blocking base. This is excellent for those who do not have a place or room to lay pieces on table, bed or floor until dry. Use large enough pieces of carton for each piece of knitting. Draw outline of correct measurements on cardboard. Pin corners first and then evenly space edges around outline.

Using a clean spray bottle containing water, spray lightly the pinned pieces. Feel the knitting with your hand. Yarn should not be wet but only damp enough to dry into shape. Stand pieces of carton out of your way, but not on top of each other, and let dry overnight. Assemble pieces and steam seams lightly with steam iron and dry cloth.

HOW TO BLOCK KNITS AFTER ASSEMBLED

In blocking assembled knits, wet the entire garment. Remove as much water as possible by rolling in towels to absorb moisture. Keep knitting very close together under your hands so it will not stretch.

1. Lay flat and shape between two towels. Do not remove until entirely dry.

2. Or, lay flat on towel. Pin to shape and let dry.

3. Or, quick dry on a nylon net sweater dryer. This is a net on a metal frame raised off the table which allows knits to have all sides exposed to the air. This quick dryer comes in two sizes and can be purchased at yarn and notion departments.

RIBBON

GROSGRAIN

Grosgrain ribbon is applied and sewed in the same manner whether (1) for reinforcing for buttonholes, (2) used for facing edges or (3) sewed for outside trim.

PREPARING RIBBON

Ribbons that are all nylon or rayon are ready to use. Grosgrain and any other ribbon that contains cotton or a material that might shrink when washed should be preshrunk before using. To do this:

1. Wet thoroughly and iron dry.

2. Or, if by any chance ribbon is soiled, wash and iron dry.

3. Or, iron using steam iron only. Sometimes this is satisfactory but I have had some steam-ironed ribbons still shrink after washing.

SHOULD GARMENT BE BLOCKED BEFORE RIBBON IS APPLIED?

I personally prefer to have garment completely finished before blocking. I do not block pieces, except some ribbon knit dresses. However, if you have sources for blocking, learn their preference.

If you are going to do all the finishing yourself, it would be easier for you to block the pieces before assembling, BEING VERY CAREFUL ON CARDIGAN FRONTS THAT YOU DO NOT STRETCH THE EDGES.

SHOULD EDGES BE CROCHETED?

It depends on the edge. On any pattern stitch that creates a rough edge, the crochet will give an even and firm edge to sew to.

On Stockinette stitch, without crochet, the edge stitch will usually roll to the wrong side when faced with ribbon which eliminates any rough edge and will lay flat and block well.

Ribbed edges are not crocheted.

FITTING RIBBON (Fig. 99)

Garment should be completely knitted and assembled.

Lay garment flat on table so shoulders are even. Allow any extra length from borders to fall below edge of back (A). This will show you how much extra length must be eased under ribbon. Usually the edge of the sweater is from 1-1/2" to 5" longer than correct length for ribbon (C to D).

Ends of ribbon will have turn under of 3/4" to 1" (C and D). Pin one turned under end below top row at neck (C). Lift bottom edge of sweater and lay parallel to bottom edge of back (D). Measure ribbon flat to bottom edge of back, turn under ribbon and pin one row from bottom (D).

THIS IS WHERE MOST PEOPLE MAKE THEIR MISTAKE WHEN FITTING RIBBON. Ribbon should not be the length of the border (A to C) BUT SHOULD BE THE LENGTH OF THE FRONT EDGES FROM THE TOP OF NECK TO THE BOTTOM EDGE OF BACK (C to D). Don't worry about the excess material in between for it will all ease in and yarn will steam in flat.

Ribbed borders knitted along with the sweater are often quite long on the edges and although it looks as if the stitches could never be eased in, they can be but it is slow and tedious work.

Beginning at the middle of ribbon and edge of knitting (E), pin ribbon to edges until all stitches have been evenly eased in. If edge is crocheted, pin ribbon along bottom of last row crocheted. If edge is not crocheted, pin ribbon along edge of knitting. Pin ribbon to other border edge in same manner.

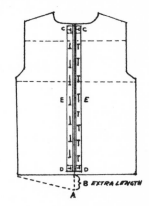

Fig. 99

Try sweater on owner of garment, if possible, to see that front edges are not too short or too long and that bottom corner of sweater hangs square. Should sweater be for a person who takes up length in the front of garment, allow 1" to 2" more in the ribbon length. To refit, remove all pins except top one and pin as before. Keep repeating this until fit is correct. Cut off any excess length of ribbon.

If you work the button side border first, you may have to do it again because borders may not match in length since the stitching on the buttonhole side often shortens the border by 1/4" to 1/2".

Therefore, work the buttonhole side first (right front for women and left front for men). Then fit and sew button side border same length.

IF THERE ARE HORIZONTAL PATTERN STITCHES, STRIPES OR COLORS IN GARMENT, BE SURE THEY MATCH ON FRONT EDGES BEFORE SEWING.

SEWING RIBBON

Using regular sewing needle and thread in color to match YARN, sew by hand.

On Stockinette stitch some knitters leave the inside edge free but I prefer to always sew around all four sides of ribbon.

Begin sewing right front at top neck edge (C) and left front at bottom edge (D). When outside edge is sewed, lay piece flat and pin inside edge of ribbon along entire length. Be sure that horizontal line of stitches are straight into ribbon. Check this frequently as you sew.

Stitches are sewed (Fig. 100) in each nub on edges (every other **row**) and in each stitch horizontally. To hide thread, I run the needle through the top of yarn between stitches. Make stitches in ribbon on the very edge.

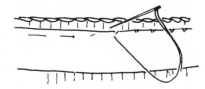

Fig. 100

About every other stitch, when you bring your thread through ribbon, place another small stitch in the same spot. This will lock the thread in and if it should break, ribbon facing will not fall off.

RIBBON AS TRIM

If using ribbon on outside as a trim, as when altering a pullover into a cardigan, fit ribbon, baste and machine stitch on outside edges. If button-holes are to be made, stitch them on the outside.

When sweaters are trimmed with ribbon, braid, beads, sequins, embroideries, etc., the ribbon is often the base for this trim. Since flat ribbon will not stretch or shape itself, as around a neck, to fit and sew, keep garment flat on table and sew the bottom edge first, then ease in top edge around neck or gather where necessary.

USE OF NETTING

This comes in different sizes and content and is used to reinforce knits that are sheer and luxurious where grosgrain ribbon would be too heavy and show through to the outside. The number of thicknesses of netting will depend on the garment. It can be cut and sewed to shaped edges, as for scallops.

RIBBONS FOR HANDKNITTING

Ribbon yarns can be knitted or crocheted. Knitting may be done in combinations of ribbon and yarn. Crocheting can be done regular, afghan stitch or hair pin lace.

Most of these ribbons come in spools of 100 yards each and are 3/16" and 1/4" in width. They are made of rayon, silk, organdy or combinations of these—often interwoven with metallics in gold, silver and colors.

Ribbon is not easy to work with. It is not for beginners. Ribbon is just a different medium—a material that has to be handled in a different manner but can be learned with patience.

The success of several of the stitches depends on special handling. Recent patterns have been designed to eliminate the necessity of keeping ribbon flat. However, those companies putting out ribbon patterns will indicate manner in which stitches are to be made, whether the ribbon must be kept flat, and whether it must always have the same side of ribbon on top.

The easiest patterns in ribbon are those alternating two rows of ribbon and two rows of yarn, such as dress yarns, light weight mohairs, sport and sometimes knitting worsted.

Although not in fashion at this time, a silk organdy ribbon garment, crocheted or in hair pin lace, is probably the most fragile, luxurious and beautiful garment one could own.

Swatches for ribbon should be made larger than for yarns and blocked before measuring gauge. Often after correct gauge is determined, ribbons can be knitted by rows instead of measuring inches.

Be patient with ribbon and give yourself plenty of time to practice before starting a garment.

ZIPPERS

PREPARATION AND SEWING

Zippers for knits I put in by hand. Edges should have a row of single crochet. Ease in edges of yarn to zipper and pin. Zipper must not be "rippled". If in doubt as to fit, baste and try on.

To sew, back stitch on the right side of garment, immediately under the two threads of the top of crochet stitch. I use a double strand of sewing thread, the weight depending on the garment. When finished, turn garment to wrong side. Tuck under top ends of zipper and overcast edges to knitting.

IN CARDIGAN OR JACKET SWEATERS

It is better to have a too short zipper than a too long one. Fit it correctly at top and allow any extra length on front edges to hang free.

Often there are 1″ to 2″ at the bottom edges not covered by the zipper and this is quite satisfactory for wearing.

IN DRESSES OR SWEATERS

In the back of a garment, do not worry if the zipper is longer than opening. To stop zipper at bottom of neck opening, sew over the teeth several times. Let any excess from zipper hang free on inside.

IN SKIRTS

Zippers do not go into skirt seams well on yarn only.

Seam should be (1) faced with grosgrain and zipper stitched by machine; or (2) if skirt is to be lined, treat the material like regular fabric and finish or have finished by a good seamstress.

COATS

Coats are easy to make and wonderful to wear. Hesitant knitters say, "Oh, I could never make a coat! I'd never get it done!" I think of coats as long sweaters and the only difference between the knitting of coats and sweaters is about 10″ to 12″ of straight pattern stitch on the bottom of the back and fronts. They are easy to do, have little shaping to make and don't take much time.

My policy in making coats is this: They should be knitted with sufficient tension and in a pattern stitch that pieces will hold their shape.

If material is so fragile and thin that it requires netting, underlining, iron-on materials, finishing should be done by an experienced seamstress.

In this instance, treat the knitted pieces entirely as fabric and assemble as any fabric garment.

Most knitters wish to do their own work and it is also difficult to find a seamstress who knows how to handle hand knits.

To me all the softness and loveliness of the knits is lost if stiff reinforcing and machine work is necessary. I never machine sew knits together (exceptions: alterations and one ribbon dress). Even if front borders and occasionally across the back of the shoulders needs reinforcing, I hand-sew seams to give the elasticity and flexibility the knitted fabric needs for good fitting.

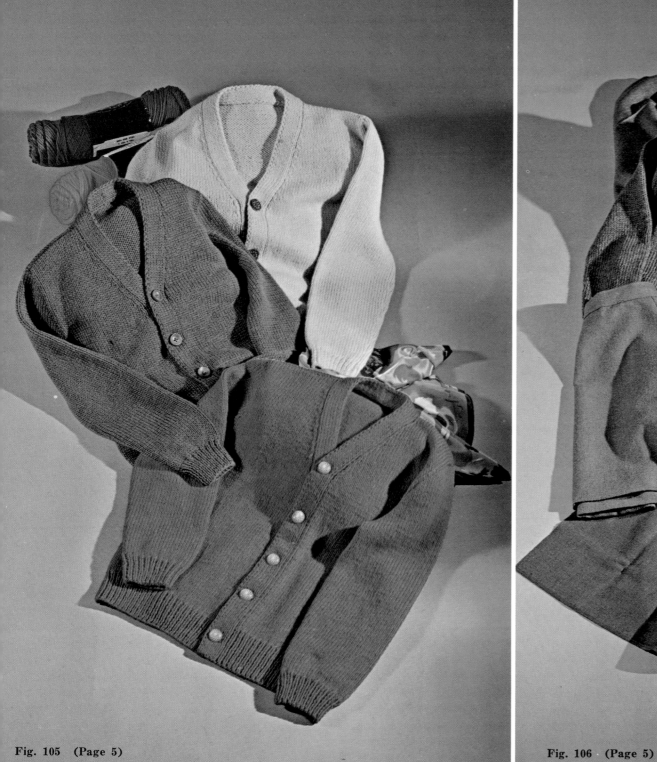

Fig. 105 (Page 5)

Fig. 106 . (Page 5)

Fig. 107   (Page 92)

Fig. 108   (Page 92)

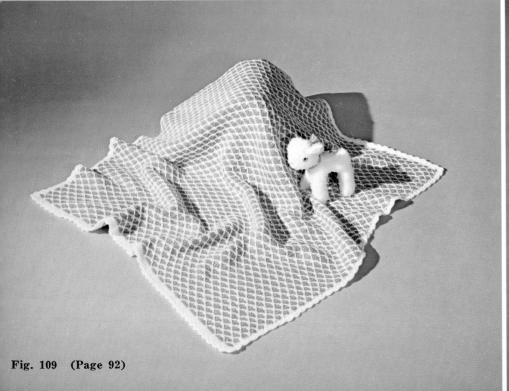

Fig. 109   (Page 92)

Fig. 110   (Page 96)

Fig. 111 (Pages 97-98-99)

Fig. 112 (Page 93)

Fig. 113 (Page 94)

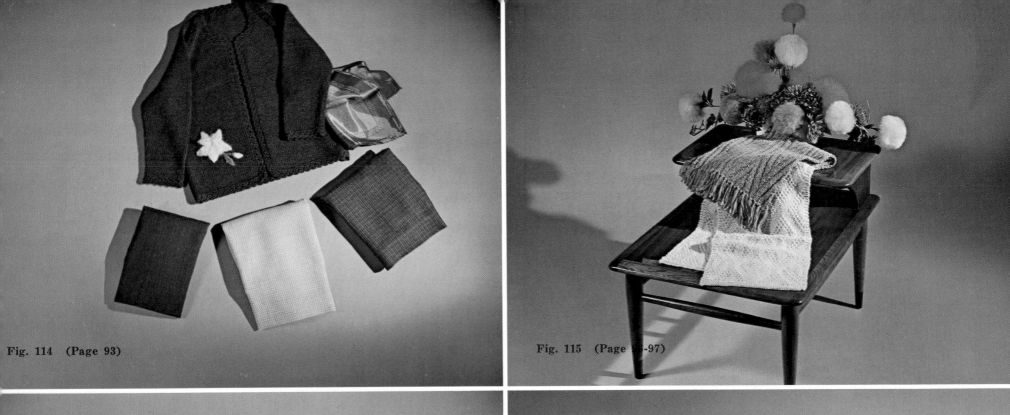

Fig. 114   (Page 93)

Fig. 115   (Page 96-97)

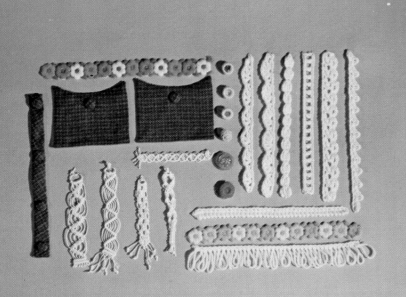

Fig. 116   (Page 94)

Fig. 117   (Page 96)

WIDTH (GAUGE) OF COAT

If you have already learned the contents of the Knitting Manual and Book 2 up to this point, you have the knowledge to pick the correct size coat for you and to knit to gauge for the proper width of the garment.

However, I believe the old saying, "Forewarned is forearmed" applies to knitting all the time. Anything I can do or learn not to make mistakes, I do. By telling you some of the extreme things that happen, what to watch for and how you can adjust your knitting for excellent results, will make you more aware of probable and possible problems and save much time and energy eliminating errors before they happen.

I must tell you about a coat that was brought to me by a knitter who several months before had purchased one of the very best yarns available for the coat. She called to ask if the pieces should be blocked before assembling. I suggested that she baste the pieces together and bring them in for me to be sure coat was not too long. I had not seen a swatch, checked measurements nor had anything to do with the coat. It is my policy that the knitter decide, at the time of purchase of yarn, if they want supervision or not. If they do, then I wish to see the pieces at specific times during the knitting, which eliminates about 99% of any problems.

Most yarn shops are very unhappy if knitters do leave their shop with a poorly made knit, not finely finished. The best shops pride themselves and build their business on top quality results. They will literally knock themselves out for you but YOU must ask for instruction, information and show up at their place of business for any instruction needed. It is very difficult and most of the time impossible to give knitting instructions over the telephone.

As the coat knitter came through the door, she remarked, "I think this coat is a catastrophe!" Her coat was the correct length but it was so wide both of us could have done a dance in it. In a way it was funny but still so tragic and so unnecessary.

Why was it so big? She was afraid of stretching the yarn! How can anyone expect to make a knitted fabric without having tension on the yarn?

Her gauge called for 4-1/2 sts to 1" and she knitted it 3 sts to 1". You might think by looking at the yarn and gauge that a No. 8 or 9 needle would be used but this is not basic yarn and a No. 6 needle is the correct size, as pattern designated.

In this case, there was no possibility of even altering the garment and the tension was so loose that if the pieces had been wet (the way some people block), they would have dropped at least one-fourth their length. Pieces were unravelled, kinks steamed out of yarn and coat re-knitted.

Why did this occur?

First, although the needle size designated was correct, this could have been an example of a pattern that did not indicate the correct needle to get gauge, since she felt she must use a No. 9 instead of a No. 6 needle.

Or, second, as I believe, swatch was not measured correctly. A swatch on knitting worsted showed that she could knit evenly (which she did not do on coat), with a normal tension and should use needle size indicated in pattern OR PERHAPS ONE SIZE SMALLER THAN PATTERN MIGHT CALL FOR TO GET GAUGE.

Third, garment should have been measured at SECOND CHECK POINT at bottom of back. ANYTIME A GARMENT IS TOO WIDE WHEN FROM 4" TO 8" AT THE BOTTOM ON BACK, FOR GOODNESS SAKE, STOP! THE WIDTH OF THE GARMENT MUST BE CORRECT OR THE PROPER LENGTH IS IMMATERIAL. You must get the correct stitch gauge and with sufficient tension to make good knitted fabric—not limp and loose but one that springs back and holds its shape.

LENGTH OF COATS

Usually when you say a coat, you think LONG. I think of a coat as being a long sweater which makes me think SHORT. This will help to guard against knitting "too long", which is the most frequent error in knitting coats.

Since most coats are raglan or set-in sleeves, proper length to be knitted and then blocked to finished length can be determined.

However, I cannot tell you exactly how much to allow for dropping because this is determined entirely by the pattern stitch and the tension you use in working.

Characteristics of stitches also will be a factor in length, like Stockinette stitch or patterns built on it which have a tendency to drop; ribbings and cabled patterns which not only drop but become more narrow; Seed stitch which can spread both in width and depth; and Garter stitch which spreads in width.

If you feel that there is any chance of your pieces dropping more than 1" to 2", try either of the following before assembling:

(1) If tension is medium or loose, and IF YOU ARE CAREFUL NOT TO STRETCH THE EDGES and keep the correct width, fronts and back can be blocked down until the "drop" is out of pieces. I have seen coats be as much as 10" too long. One was knitted so loosely that I could almost put my little finger through the stitches. But whether 1" or 10", it is still too long. This means that you may have to shorten at the bottom and knit facings on again before assembling. But it is better to save future time and energy and to correct this here than to finish the entire coat and find it unwearable.

(2) Another idea some knitters use is to fasten the top edges of knitted pieces to a hanger or baste entire coat together and allow to hang for several days, which will allow the knitting to drop from its own weight.

KNITNOTE: DO GUARD AGAINST OVERCOMPENSATING

AND DO NOT KNIT PIECES TOO SHORT.

Be aware that sometimes the neck edges of coats are quite loose and large but in finishing and lining such coats, they are held in and pulled up to fit, thus taking up some length. In planning your particular coat pattern, if this should be a factor, make allowance in the length.

TO MEASURE FOR FINISHED LENGTH OF COAT

Since lengths of garments change annually fashionwise and individual taste varies greatly, YOU decide the length coat you want.

Ladies, if you wish a correct measurement, please wear a dress (with girdle if you wear one) or a coat that is the size and length you wish for your finished knit. It is impossible, as well as unfair, to ask anyone to take measurements for dresses, suits and coats if you are wearing slacks or shorts.

(1) Measure from bone at back of neck to length desired.

(2) Or, if the knitter has a straight fabric coat she likes, measure the coat while on knitter from the top center of neck seam (no collar included) to bottom of coat.

(3) Or, have knitter wear a dress which is the desired length, and add 1″ to 2″ for the finished length of coat.

These measurements do NOT include any hem facings.

TO DETERMINE ACTUAL LENGTH OF PIECES TO BE KNITTED

If knitting is on gauge and with good tension, I usually allow 1″ to 2″ for blocking. If more than 2″ is allowed for blocking, pieces had better be blocked before assembling, because after being sewed the side seams often will not want to block down this much and will pull and pucker, while the fronts and back hang longer.

TO DETERMINE THE LENGTH OF ARMHOLE PLUS
SHOULDER SHAPING (Set-in sleeves)

We must first find out the depth of the armhole, plus the rows for shoulder shaping. With set-in sleeves, of course, you already have the measurement in inches from your pattern up to the beginning of the shoulder shaping. From the beginning of the shoulder shaping through the bind-off row of back of neck can usually be figured to be 1″.

TO DETERMINE HOW MANY INCHES TO KNIT TO ARMHOLE

We know the total length of coat. To learn measurement from beginning of armhole shaping to top, we will add the depth of armhole and shoulder shaping and subtract this amount from the total length of piece.

EXAMPLE: Finished coat length desired	37″
Actual knitting on coat length as on back, less 2″ for blocking	35″
Armhole depth per instructions	9″
Shoulder shaping	1″

Deducting the total length above armhole (10″) from the length to be knitted (35″), measurement to underarm shaping will be 25″. This method automatically takes care of any height person and any length coat desired.

TO DETERMINE THE DEPTH OF A RAGLAN ARMHOLE

Do not measure along raglan shaping (seam edge) for armhole measurement. Depth of armhole is always measured straight up about one-third across first bound-off row of armhole.

Since the row gauge varies with different knitters and the measurement for depth of armhole is not given in the instructions, it is necessary to learn the actual vertical depth of this armhole by counting the rows.

To learn this, count the number of rows worked and divide by the row gauge which gives the depth of armhole in inches.

EXAMPLE: Row gauge — 6 rows = 1″	
Coat finished length	37″
Coat sections to be knitted	35″
Rows worked:	
Bound-off rows	2
Knit decrease rows	26
Purl rows	26
Total	54

Total rows (54) divided by row gauge (6) equals depth of armhole (9″).

Coat length to be 37″ finished. Coat to be knitted, less 2″ for blocking is 35″. Subtract 9″ for armhole which leaves 26″ as the length to be knitted to armhole shaping.

KNITTING AND CHECKING GAUGE ON BACK OF COAT

Pick your coat size. Make swatches until proper gauge is secured. Work in pattern on back of coat until 4″ above hemline. Check width measurement. If too wide or too narrow, make any adjustments in pattern, needle size, tension, etc., or if necessary, start again. Work until 8″ above hemline and measure again. By this time, sufficient knitting has been done to assume this is your normal knitting, pieces are correct in width and a true count of your number of rows per inch can now be made. This row gauge will be important to figure length of raglan armhole patterns and if you are knitting by rows per inch.

To secure row gauge, measure vertically over at least a 4″ area. Using knitting worsted as an example, it is usually about 6 rows to 1″. However, your yarn, row gauge and knitting may be different, so measure YOUR work. Halves and quarters of rows are important. Don't round off the number of rows per inch. EXAMPLE: When 25 rows equals 4″, 6-1/4 rows equals 1″, not 6 rows per inch. If working by rows and this one-fourth row was ignored, there would be a difference of 1″ to 2″ in length of coat.

FINISHING COATS

I prefer to make double facing on front edges; knit in buttonholes; reinforce front with pellon or Veriform; and after lining, cut out material at buttonholes and finish edges of buttonholes with yarn. Sew on buttons.

LININGS

Should knits be lined? This is a matter of personal preference.

It has always been my policy NOT to do anything more to knits than necessary.

You can do much to keep your knits in good shape if when you sit down, you pull the knit up a little at back and ease the knit up across top of knees to take the pressure off the skirt.

Special foundations for knits and taffeta or rayon slips are available to wear under knits and will not only protect your knits but allow them to hang better.

TO LINE KNITS

When we speak of lining knits, we mean the finishing of all kinds and styles of garments, their lining, underlining, interlining and interfacing.

A LINING is made separately from the knitted garment and although lining will help to preserve the shape of the knit, it has nothing to do with the body or firmness of the knitted fabric.

Lining makes a garment more beautiful, eliminates the need for fine finishing on the inside of knitted pieces, keeps the yarn from direct contact with the skin, helps prevent unnecessary stretching of the knitted fabric and will eliminate the rubbing or sticking of the yarn to clothing.

INTERFACING is cut in the shape of and placed between facing and outside of garment to give body and shape and to support areas such as fronts of coats, collars, etc.

UNDERLINING (which has nothing to do with the lining) is a backing or second layer under the knit, cut to fit the pieces and catch stitched to each piece before assembling. This is to give body and create shape, to prevent stretching, the pulling of the knitted fabric, the pulling of seams, to hide seams and to prevent sagging of the knits.

INTERLINING is used only for added warmth and can be made as one with the lining or made separately and then attached to lining.

COATS

We line practically all coats because it makes them much more attractive, nicer to wear and easier to slip on and off over clothing.

MATERIALS FOR LININGS: These should have enough body to drape and hold their shape since they hang and are not sewed into seams. You may select any lining you like but I prefer peau du soie and miliums for medium to light weight coats. For a heavy winter coat, a good lining is a rayon satin fabric backed with a cotton fleece, which comes in many attractive colors.

TO PREPARE FOR LINING COATS: Block individual pieces of garment. Cut a brown paper pattern of each knitted piece making the following allowances:

(1) ½" to 1" for seams
(2) A 2" box pleat in center back
(3) The depth of hem
(4) In raglan sleeves, two ½" pleats at top of each sleeve

SHOULDERS: Reinforce if needed. Ordinarily, these do not need to be reinforced but should shoulders sag or be too wide, shoulder seams can be pulled and held into shape by sewing on a woven edge seam binding (binding as used for hemming a skirt).

FRONT BORDERS: Interface. There are many satisfactory materials you can purchase in fabric shops to use for interfacing, such as Veriform, pellon, Formite, firm Super Siri, etc.

SLEEVES: No dart is needed at the elbow if sleeves are straight. Lining can be eased in a little and tacked along the underarm seam, which shaping takes the place of a dart.

UNDERLINING OF COATS

For sheer, fine, light weight knits or those that are loose and will not hold their shape, underlining can be used. Netting, Veriform, Si Bonne, Super Siri, pellon, silk or even nylon curtains are all good underlining materials.

Some knitters have bonded iron-on materials directly to knitted fabric. This makes the pieces heavier and stiffer and they will then need to be assembled as a fabric by machine stitching. I do not care for this finishing because the softness and elasticity of the handknit is lost.

TO UNDERLINE: With the netting or selected material, catch stitch underlining to knitted fabric over all pieces. Sew by machine. If underlining is cut to within ½" of edges, seams may be sewed by hand. Although this is a little more difficult to handle, it will give a little more elasticity to the garment.

An underlining is necessary where seams and raw edges of lining would show through, as on a thin white mohair coat.

TO LINE SKIRTS

Although I have never lined a knitted skirt, there are several ways to do this.

1. A knitted skirt can be lined and assembled as any other fabric with side zipper opening and machine stitched. Allow lining to hang free from hips down.

2. If lining is sewed into the seams, after dry cleaning I have seen sewing thread shrink and pucker the seams and the rest of the knitting sag and drop down so badly that the garment could not be worn again. Seams had been cut and trimmed like fabric which would not allow further alterations. Even with a finished edge on knitting, after being machine stitched, it is doubtful if seams could be undone safely since the yarn would be frayed or cut through by the sewing thread.

3. If an underlining is used, be sure it is dry cleanable. Some underlining materials are Veriform, Si Bonne, sheath lining, Super Siri and Formite. A new material called "thimble knit fabric" can be used for knits. It is made of rayon and will stretch to the sides but not up and

down. The direction of the stretch can be placed horizontally or vertically.

To LINE: For a two-piece skirt, catch stitch underlining to pieces and sew. Back of skirt only can be lined if desired.

4. For a circular skirt with elastic waistband, cut a shallow U-shape in the top edge of the lining on each side of skirt (Fig. 101). This will free enough of the elastic waistband to stretch and allow skirt to go over head or hips.

5. Some knitters buy a taffeta or rayon slip or knitted garment foundations and sew knitted skirt permanently to slip at the waistline. This is particularly helpful where a figure problem is present or where no pressure is wanted across the abdomen.

DRESSES

I personally do not like zippers in dresses or skirts and try to finish them in a manner that is satisfactory without them. A very successful dress is lined with Veriform and finished leaving the left side seam of lining open to allow dress to stretch enough to go over head and shoulders. Lining edges are closed with snaps.

Dresses can also be underlined and finished by machine stitching.

SWEATERS

Knitters frequently like their sweaters lined because it makes them much more luxurious, makes a handsome custom knit, helps to give sheer knitting shape and keeps yarns that might irritate from touching the skin.

MATERIALS: These should feel good to the skin. Crepes, Butterfly, chiffons, Whisper, sheath lining, silk organza, shantung, surah and prints or any of the new synthetic materials of similar nature are lovely.

TO LINE: Pattern for lining is cut and sewed in the same manner as for coats. Some linings are tacked at the bottom of the sweaters, some at top of ribbing and some not at all. Although cardigans usually look better if allowed to hang free at the bottom, it depends entirely on the style of sweater and bottom edge.

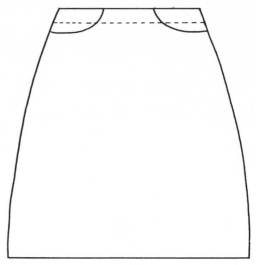

Fig. 101

BORDERS

MAKING VERTICAL BORDERS

On cardigan front edges there are four methods of making borders:
1. Knit borders and body at the same time in one piece.
2. Knit separate borders and sew them on.
3. Pick up edges and knit to width desired for borders.
4. Crochet borders.

The purpose of borders is not only for trim but to keep the edges of the garment flat, to keep bottom corners from sagging, to hold the knit into shape and if needed, to supply a base for buttons and buttonholes.

FINISHING KNITTED BORDERS AND BODY IN ONE PIECE

STOCKINETTE: This edge will have to be finished with ribbon, crocheted or knitted with double facing.

DOUBLE FACING: This is excellent for the Stockinette edge and sewing of facing and buttonholes gives fine results.

If garment instructions are not written to include double facings, and you wish to make this kind of border, you will cast on additional stitches in the amount of one stitch to slip for turning edge and one inch of stitches, as, with a gauge of 5 sts = 1″, a basic front would add a total of 6 sts.

Often, we have suits and double-breasted coats that have buttonholes much further from the edges than on a basic knit. For double facing, be sure to add sufficient stitches to allow room to make matching buttonholes plus 1″ of stitches for outside edge. It is much easier to knit these double facings than to reinforce with strips of ribbon or fabric. This facing would not be recommended for double-breasted garments using bulky or gigantic yarns.

For sewing facings, see page 28.

RIBBING AND SEED STITCH: These will usually be from 1-1/2″ to 3″ (sometimes 5″) longer than a corresponding number of rows of Stockinette stitch.

If using ribbon to shorten and hold ribbing in shape, it is a difficult job and can be done but results are not always satisfactory since edges may "crinkle" a little. Blocking will help some.

Slipping the first stitch at the beginning of the border edge (every other row) will help hold this in shape.

Or, the first stitch on border can be twisted by knitting or purling in the back of the stitch (Figs. 47 and 78).

CROCHETING: Finish on outside edges with sc or other pattern stitch, or, on wrong side work a slip stitch just under edge to hold the edge rigid.

SEPARATE BORDERS

Some borders are sewed up to the neck edge and stitches placed on a holder to be used later for ribbing around neck.

Some work the bottom ribbing and then separate border to neck edge.

Some of the knits use a one-piece border, up front, around neck and down other front. These can be knitted (1) in one long piece by casting on sufficient stitches for complete length of border and knitting for 1″ or width desired but this is difficult to accurately get correct lengths.

Or (2), it is easier to cast on the width of border and work back and forth, beginning the end with buttonholes first. Should there need to be any adjustment in length, this can be done from bound-off edge and will not disturb the buttonhole side. Always begin sewing at the buttonhole end of border.

WHY ARE BORDERS MADE SEPARATELY?

The nature of the stitches cause the edges of the border to stretch or spread more than the main pattern stitch.

Regardless of the size of yarn, needles, pattern, a too large or loose border, as happens with ribbing or seed stitch, border will be approximately 1-1/2″ to 2-1/2″ longer than a like section knitted in Stockinette stitch on the body of the garment. This, of course, defeats the purpose of the border which is to hold garment edge flat and in shape.

To eliminate this extra length, these borders should be separated from the top of bottom ribbing of garment, worked separately and sewed on. When your instructions say, "Knit your border up to the same length as the front of the garment", DO NOT MEASURE THE EDGE OF THE GARMENT because edge is invariably longer, stretched and rolled under to such a degree that a correct measurement could not be made. Measurements should be taken at least 3″ in from edge from bottom up to and even with first row of neck shaping. Make border equal to this length.

Pin border at bottom and even with top of neck shaping. Always easing in the middle of the sections first, pin and ease in edges to border in preparation for sewing. If bottom corner does not dip down into a point but hangs exactly square, you have the correct length. There may seem to be a lot of knitting to be fitted to the border but it will ease in as it is sewed and will block well.

SEPARATE V-NECK BORDER FOR PULLOVER

Cast on number of stitches required for around V-neck, beginning pattern at top of back left shoulder seam. This can be knitted working back and forth, mitering V and sewing ends together after knitting. Or, knit border on a circular needle mitering for V. Border is sewed to sweater in the same manner as for other separate borders.

SEWING SEPARATE BORDERS

RIBBING: These borders are usually assembled on the right side of garment by alternately picking up two threads on edge of body and edge of border, easing in any fullness from body edge. See Fig. 45.

Since this kind of seam can easily become rigid, pull sewing yarn up only until seam is closed, checking frequently the way border fits and the elasticity of the seam.

If this seam was overcast, it would spread and show sewing stitches.

If sewed with a back stitch, seam is much too thick and border has a tendency to flop open with wrong side out.

SEED STITCH: Handle in the same manner as ribbing border but there will not be as much extra length to ease in. If ribbon and machine buttonholes are used here, buttonholes can be made horizontally or vertically.

GARTER STITCH: This is an excellent opportunity to knit in horizontal buttonholes. No ribbon is necessary. However, if ribbon and machine buttonholes are to be used, in this instance, you may have to pull border DOWN to correct length for finished front border.

PICK UP AND KNIT BORDERS

Pick up stitches on edges (three out of four rows on edges and every stitch on horizontal rows), work and bind off in pattern. If buttonholes are to be knitted in, use the two middle rows of band.

CROCHET BORDERS
ON VERTICAL EDGES

Applying crochet to knits is an entirely different problem than doing crochet patterns. It must be done not too tight nor too loose. It should not be "hard".

Edges of a garment can be crocheted with many different kinds of pattern stitches (Fig. 116).

SINGLE CROCHET: Garments should have one row of single crochet (sc) to properly shape and size edges and provide a base for the trim.

SLIP STITCH: This stitch does not build in height and will not cover edges and should be used only along wrong side edge to hold piece in shape. Beware of working slip stitch too tight!

TO CROCHET BORDERS

If you do not know how to crochet, get a basic crochet manual and teach yourself.

You must know the following to finish knits:

1. Basic crochet stitches like, ch, sc, sl st, dec, sp, dec. skp, inc, yo, etc.

2. How many ch to make when turning at end of a row or a corner for your pattern.

3. How to ch and skp sts to make buttonhole.

TO CROCHET FRONT BORDER FOR BUTTONS

TO WORK: Crochet side for buttons first—left front for women, right front for men.

SIZE HOOK: Your pattern will give you a recommended size crochet hook although this will not necessarily be the size that is correct for you. I have often tried three sizes before finding the one that gives me the correct length of border.

If you have a tendency to work tight, buy sizes recommended plus the next two larger sizes. If you have a tendency to work loosely, buy recommended size plus the next two smaller sizes.

PATTERN STITCH: Single crochet (sc).

ROWS: Five on each border edge, last row right side, crochet left front beginning at neck and right front beginning at bottom.

OPTIONAL ROW 5: After 4th row, cut yarn and pull through last stitch. Join in first stitch of first row made an sc across end of border. Work 3 sc in corner, sc in each sc of previous row along border edge, 3 sc in corner and sc along end of border. This gives a much nicer, complete and finished appearance. Weave in ends.

WHERE TO MAKE STITCHES: Always crochet under two threads and in nubs (tight stitches).

HOW MANY STITCHES? This can be done in two ways.

1. I use a large enough hook that I can work a sc in each nub (every other row) and get my correct length.

2. Or, you can try this: *Work 1 sc in the first nub and 2 sc in the next nub. Repeat between *'s on edges.

LENGTH: KNITNOTE: THESE SINGLE CROCHET BORDERS (which should not be so tight they are rigid) WILL STRETCH DOWN IN BLOCKING. CROCHETED LENGTH SHOULD BE SHORTER THAN FINAL LENGTH AND EDGES WILL BE SLIGHTLY CURVED IN. (Fig. 102) AFTER BLOCKING, BORDER SHOULD BE EXACTLY RIGHT LENGTH AND CORNERS HANG SQUARE. AS YOU WORK, PULL EDGES DOWN TO SEE IF THEY WILL STRETCH CORRECTLY TO BLOCK TO RIGHT LENGTH.

TO CROCHET FRONT BORDER FOR BUTTONHOLES

Assuming you have knitted the same number of rows on right front edge, it is easy to space for buttons and buttonholes, working with the left front.

TO MARK FOR BUTTONHOLES: Place a pin horizontally in the center of a sc for a button at bottom and one at top of garment. BOTTOM EDGE OF BUTTON should be about ¾" to 1" from bottom edge. Top buttonhole should be about the third or fourth sc from top.

If you are using 6 buttons, count the number of sc on edge between top and bottom buttons. Subtract the number of buttonholes yet to be spaced (4 in this instance). Divide the remaining stitches by 5 (spaces). It if does not divide evenly, stagger the spacing as we did for increasing (Fig. 148). One sc difference between buttonholes will not be noticeable.

SIZE BUTTONHOLES: Unless on 3 ply or very fine yarn, I skip only one single crochet for a buttonhole. Many patterns call for skipping 2 sc, etc. Using knitting worsted and its correct size hook, you could use a button 1-½" wide in these. This makes the buttons much too large and the buttonholes much too loose.

Crocheted buttonholes require no finishing and have a great deal of stretch. Therefore, they can be smaller than in knitting.

TO WORK BUTTONHOLE BAND:

Row 1: 1 sc in each nub. Ch 1. Turn.

Row 2: 1 sc in each sc. Ch 1. Turn. Check length with left front. Make any adjustments to get same length.

Row 3: 1 sc in each sc up to spot for first buttonhole, ch 1, skp 1 sc *1 sc in each sc to next buttonhole, ch 1, skp 1 sc, repeat between *'s across row ending 1 sc in each sc. Ch 1. Turn.

Row 4: 1 sc in each sc and in each ch-1 sp.

Row 5: Same as Row 2.

OPTIONAL ROW 5: Work row the same as for left front.

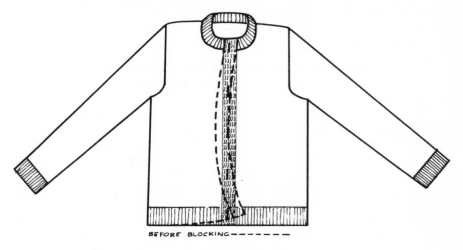

BEFORE BLOCKING – – – – – – –

Fig. 102

ON HORIZONTAL ROWS

CROCHETING AROUND NECK

If working a neck only with 5 rows of crocheting, usually the first two rows do not have any decreasing for shaping.

TO WORK:

Row 1: Sc around edges to fit.

Row 2: 1 sc in each sc around.

Rows 3-4-5: Continuing working in sc, decrease 4 or 5 sts in each round. EXAMPLE: I would make these decreases, one in each curve of neck, one at top of each shoulder seam and one in back of neck.

SHAPING WITH CROCHETING

WHEN CROCHETING FRONTS AND NECK IN ONE PIECE OR ENTIRELY AROUND THE EDGES OF A SWEATER, remember if shaping goes OUT (as on corners), you INCREASE and if shapings go IN, you DECREASE (around neck). Where and how much this is done depends on the shaping and how much fitting is needed.

DECREASING ON HORIZONTAL ROWS

Since I wish to use the same size hook for both vertical edges and horizontal rows, the hook makes the stitches or horizontal rows much too large, thick and "ruffly".

The rule, to eliminate this, is to decrease 1 st in every 3rd, 4th, or 5th stitches. This depends on the yarn, size hook and your tension. I find crocheting 3 sc and working the next 2 sc tog. (1 decrease in 5 sts) is the basic rate of decreases I use the most.

Again the edges, before blocking, should curve and be little shorter than final length. You can stretch the crocheted edge and very easily see if it is going to be too loose, too tight and not hold exactly in shape.

Fitting crocheting to knitting is a matter of trying, practicing, adjusting and a little experience in doing.

POCKETS

KINDS OF POCKETS

There are many kinds of pockets that can be made for knits.

Patch pockets: If you have no pattern for these, cut out a paper pattern in the shape and size you wish and place and pin to garment before knitting to the paper pattern.

Inset pockets: These are pockets where you knit the pocket linings before beginning the fronts of the garment. On the row for top of pocket, work to spot for pocket; bind off the number of stitches in the pocket lining (or knit across this number of stitches and place pocket stitches on a holder); continue across row. On next row, when you reach the pocket opening, pick up and knit the pocket lining stitches; knit across balance of row. Top of pocket edges can be picked up and ribbed, or faced by making a turning edge and hem or crocheted.

False pocket: This is just a strip of trim sewed to garment to simulate the appearance of pockets.

Slanted pockets: These are seldom used in this country but can be worked by short rows or decreasing or increasing edges of pocket opening for shape.

Side Seam pockets: These are made by leaving part of side seam of garment open, usually on coats or jackets, and knitting back lining of pocket with yarn or making the entire pocket with fabric.

BASIC PLACEMENT OF POCKETS ON CARDIGAN FRONTS

Divide number of stitches on front (not including borders) by 5. Pocket will be width of two of these sections or 2/5 of the width of the front and is placed in the second and third sections nearest the underarm.

If ribbing is on the bottom of sweater, the bottom of pocket starts at top of ribbing. Pockets sewed to ribbing either on the outside or inside, never seem to lay nicely.

If sweater has a hemline, bottom of pocket should begin above top of hem facing.

SEWING KNITTED POCKET LINING

Smooth the inside of pocket flat and place a pin at the bottom row and at each corner. To do an exact job, count rows down and stitches horizontally.

To be able to keep a straight line in sewing edge of lining to body of garment, outline the pocket as follows: Using a contrast color cotton sewing thread and on the outside of the body piece, baste in and out through the vertical line of stitches where each side of pocket lining will be sewed and across the bottom row.

Using a long enough piece of yarn to sew entirely around pocket, overcast every other row of edges to body and every stitch at bottom edge. Fasten and weave in all ends.

If there is a pocket trim on the right side that must be sewed, leave a good long end at both the beginning and end of sewing pocket to sew the outside trim.

If top of patch pocket is faced, sew down hem facing before sewing pocket to garment.

PICKING UP STITCHES

To pick up stitches means to go through the knitting, pull up a loop of yarn and place on the needle for knitting, making a row or round of stitches which is the base for working a piece of knitting usually shaped in a different direction than piece where stitches were picked up. This is to be done in such a manner that these extra pieces or sections look like a continuation of the basic knitting, without "holes" or loose seams in the knitting.

The method of picking up stitches is the same (1) for flat pieces, worked back and forth using two needles, or (2) for circular knitting of body pieces or borders as on round and V-necks, around entire edges of a cardigan, for armholes, etc. Circular knitting can also be done satisfactorily on four or five double-pointed needles but the difference in price between double-pointed and circular needles is so little, I prefer the circular. Many knitters have undesirable loose places between needles where moving from one double-pointed needle to another.

Some of this knitting is worked in small pieces as for borders on armhole edges of sleeveless sweaters, vests, neckbands, cardigans or on any and all edges of blankets, etc. Some are picked up for making complete sections of a garment as for seamless or one-piece garments where body is worked on circular needles and sleeves are picked up around armholes and worked from top down in circular knitting. Since stitches can really be picked up ANYWHERE on a piece of knitting, they can be picked up in a design and worked into lovely trims and ruffles, welts or laces making your garment one of a kind.

When picking up stitches, they (1) may be worked one by one as they are picked up or (2) all the loops placed on needle before working.

It is not difficult to actually pick up the stitches but WHERE, HOW AND HOW OFTEN determines the results. Several methods are listed and you will probably at some time use all of them. My method is listed last. I have used this exclusively for several years. Try the different methods and use the one that works best for you and gets the best results for strength and support needed at that particular spot.

Do you have to pick up more stitches when you use double-pointed needles than circular? The kind of needles has no bearing on the number of stitches to be used. Use the needle size indicated on your knitting instructions or if using my method, use knitting needles two sizes smaller than those used on the body of garment.

No definite size needs to be indicated for the crochet hook, but size 5 or 6 aluminum hook will take care of picking up stitches on most yarns of all weights.

PICK UP AND KNIT METHOD

The following example of instructions often confuses many knitters. EXAMPLE: "Pick up and knit 80 sts on armhole edges for border . . . ." This means that you insert needle through knitting, wrap yarn around needle and pull through like a knit stitch (Fig. 103). Continue to pick up stitches evenly spaced, until number desired is obtained.

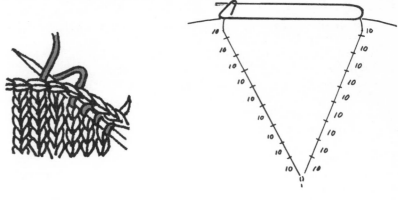

Fig. 103   Fig. 104

This is much easier to do if a little time is spent in preparation before any picking up of stitches. It is advisable to divide the edge into sections, marking with pins (Fig. 104), which will allow you to pick up exactly a certain number of stitches evenly spaced in each section. EXAMPLE: If you need to pick up 180 sts on front neck edges, divide the edges into 9 sections with 10 stitches in each section.

This will eliminate picking up incorrect number of stitches, getting stitches too close together, too far apart, or having to re-do the work, which results in the stretching and sometimes spoiling of edges. In fact, I have seen edges that has been "tried" so many times that I could put my little finger through the holes made in the knitting. Unfortunately, this kind of thing makes it necessary to move into the body of the piece further to pick up stitches making extra and thick seams which causes some problems with size, shapings, etc.

Picking up stitches is probably the most difficult thing to do WELL in knitting. Take your time. Be particular and try to do good work on the first try.

WHERE AND HOW MANY THREADS TO PICK UP

For the "pick up and knit method", needle is usually inserted under two threads or strands of yarn.

In my method I usually pick up only one thread on edges or one side of a stitch. There will be instances however, where you will need to use your own judgment as to whether to insert needle under one loop or two.

Some exceptions to picking up one thread on edges are:

1. For stronger seam around armholes, I pick up under two threads if knitting sleeves from top down or for some border bands.

2. If edges are rough, loose or have "holes", move in at least a row to pick up stitches.

3. If shaping along edges is badly done, pick up INSIDE this edging. This kind of problem makes you aware of how important the neatness, method and direction used is to get shapings. Think ahead whenever shaping. How are you going to use edges? What kind of edges do you want? Are they leaning in the right direction?

A classic example of printed instructions of matching decreases and kind of decreases are: A round neck with a PSSO decrease on one side and a K 2 tog on the other (Fig. 118). The K 2 tog will pick up fine and not show holes but just try to pick up on the edge the PSSO stitches without leaving loose threads or holes. You will have to be satisfied with this or move inside the decreases, which will change the looks of the seam.

You now know how to match decreases. YOU change your instructions to work correctly (Fig. 119 or 120). I would use the tighter matching K 2 tog decreases on this neck edge to allow good picking up of stitches. (Manual, page 47)

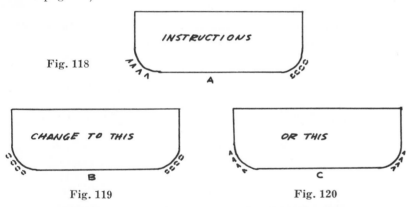

Fig. 118

Fig. 119   Fig. 120

METHOD OF PICKING UP STITCHES WITH CROCHET HOOK (Fig. 121)

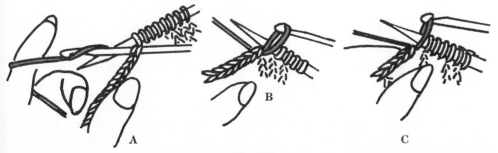

Fig. 121

This is similar to picking up with a needle and knitting except you insert crochet hook under loop or loops, pull yarn loops through knitting and place on needle. Do your preparation work and space stitches evenly.

PICKING UP STITCHES WITH KNITTING NEEDLES IN EVERY ROW ON EDGES

Some knitters pick up a stitch in every row on edges and on next row decrease evenly spaced to the proper number of stitches. This is done basically to eliminate "holes". It is the least desirable method, doesn't look very good, except possibly on fine knitting but can be useful and solve special problems as on page 80.

MY METHOD OF PICKING UP STITCHES ON EDGES OF KNITTING FOR BORDERS

1. This requires no pattern instructions.
2. This requires no definite number of stitches.
3. Two rows of preparation are necessary to get exactly the correct proportion of stitches before beginning pattern stitch.
4. The principle of Method No. 3 Inc. is used to eliminate "holes".

At this time, ignore your knitting instructions and the number of stitches indicated to be picked up. If I refer to the pattern instructions at all, it is only to give me a general picture of what happens to the picked-up stitches.

You do not need to know an exact number with this method. I have seen women almost have a nervous breakdown because they couldn't find exactly the number of stitches instructed to be picked up. If you wish to compare number of picked-up stitches ON A WELL DESIGNED PATTERN with the resulting number of stitches using my method, you will find the total number of stitches very close in number to the amount indicated in instructions.

My method eliminates the problems and hazards of poorly designed patterns that pick up too few stitches or too many stitches which result in an unsatisfactory, "ruffly" edge or where 20 to 30 stitches more are asked for than possible to pick up.

If you follow this method as instructed, pieces will fit, be easy to do and take the pressure off you for an exact number. For the knitter who is designing her own garments, this is a fool-proof method.

PATTERN STITCHES AND THEIR MULTIPLES

Border bands are usually worked in ribbing, Stockinette, Seed or Garter stitch. This method of picking up stitches applies to all patterns.

However, you will need to have the right multiple of stitches to make pattern stitch work, which usually means an adjustment of one or two stitches, more or less. Any difference in amount of stitches needed is adjusted on the (2) INCREASE AND KNITTED ROUND.

DEVELOPMENT AND RULE FOR MY METHOD

Many times knitters bring in garments for borders to be worked, particularly V-necks, but forget to bring their instructions. If you do not know the correct number of stitches to be picked up and if you pick up edge of every row and use every stitch, you will have "ruffly" edges, resulting in too large and loose a border, which defeats the purpose of the border in the first place.

If you used only every other row for picked-up stitches, borders would be too small, pucker, certainly not fit and again be unsatisfactory. After working out and knitting many of these borders without instructions, I found the picking up of the correct number of stitches fell into an orderly pattern, with rare exception.

RULE: PICK UP EVERY STITCH HORIZONTALLY AND PICK UP STITCHES ON EDGES OF THREE OUT OF FOUR ROWS VERTICALLY.

HORIZONTAL STITCHES can be slipped from unfinished edges which have been put on holders, can be picked up by using the outside edge of the cast-off stitches (Fig. 122) or one loop from each stitch (Fig. 123).

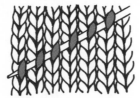

Fig. 122   **Fig. 123**

ON EDGES OF ROWS, I pick up only one thread or strand of yarn, which allows the garment to lay flat, smooth and with the same soft feeling and knitted thickness throughout all of garment—none of those extra lumps, ridges or junk under picked-up stitches.

I recommend neckbands to be knitted around and around in one piece. Some patterns have you knit ribbing on each piece before assembling. Patterns are written in this manner usually to save knitters the price of a circular needle. I have seen few people who can sew ribbing together well at the top of neck edges and truly believe it is worth the price of a circular needle for a fine finishing result. The illustrations are shown with double-pointed needles for easier explanation.

Although the same rule and principles are used for picking up stitches anywhere, to learn this method we will use the following example and circumstances:

A V-neck pullover sweater (Fig. 124)
Picking up stitches for neckband
Border to be worked in K 1, P 1 pattern for 1"
Miter at V with one K st at center
Decreases to be made in matched PSSO
Stitches at back of neck on stitch holder (Fig. 126)

24" circular needle, two sizes smaller than for body of garment

(1) PREPARATION ROUND
(2) INCREASE AND KNITTED ROUND
(3) FIRST PATTERN STITCH ROUND

Since it is difficult to pick up on the edge three out of four rows in succession, to eliminate "holes" we will pick up the TIGHT stitches (nubs) first (Fig. 125) in (1) PREPARATION ROUND. Each nub is really the end of every second row. Then pick up the balance of stitches needed, evenly spaced on (2) INCREASE AND KNITTED ROUND.

If sweater has set-in sleeves, sew shoulder seams. If sweater is raglan, sew in sleeves.

(1) PREPARATION ROUND

TO WORK:

Place a thread or yarn marker around entire single center stitch at V and leave in place until band is finished (Fig. 124). This stitch will be worked to appear as a knit stitch on the right side of garment and have a decrease on each side every row at miter V.

With garment right-side out and beginning at back left shoulder seam and working counterclockwise, slip stitches from back of neck to needle (Fig. 127).

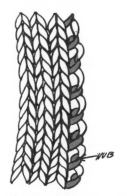

Fig. 124   **Fig. 125**

Turn sweater and with fingers, roll wrong side of the right front edge to outside and insert needle in each "nub" (Fig. 128), which is picking up a loop in each tight stitch along this edge.

Pick up center stitch at V.

Turn sweater again, roll out edge and repeat picking up one loop in each "nub" up left side of neck edge. PREPARATION ROUND is completed (Fig. 129).

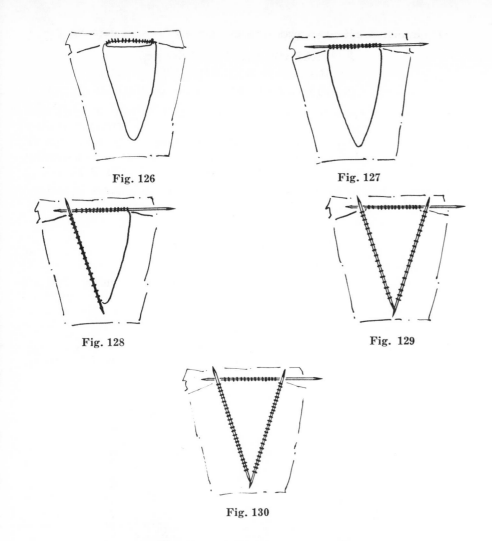

Fig. 126

Fig. 127

Fig. 128

Fig. 129

Fig. 130

(2) INCREASE AND KNITTED ROUND

All circular knitting will now be done on OUTSIDE of garment and from right to left (clockwise).

KNITNOTE: HORIZONTAL STITCHES DO NOT CHANGE IN NUMBER. BALANCE OF STITCHES NEEDED ARE PICKED UP ON EDGES OF ROWS ONLY.

Notice in Fig. 125 that end of one row has a "nub" and there is a straight, loose thread at the end of the next. Of course, if we pick up the loose thread and knit regularly, we will have a hole, which is just what we do not want.

THE SECRET OF THIS ENTIRE MANNER OF PICKING UP THE BALANCE OF STITCHES NEEDED IS TO PICK UP THE LOOSE THREAD AND TWIST THE STITCH BY KNITTING IN *BACK OF*

THE STITCH. THIS IS UTILIZING THE PRINCIPLE OF METHOD NO. 3 INC. (Manual, page 42), WHICH TWISTS THE YARN, MAKING A TIGHT STITCH WHICH LEAVES NO "HOLES".

Please notice that anytime you twist stitches, you make the piece more narrow. Therefore, you would never twist every stitch. Also there are places to pick up these extra stitches which are tight enough and do not need to be twisted. Only twist a stitch when stitch would leave a hole.

This INCREASE AND KNITTED ROUND could be picked up in pattern, which in this instance is K 1, P 1, but is worked in the knit stitch because (1) it is easier to see and keep track of your increase stitches; (2) the knit row does not show after band is completed; (3) and if band is to be worked in another color, this eliminates the purls showing two colors after being worked.

As you picked up these neck edges, you probably noticed that one side picked up easier than the other and sometimes the loops did not lay on needle with the right side of loop on top. Do not worry about this for as you knit these, knit flat into the CENTER of the loop regardless of the direction it lays on needle. In other words, stitches picked up in tight nub are worked off flat and not twisted.

Since the tight stitches at the ends of every other row are already on the needle, one more stitch needs to be picked up in each four-row section. I skip the end stitch of every second row and pick up end stitch of every fourth row, working as follows:

TO WORK:

From right side of garment and beginning at back left shoulder seam and working down left front edge, *Knit first loop on needle; knit next loop on needle; pick up one stitch (an increase stitch made by picking up thread or bar before next stitch and KNITTING IN BACK OF STITCH). Repeat between *'s to center K stitch for V.

Knit center stitch.

Repeat between the *'s again up right front edge.

Knit across each stitch of back of neck (Fig. 130). (2) INCREASE AND KNITTED ROUND completed.

Sometimes it is difficult to insert needle into back of stitch because yarn is tight or will split. A very simple way to work this is: Insert needle straight in (as if to purl) AT THE FRONT OF THE WORK. Keeping needle in stitch, roll right needle over TOP of left needle to back of work. You are now at back of stitch. Knit. I pick up all Method No. 3 increases in this manner which makes neat, clean pickups without "frazzling" my nerves.

The number of stitches on right and left front edges should be the same or within one or two stitches of each other.

It is wise to check how the number of stitches work out in pattern before you finish round across back of neck. If there are too many stitches to make pattern work correctly, decrease by knitting 2 tog. at top of a seam or where a loose stitch can be worked with a tight one.

I often go back a few stitches on the side edge and drop one of the picked up stitches rather than decrease in the middle of the back of neck.

Should you be using K 2, P 2 ribbing pattern and are one stitch over the multiple of four stitches, decrease one stitch. However, if you are two over, use your own judgment as to whether you need to increase two stitches or decrease two stitches. These can be done evenly spaced across back of neck or at shoulder seams.

(3) FIRST PATTERN STITCH ROUND

TO WORK:

Round 1: Using the basic K 1, P 1 ribbing pattern, work in pattern stitch to within two stitches of center K stitch, PSSO (decrease to left), K 1 (center stitch), PSSO (decrease to right), rib in pattern up right side of neck edge and across back of neck. Repeat Round 1 until neckband measures 1″ or depth desired. Bind off in ribbing pattern.

If ribbing is ever bound off with the knit stitch, it is only (1) if you wish edge to be outlined with a straight line for looks or (2) if for some reason neck edge was worked too loosely or had too many stitches, it needs to be held in place with a firm edge. This edge will not have the elasticity nor will it stretch to the same size as a ribbed bind-off.

MITER

A miter is "to shape on a slanting line on a corner". In knitting, this shaping is done by increasing or decreasing stitches, usually two stitches each row or round at the place of miter.

Note that miter decreasing is done in EVERY ROUND to make a nicer fit and eliminate V puffing out (Fig. 124).

MATCHING PATTERN STITCH ON EACH SIDE OF V MITER

In matching the pattern stitch on each side of the miter section, if the last stitch before the miter is a knit, start with a knit after the miter or if a purl stitch, start other side with a purl.

MITERING PATTERNS

Any combination of pattern stitches with a decrease on each side can be used. One stitch at center is basic. Two or three stitches are often used but are a little more "sporty" in style.

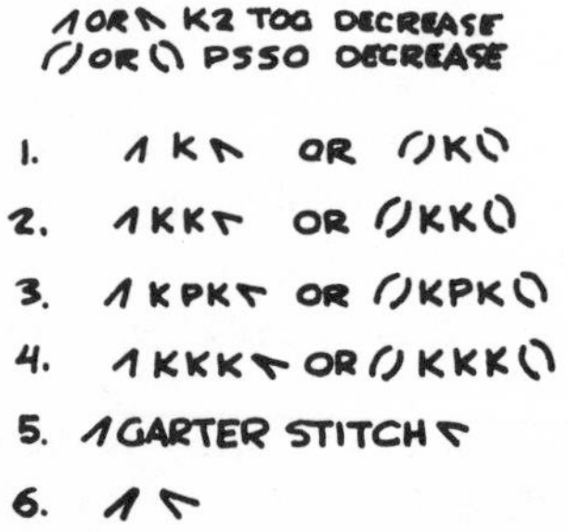

⌐1 OR↖ K2 TOG DECREASE
()OR() PSSO DECREASE

1. ↗K↖ OR ()K()
2. ↗KK↖ OR ()KK()
3. ↗KPK↖ OR ()KPK()
4. ↗KKK↖ OR ()KKK()
5. ↗GARTER STITCH↖
6. ↗↖

Fig. 131 gives some ideas and variations for miter patterns and indicates that the decreases should be matching K 2 tog., one to left and one to right or PSSO, one to left and one to right (Manual, page 47).

Fig. 131

DOUBLED RIBBED BORDER BANDS FOR ROUND OR V NECKS
(For flat or circular knitting)
BASIC DOUBLE BAND

Knit the band until 2″ to 3″ in depth. Bind off EASY. Leave a long end of yarn to sew around neck. Keeping line of knitting straight, turn edge to inside, pin and overcast to first row of band, SEWING EASY, either every stitch or every other stitch. Do not fasten off until you are sure sweater will go over the head. If too tight, usually band has been bound off too tight and will have to be bound off again.

DOUBLE BAND WITH TURNING EDGE (Hemline)

There will be an equal number of rows or rounds on the outside of band and inside of band, with one row of hemline in the middle at turning edge, plus the bind off row.

Pick up stitches at edges and work in pattern until 1″ or width of outside band. WORK NEXT ROW SO A ROW OR ROUND OF PURL STITCHES WILL BE ON OUTSIDE OR RIGHT SIDE OF PIECE. Work in pattern for number of rows or rounds to match those on outside band. Bind off EASY.

DOUBLE BAND FOR V NECK

(1) BASIC DOUBLED BAND IS MADE WORKING A DECREASE MITER AT V FOR ½ of BAND and INCREASE MITER IN LAST ½ of BAND.

(2) DOUBLE BAND WITH TURNING EDGE is made with decrease miter at V to turning edge. MAKE A PURL ROW ON OUTSIDE OR RIGHT SIDE OF PIECE. No decrease is made in hemline row. Continue in pattern stitch making an increase miter (Fig. 137) for number of rows or rounds to match those on outside band.

KNITNOTE: Since these sewing edges will not have to curve and stretch as for a pullover, bind off and sew with a basic tension, which will give a nice, firm fit and still sufficient elasticity.

ROUND NECK PULLOVER

Stitches are picked up in same manner as before, except there is no mitering (shaping) as for V neck.

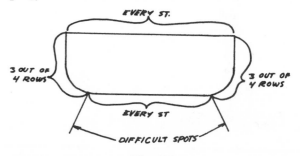

Fig. 132

The most difficult spot to pick up and work stitches to get a smooth, continued line is where curve on neck edges begins (Fig. 132).

Here you may need to pick up extra stitches in order to eliminate "holes", and you may need to go down a row or even two rows to pull up a tight stitch or thread that will fill in.

You may pick up a stitch and it will not work off flat or look good. Drop it and try another thread. You may find a "nub" that is loose and needs to be twisted by knitting in back of the stitch.

KNITNOTE: KNIT IN BACK OF LOOSE STITCHES AND PICK UP WHEREVER YOU CAN GET GOOD STITCHES THAT WILL FIT IN WELL. Twisting the stitches can be used anywhere needed but remember when you twist a stitch, it makes piece more narrow and row tighter, so, don't over-use it.

Don't be discouraged if you are not satisfied with your work on the first couple of garments. It is a difficult process to show a knitter how to do this on a garment and certainly is even more difficult to write. But after you work this method one or two times, you will understand the instructions and work more easily. The results are quite worth your efforts.

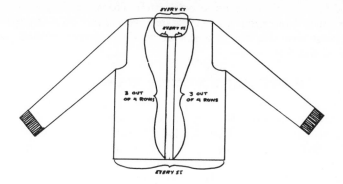

Fig. 135

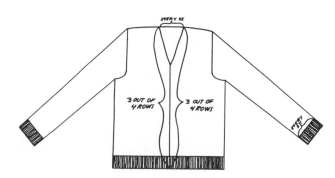

Fig. 133

Fig. 136

Fig. 134

V-NECK CARDIGAN BORDER

For a one-piece border around fronts and neck, pick up stitches as instructed before (Fig. 133). You will need a circular needle of sufficient length for stitches and will work back and forth in rows.

Because ribbing worked in this manner will pull up a little from edges at the bottom, pick up a stitch in EVERY ROW for the first few rows which will fill this in and allow edge to hang squarely after blocking. (Fig. 134)

ROUND NECKED CARDIGAN, MITERED CORNERS

When working ribbing around entire sweater edges, begin picking up stitches at the bottom of right underarm seam. (Figs. 135 and 136)

Note where there are square corners at top and bottom of fronts, it is necessary to miter corners or edges will pucker and roll under. These miters are INCREASE miters (Fig. 137). Mark corner stitches, keep one knit stitch in center and increase 1st on each side of knit stitch on every round. There will be 4 miters in this border band.

If cuffs are knitted circularly, they would have to be done on double-pointed needles to get short enough needles to work. Any length under 16″ circular is difficult to handle easily and in my opinion, not worth the trouble.

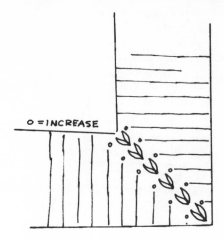

O = INCREASE

Fig. 137

COLLARS

PICKING UP STITCHES FOR COLLARS

If neck edge shapings are even and smooth, they can be picked up for collars satisfactorily.

If neck edge is too large, pick up stitches as usual and on the first row of pattern stitch, decrease evenly to the size desired. Most of this decreasing is needed in the curves on the neck fronts.

If neck has irregular edges or you do not wish to fit by decreasing as above, work one row of crocheting, holding in to fit. Edge of the crochet stitches can be picked up for knitting.

SEWING

Since firm edges that do not stretch out of shape are needed around the neck, work collar separately and sew to neck edges with overcast stitch.

It is frequently necessary with soft yarns to reinforce the neck edges with silk seam binding.

SUBSTITUTING COLLAR FOR RIBBING

If you wish a collar instead of ribbing on a neck edge, bind off all stitches instead of putting them on holders and do not work ribbing. Make a separate collar and sew on.

ABOUT NEEDLES

Since retail outlets selling yarn are well equipped today with all kinds and sizes of needles and accessories, space will not be taken to repeat this information. To help those using circular, jumper or double-pointed needles for the first time, here are some thoughts that might make easier knitting and save some time by eliminating possible errors.

If a knitting pattern is put on the market which uses a new needle or accessory, it will be made available for your use.

CIRCULAR NEEDLES

A circular needle (Fig. 138) is one piece of flexible material with a

needle point at each end. These come in all sizes from 0 through 15. Lengths can be from 11″ to 36″ but not every length is made in every size as shown below.

Length	Sizes
11″	0 - 10½
16″	0 - 10½
24″	0 - 10½
29″	0 - 15
36″	4 - 15

Fig. 138

The length of a circular needle used must not be longer than the stitches would measure if laid out flat to gauge.

EXAMPLE: Gauge 5 sts = 1″, 80 sts = 16″. You would not try to spread and work these 80 sts on a 24″ circular needle, for it would stretch yarn and stitches out of shape, make the knitting loose and piece too big. Fitting the correct length needle to the number of stitches is the reason some one-piece pullover sweaters with yoke patterns use two different lengths of circular needles, one length is needed for the body and a shorter length for the yoke.

It is usually better to have a too short circular needle than a too long one. When circular needles get under 16″ in length, they are difficult to handle and many times a set of double-pointed needles is substituted for the circular needle.

Circular needles are used (1) to work round knitting which eliminates seams and (2) to work flat knitting.

Circular knitting can be done beginning at the top or the bottom of a garment.

If beginning at the bottom, be sure pattern stitch is one that will not twist but keep in up-and-down line. The sleeves would probably be started on a double-pointed needle, changing to a circular needle when sufficient stitches are available for circular needle further up the sleeve. These sleeves could also be made flat and sewed with an underarm seam.

ROUND KNITTING ON CIRCULAR NEEDLES

Round knitting is done by casting on stitches on a circular needle or a set of double-pointed needles which make a circle by joining. Take the first stitch cast on in left hand and with right hand, knit with yarn and end of needle at last stitch cast on (Fig. 139).

Knitting is worked around and around in a clockwise direction, from right to left and on the OUTSIDE of circle, the right side of knitting facing you and the wrong side of garment inside of needles. KNITTING ONCE AROUND THE CIRCLE IS CALLED A ROUND.

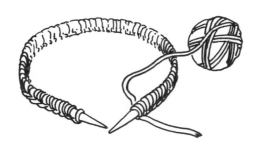

Fig. 139

Beginners, or those who have not used circular needles, often ask how you can knit every stitch and end up with Stockinette. In circular knitting the knit or right side of the garment is constantly turning but always facing you and since you place knits over knits, you will be making Stockinette stitch pattern.

If you wish to make a purl round, bring yarn to front between needle points and purl. If you wish to work Garter stitch, mark the beginning of the rounds and alternate one knit round and one purl round.

TO ELIMINATE TWISTING OF STITCHES

GREAT CARE MUST BE TAKEN IN JOINING THE FIRST ROUND OF CIRCULAR KNITTING THAT ALL LOOPS LAY FLAT ON TOP OF NEEDLE AND NO CAST-ON STITCHES ARE TWISTED OVER TOP OF NEEDLE.

There are times, as for casting on a circular skirt or dress, where there are 400 to 850 stitches and the yarn is fine and possibly of a nubby texture. This is difficult to cast on, count and be sure first row is not twisted.

A trick that eliminates the possibility of twisting stitches and saves many hours of work, is to cast on several stitches, placing a thin marker after every 25 to 50 stitches. Then take a piece of seam binding, tape or strip of fabric, spread the stitches loosely across the edge of tape and baste loosely to bottom edge of all cast-on stitches. Repeat this around. Fasten thread and cut off excess tape. Join and knit around and around (Fig. 140).

Leave this tape on bottom for two reasons. (1) Tape will show you instantly if cast-on round or any row is twisted. If tape hangs in a complete untwisted circle at bottom of stitches, continue knitting. If at any time tape LAYS ACROSS TOP OF NEEDLE, STOP AND CORRECT, ANY TWISTED ROUND WILL NEVER BECOME UNTWISTED BY CONTINUING WITH THE KNITTING. (2) This tape can be removed at any time but it will help to keep bottom edge of garment clean.

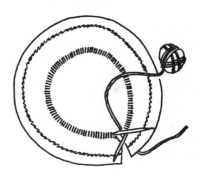

Fig. 140

ALTERNATE METHOD OF BEGINNING CIRCULAR KNITS

A second method is to work back and forth for a few rows, or through a border pattern, and then join into a circle and knit around and around. This will give you a piece of knitting that is wide enough to see that when joining you do not twist material. The edges of these first rows are later woven together flat on the outside.

TUBULAR TIES

It would be very difficult to knit tubular ties on double-pointed needles using only 5 or 6 sts. Usually these are worked on a knitting spool often made with nails and empty wooden thread spools used in handicraft classes. A commercial item called a knitting nobby has been on the market for many years and it can be found with the yarns and accessories. Should you like to make your own knitting spool, check the hobby books at your public library.

However, another way to make a narrow tie is to cast on the entire length of piece needed and work in Stockinette stitch for three rows. Bind off and overcast edges together using the purl side out. This will give a rounded tie that will not stretch too much.

FLAT KNITTING ON CIRCULAR NEEDLES

Circular needles can be used at any time to knit back and forth but are usually used for flat knitting when more stitches are needed than can be put on straight needles, as for making afghans and one-piece cardigans.

JUMPER NEEDLES (Fig. 141)

These come in pairs and are like a circular needle cut in two, with stoppers on the cut ends. These come in sizes 1 through 15.

There are several advantages with jumper needles. They can be substituted for and will hold more stitches than straight needles. There is no pressure from needles against your hands as with circular or straight needles and you can keep hand motions to a minimum and your knitting in a very small working area in front of you. Jumper needles are very convenient for knitting when traveling.

Fig. 141

I find jumper needles sometimes bother new knitters because the ends become entangled in the yarn frequently while knitting. This is easily undone. When row has been finished, pick up empty needle from bottom or stopper end and carefully pull out of material.

DOUBLE-POINTED NEEDLES (Fig. 142)

These come in sets of four needles with points on each end, three to hold stitches and one to knit with. In Europe, five or more needles are often in a set. If you wish to use more than four needles, do so as long as they are the same size.

Length	Sizes
7"	0 - 8
10"	1 - 15

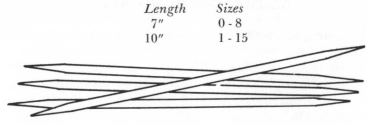

Fig. 142

When casting on on double-pointed needles, it is difficult to try to cast on all three needles in succession. If one needle will hold all the stitches, cast on on one needle (Fig. 143), then divide and slip one third of stitches to each of the other two needles (Fig. 144). It is a little easier to work around and around if you arrange stitches so the first stitch to be worked on each needle is a knit stitch.

If all the stitches won't cast on on one needle, put on as many as you can and then transfer one-third of stitches to other needles as necessary.

To knit around and around on double-pointed needles, join in same manner as for circular knitting. Hold first cast-on stitch in left hand and yarn and needle with last cast-on stitch in right hand (Fig. 145).

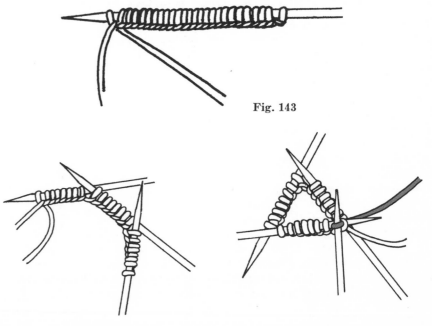

Fig. 143

Fig. 144

Fig. 145

ELIMINATING LINES AND LOOSE SPACES BETWEEN DOUBLE-POINTED NEEDLES

Where knitting moves from one needle to another, many knitters have "lines" or loose spaces, particularly obvious on Stockinette stitch.

This seems to be a "human" factor and there is no sure method of eliminating this. The only method that has been successful in solving this to any degree is to keep moving the needles forward a few stitches on each round as follows:

Knit across first needle. *Using this first needle, knit two, three or four stitches off next (second needle). Pick up free needle and knit across balance of stitches on second needle. Repeat between *'s in the same manner using second and third needle and then third and first needles. Repeat for each round of work. Be very neat and careful to keep knitting smooth and even.

KNITTING ACCESSORIES

Knitting accessories are necessary for your knitting. They are called tools, knitting aids and sometimes equipment. Buy your knitting tools as you need them. As you knit more and more items, you will gradually accumulate complete sets of all sizes of needles, several sizes of crochet hooks, stitch holders, markers, etc. Unless you break or lose them, they will last many years.

For an adult beginning knitter, the following accessories are basic and advised for learning to knit:

1 copy THE RIGHT WAY TO KNIT, A Basic Manual For Knitting
Knitting worsted yarn
1 pair. No. 8 knitting needles
Notebook, paper and pencil
Tape measure
Row counter
Stitch markers
Cable holder
Stitch holders
Scissors
Rustproof straight or T pins
Yarn needles, 1 large and 1 small
Crochet hook, 5 or 6 aluminum
Bobbins
Carry-all for materials
Pattern, yarn and required needle size for first knitting project

Some other items that you may purchase when desired are name labels, ribbons, buttons, trims, needlecases and knitting bags.

There may be times when you will not have your tools with you and it is necessary for you to improvise. A hairpin, paper clip or pencil can act as a cable holder. A piece of thread, string or small plastic curtain ring can act as a temporary marker. As an emergency stitch holder, try a hairpin, paper clip or a piece of wire. It is very interesting to learn how ingenious you can be when necessary.

These emergency tools are not recommended for regular use because their edges are not smooth, will split and fray the yarn and have not been engineered to the proper sizes for good or easy knitting.

KNITTING MACHINES

Knitting machines are called accessories by some but to me they are in an entirely different field of work and a class all their own.

Knitting machines come equipped with tools and instruction book. Most people are able to teach themselves. Numerous additional accessories and excellent pattern books are now available and the machine knitter can choose from a simple basic to the most complex pattern.

Since our time is precious today, many hand knitters, to save time doing "straight" knitting, use the machine for fine and Stockinette stitch work. Machine knitting can be done very quickly but allow yourself plenty of time to learn to operate the machine to get as good results as you would if hand knitting.

Many people who purchase knitting machines have never learned to hand knit and are NOT trying to do hand knitting on the machine. Hand knitters must guard against the frustration of trying to work all yarns on machines when there are many bulkies and novelty yarns you can work better and quicker by hand. Do not expect the machine to do all kinds of hand knitting and do not expect your hand knitting to imitate machine knitting. In other words, let each work in its own medium. They both make knitted fabric. They both can be highly successful and unlimited in scope and each has its place in art handicrafts.

DECREASES AND INCREASES

For basic information concerning how to decrease and increase, please refer to Manual, since space will not allow repetition here.

DECREASES

Most decreases in knitting are done on every other row and on the right side of garment. But there are many shapings as on the front of a scoop neck dress, in which we wish to make a shallow flat neck edge which means taking stitches off faster than every other row.

DECREASES "EVERY ROW"

You will find instructions written, "Decrease one stitch at the neck edge EVERY ROW . . . times." This means, if you are beginning to knit the row at a neck edge, you K 2 tog. and as you work back the next row to the neck edge, decrease the LAST two stitches by K 2 tog. This places decreases at the neck edge on top of each other. Repeat thse two rows until all EVERY ROW decreases have been made. Two, three or four of these EVERY ROW decreases are usually followed by the EVERY OTHER ROW decreases.

Well-written instructions will have the words "EVERY ROW" underscored, in bold type, italics or written in some manner to call your attention to this exception, so you will not get it confused with EVERY OTHER ROW.

DECREASE IN PATTERNS

You would be surprised how many knitters expect every stitch for every row under every circumstance to be written out. This is impossible to do. It would be an unending job but most important, the time and cost of printing involved would be most prohibitive.

To clarify the following explanation, PLAIN ROWS are those containing all knits or all purls; those that make fancy or lace stitches are called PATTERN ROWS.

Any interruption of a motif, lace or pattern stitch or design in color knitting is called a broken pattern. Our greatest problem is keeping pattern when decreasing regularly across a design or at the beginning and end of rows.

HOW TO DETERMINE FIRST STITCH ON BROKEN PATTERN ROWS

Often on fancy or lace patterns it is difficult to decrease at the beginning and end of row and then pick the proper stitch to start next pattern row, particularly since each decrease changes the beginning stitch of each pattern row and first the two stitches will be used in the decreasing. Therefore broken pattern stitch must then be started on third stitch on left needle.

Try decreasing regularly on the plain rows. It does not matter if they are on the wrong or right side of the garment. This allows you to keep a more accurate count of the decreases and also helps you to ascertain more easily the kind of stitch to begin pattern row. The first pattern stitch of the row is the most important and must be correct because if first stitch is worked incorrectly, the entire row is wrong. If row is correct, decreases at end will automatically fall into pattern.

Should you have a pattern that changes on every row, both right and wrong side of garment, it is important that you know pattern very well and be patient in the working. Check motifs every row and count if necessary.

In working out any kind of problem, first you take what you know and go from there. Any knitter who has worked a garment to the armhole in a pattern stitch, no matter how difficult or complicated, should be able very quickly to figure out what stitch starts any row of any broken part of row. You have probably already noticed that certain stitches fall regularly over other stitches as you build row upon row. Therefore, pick out one of these stitches on left needle you know and find what NUMBER OF STITCH this is in your pattern row.

FOR EXAMPLE: A certain knit stitch is number 5 in the row. Now find which stitch is number 5 in the row to be knitted. If you have four stitches on the needle and the 4th from the point of the needle is number 5 of the pattern row, stitches will be numbered 5, 4, 3 and 2. If you have a decrease to make, use stitches numbered 2 and 3 to make decrease and begin broken pattern with stitch numbered 4 of that pattern row. This sounds confusing but try it and you will find it will work on any pattern or combination of stitches.

Should the row begin with a Yo, I do not think it advisable to use this on an armhole edge since you need better and stronger edges here than that. I would work this as a plain knit or purl.

Sometimes adjustment in the required number of stitches is necessary, omitting a decrease on edges or picking up a stitch on edges to keep the the correct number of stitches or to allow pattern to work.

Frequently we have trouble with shaping a pattern like Popcorn which is difficult to decrease without gaining stitches.

First, do your decreasing on a plain row if possible and count the number of stitches after each pattern row to be sure you have the correct number. If there are two stitches too many, do not make a first and last popcorn in a pattern row until stitches are adjusted to correct number. The edges of the armholes in this particular pattern are often uneven and different lengths on the edges but will sew together satisfactorily with a back stitch seam.

Another difficult pattern to shape is the "Yo, Sl 1, K 1, PSSO" pattern. I do not think this one is worth the trouble. There is no easy or basic answer, except to count stitches each row and be sure you have decreased.

INCREASES

The same principle of determining the first stitch on broken pattern rows applies if a knitted piece is being increased in either a flat or circular piece. Note that when an increase is done on pattern row, the first stitch will be used to make the increase and broken pattern will begin on SECOND stitch.

BROKEN PATTERNS ON CIRCULAR SLEEVES

On sleeves knitted with double-pointed or circular needles from the bottom up, place a marker where underarm seam would be if it was a flat piece. There are several ways this can be worked. Try the different ways and use what looks best.

(1) You can increase in the stitch before marker and stitch after marker by knitting in front and back of stitch (two increases); pick up broken pattern and continue.

(2) Or you can leave one knit stitch only as a seam and increase on each side; pick up broken pattern and continue around.

(3) Or you can keep two seam stitches, one stitch on each side of marker, always knitting these two stitches. Increases are made on each side of these two stitches and will allow you to increase in whatever method you prefer. Pick up broken pattern and continue.

NOTE: It is seldom that you can start broken pattern in the increase stitch. On all rounds between increases, pattern will be worked on all the stitches, except where knit seam stitches are used, being careful to begin row with correct stitch for broken pattern.

INCREASING EVENLY SPACING ACROSS ROW

This creates a problem to some knitters as how to space evenly and how to increase without leaving holes.

As an example, where you are to increase at the top of the ribbing before starting pattern for body of garment, instructions might read: "On 90 sts of ribbing, increase 8 sts evenly across row (98 sts)."

To place 8 sts across piece of knitting, you will have 9 spaces around them (Fig. 146). Divide the 90 stitches by 9 (spaces) making an increase in or after every 10th stitch 8 times only across row. Should the number in the spaces not come out evenly, divide the extra stitches and add to space before the first increase and after the last increase (Fig. 147) or stagger extra stitches evenly across row (Fig. 148). The number of stitches between increases does not have to be exactly the same. One, two or even three stitches difference is not unusual.

In increasing evenly across row, it is very important that the smoothest kind of increase be used to eliminate "holes". If your pattern says increase in the top row of ribbing, you may use Method No. 1 of knitting in the front and back of the KNIT stitches as you work across ribbing. However, if you wish to increase these stitches evenly across in the first knit row of body of garment, use Method No. 3 (between stitches) which will not disturb the smoothness of the pattern or leave holes. Method No. 2 of picking up loop at the back of the next stitch could also be used and is most effective with bulky yarns.

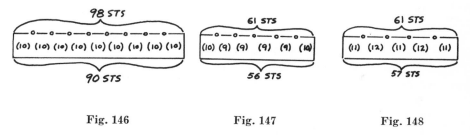

Fig. 146   Fig. 147   Fig. 148

DARTS

Darts are not usually used in knits because the natural elasticity of the knitted fabric allows it to mold to the body. But there are designs and figure adjustments that require more fitting than the flat pieces can give and therefore, darts are necessary.

Darts are often used in patterns for fine tailoring, as in well-designed suits, jackets, where there may be an open vertical dart under the bustline, as well as a small dart at the underarm.

Since few people have standard body measurements, darts are used to make wider, longer and more narrow sections.

One of the frequent figure problems is fitting a person who has a large bustline and narrow shoulders. Horizontal darts can be made to give more room at the bustline and vertical darts to narrow the shoulders.

Often people need horizontal darts to give more length to cardigans because the shape of the body consistently hikes up the fronts.

HOW DARTS ARE MADE

In knitting, these can be made (1) by using increases and decreases, (2) by shaping open darts, or (3) by sewing by hand with yarn or machine stitches as with fabric. The manner of working darts is decided by the direction they are to be placed in the knitting—horizontally or vertically.

HORIZONTAL DARTS

The horizontal dart used depends on the figure problem of the individual. If more length on front pieces is needed, try the gathered dart. If more width is needed at underarm bustline, try the closed or knitted-in open dart.

GATHERED UNDERARM DART

Work front pieces 2″ longer than back to underarm and ease in this extra length within the top 3″ to 4″ of the underarm seam (Fig. 149).

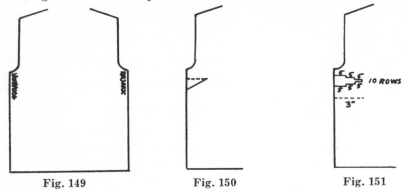

Fig. 149   Fig. 150   Fig. 151

CLOSED UNDERARM DART

Work front piece 2″ longer than back and make a folded dart by sewing with yarn about 2½″ below armhole shaping (Fig. 150).

KNITTED-IN OPEN DARTS

A basic dart here is worked 3″ into the knitting. The stitches are divided into sections and bound off one section at a time like the shaping of a shoulder and immediately cast back on again in the same number of sections and stitches. Dart is then sewed with back stitch seam (Fig. 151).

EXAMPLE NO. 1: Knitting Worsted, 5 sts = 1″, 6 rows = 1″

A 2″ dart will need approximately 1-½″ of extra rows.

From underarm edge, bind off 5 sts 3 times (every other row) and immediately from center of dart, cast on 5 sts 3 times (every other row), which will use 10 rows of knitting and with seam sewed, make a 2″ dart.

EXAMPLE NO. 2: 3 ply yarn, 8 sts = 1″, 12 rows = 1″

A 1-½″ dart will need approximately 1-¼″ of extra rows.

From underarm edge, bind off 6 sts 4 times (every other row) and from center of dart, cast on 6 sts 4 times (every other row), which will use 14 rows. After sewing, this will make a 1-½″ dart.

When you have decided the size dart you need, the number of rows and the width, use the above examples as a guide. BY ALL MEANS, ELIMINATE THE JOGS AND THICK SEAMS BY BINDING OFF AS IN THE SLANT SHOULDER SHAPING ON PAGE 14.

VERTICAL DARTS

These are made by regularly decreasing or increasing (1) a single stitch at a time or (2) deeper darts with double increases or decreases.

INCREASE DART

For extra room under bustline, a single increase dart could be used here but usually if a dart is necessary, the double increases are used to give more stitches quickly.

When about 3″ under the bustline, divide stitches for front into four sections, placing as markers pieces of white thread around both threads of a stitch where these sections divide. Darts will be made at the markers closest to the sides and should contain the same number of stitches from the underarm edges. Center marker will not be used (Fig. 152).

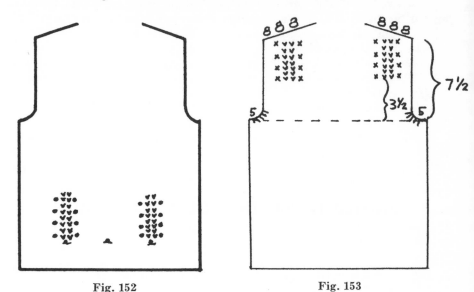

Fig. 152   Fig. 153

DOUBLE INCREASE DART

I believe it is easier to do and make smoother knitting if two knit stitches are allowed between increases. The following example is made in this manner using Stockinette stitch and Method No. 3 increasing. Increases are made every ¾″ for a 4 st-increase dart, and on each side of the marked knit stitches as written below.

EXAMPLE: Directions read:

INCREASE ROW: *Knit across row to marker, increase 1 st (Method No. 3), K 2 sts, increase 1 st (Method No. 3); repeat between *'s one time. Knit across balance of row.

Work even until ¾″ (or desired distance between increases) and repeat the increase row 3 times more (or desired number of increase rows.)

In this instance 4 sts have been increased in each increase row 4 times, totaling 16 sts, giving an additional 2″ in width of garment.

Adjust this example to your individual needs. You may want darts more toward center, smaller, larger, etc. On cardigans fronts darts are placed in center of piece, excluding border or overlapping edges.

DECREASE DARTS

These can be used to eliminate extra increased stitches before shoulder shaping or to make shoulder pattern more narrow.

If pattern stitch is fancy or so complicated that it can not be interrupted with decreases, use a smaller needle for knitting, beginning 3-1/2″ to 4″ from first bound-off row of armhole.

WHERE TO MARK FOR SHOULDER DART (Fig. 153)

Dart decrease will begin 3″ to 3-1/2″ straight up from first bound-off row of armhole. It is worked on the center stitch or stitches to be used for shoulder shaping.

To find the stitches to mark for dart, armhole shaping would be completed and you would know that the next 24 sts, as an example, are the stitches that will be used to shape shoulder. Therefore, mark the 12th and 13th stitches (center) from armhole edge. Dart decreases would be made on each side of these two stitches.

INSTRUCTIONS: (Match K 2 tog decreases, Manual page 47)

DECREASE ROW: *Knit to within 2 sts of first marker, K 2 tog. (leans to left), K 2 sts, K 2 tog. (leans to right); knit across to other shoulder dart or across balance of row. Repeat between *'s one time for other shoulder. Work 1″ even; repeat decrease row every 1″ three times MORE (or number of times desired). Continue with regular instructions. Since shoulders must have the same shape and number of stitches, darts are usually made in both back and front pieces.

MACHINE-STITCHED DARTS

Treat knitted fabric like cloth. Fit, pin and sew on machine. I do not recommend cutting or trimming of darts. If excess material must be cut out of dart, double machine stitch before cutting.

SKIRTS

KNITTED FABRIC THAT GOES DIAGONALLY

This usually happens for one of the following reasons:

1. The characteristic of the pattern stitch is to go diagonally. If it goes to the extreme, on flat knitting, stitches are increased and decreased at end of row to adjust shape and square up pattern.

If this happens when knitting circular skirt, pattern should be changed and skirt made in two pieces.

2. One side of the knit stitch is twisted more than the other. This is an individual factor and to my knowledge, there is no way of correcting or changing this any more than changing your own handwriting.

3. Some materials, like rayons, linens, cottons and summer yarns, are often smooth, slippery or spun in such a manner that when knitted they roll into a permanent diagonal line. I have had some yarns that did this and the garment NEVER blocked into a straight up and down line and even when worked flat in two pieces, the side seams may not sew or hang straight.

TWO-PIECE SKIRT WITH ALL SHAPINGS ON SIDE SEAMS

I am always unhappy with this kind of pattern and never use it. Many women wish a little more fullness at the bottom edge of skirt for ease in walking and sitting but if the shaping is made on the sides only, skirt will not stand out at the sides, as for an A shape, but will drop down and fullness will fall crookedly (or what I call "hoop in") toward front of skirt. This just never allows a skirt to have a nice clean line and hang evenly.

CORRECT SHAPING OF SKIRT

To design a two-piece skirt that will give you the line needed to hang properly, decreases should be made regularly and evenly spaced across skirt pieces.

THREE-PIECE SKIRTS

There have been a few dress and suit patterns, usually made of ribbon or fine dress yarn, that had three-piece skirts—one piece in front and two pieces in back. These pieces are shaped on the edges similarly to a sewing pattern designed for fabrics, to give a tailored and molded look so they will hang or drape with the straight (vertical line) of the knitted fabric.

SHAPING PATTERNS THAT CANNOT BE DECREASED IN THE ROW

For these skirts, flat or circular, try graduating sizes of needles, as many as three sizes in one skirt, or a combination of changing sizes of needles and some shaping at the seam edges.

CHARTING

CHARTING A CIRCULAR SKIRT

The plain Stockinette stitch skirt in matching or coordinating colors to complete ensembles with sweaters, jackets, vests, coats, etc. is invaluable to your wardrobe, not only moneywise but fashionwise. You should have several. This plain skirt is very easy to chart and if knitted properly and to gauge, it should fit exactly and needs only to be steam pressed.

PREPARATION FOR SKIRT

1. MEASUREMENTS: Take exact outside measurements at waist, hips at 7″ and 10″, Since most of us are not necessarily shaped to be measured at these spots, measure at two or three of the largest spots, listing distance down from waistline. If there is much irregularity in the hip line, a good girdle should be worn with knits .

2. WIDTH AROUND BOTTOM OF SKIRT:
Straight skirt, 2″ to 4″ larger than largest part of hip
Medium skirt, 4″ to 8″ larger than largest part of hip
Full or flared, 8″ and over than largest part of hip
Most of the skirts I chart are the straight skirt plus 4″.

3. LENGTH: This must be your personal decision. The average length today is about 21″ to 22″ for adult women. The mini skirt pictured in Fig. 106 is 18″ in length.

TO MAKE CHART FOR SKIRT

Use a large sheet of paper and draw diagram like Fig. 154.
List measurements of 7″ and 10″ below waist, or wherever they have

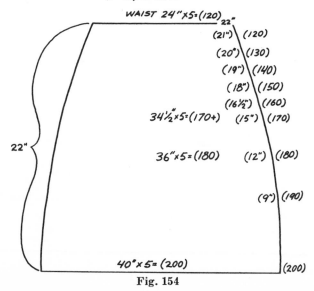

(NEW) SIZE 10

WAIST 24″ X5= (120) 22″
(21″) (120)
(20″) (130)
(19″) (140)
(18″) (150)
(16½″) (160)
34½″ X5= (170+) (15″) (170)
36″ X5= (180) (12″) (180)
(9″) (190)
22″
40″ X5= (200) (200)

Fig. 154

been taken, in center and multiply by stitch gauge placing results to the right of diagram.

List measurements in inches from bottom of skirt to coincide with measurements made from top down as, for this 22″ skirt, from waist, 7″ would be the same as 15″ from bottom and 10″ from waist would be the same as 12″ from bottom.

You now have number of stitches to be used at waist, 7″ and 10″ hip and width at bottom. Using gauge of 5 sts = 1″, fill in balance of stitches in multiples of 10 with figures closest to the measurements.

The distance between decreases should be wider at the bottom and become more narrow as they reach the waist. Divide the decreases into the number of inches remaining. Note that between 15″ and 21″ there are 6″ but only 5 decreases, so shaping would be at 1-½″, 1-½″, 1″, 1″, and 1″ intervals. Keep at least 1″ even before waistline and bind off easy, since top should stretch enough, when finished, to go over hips.

CHARTING CIRCULAR SKIRT (New) Size 10

Stockinette Stitch
Gauge: 5 sts = 1″
1 - 24″ No. 8 circular needle or whatever size necessary to obtain gauge

Measurements:		
	Waist	24″
	Hip	34-½″
	Length	22″
	Width around	
	Bottom of skirt	40″

DIRECTIONS: Cast on 200 sts. Join and knit around and around until

INCHES	DECREASE ROUND (10 sts in each decrease round)		STITCHES REMAINING
9″	*K 18, K 2 tog. (one round only)	*	190
12″	*K 17, K 2 tog. "	*	180
15″	*K 16, K 2 tog. "	*	170
16-½″	*K 15, K 2 tog. "	*	160
18″	*K 14, K 2 tog. "	*	150
19″	*K 13, K 2 tog. "	*	140
20″	*K 12, K 2 tog. "	*	130
21″	*K 11, K 2 tog. "	*	120

Work 1″ even. Bind off easy.

FINISHING: Using ¾″ or 1″ elastic, measure to fit (the average is 2″ less than waist measurements) . Overlap and sew ends together. Pin elastic inside top edge of skirt, spacing evenly around. Sew with yarn or heavy matching thread on inside top edge using blanket stitch. Crochet 1 row sc around bottom edge.

CHARTING FOR HEM FACINGS

If you wish a tailored or bottom edge with a hem facing, there are two methods of knitting this.

(1) Cast on 20% less stitches than instructions call for. Work depth of hem to within one row or hemline. Increase (Method No. 3) evenly around to original number of stitches. Purl one round. Resume knitting around and around following skirt instructions.

(2) Or, cast on number of stitches as per instructions using circular needle same size as for body of skirt. Change to circular needle one or two sizes smaller and work balance of hem facing and hemline (one purl round). Change to large circular needle and continue as per skirt instructions.

TO CHART A SLEEVE CAP

MEASUREMENTS FOR WOMEN

DEPTH OF ARMHOLE	DEPTH OF CAP
6-1/2" to 7-1/4"	4-1/2"
7-1/2" to 8"	4-3/4"
8" to 8-1/2"	5"
(Allow 2" to 3" for binding off at top of cap.)	

MEASUREMENTS FOR MEN

DEPTH OF ARMHOLE	DEPTH OF CAP
8-1/2" to 9"	3-1/2"
9-1/2" to 10"	4"
10" to 10-1/2"	4-1/2"
(Allow 5" to 6" for binding off at top of cap.)	

Decrease 1 st each side every other row for shaping, in addition to bound-off stitches at underarm.

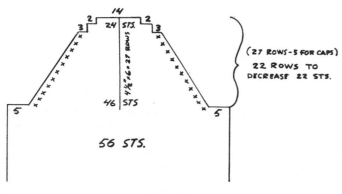

Fig. 155

If all decreases cannot be made in the required number of rows, these extra stitches can be eliminated by:

(1) Decreasing 2 sts at each side (K 3 tog.) for one, two, three or four times. This double decrease should be done immediately above the first bound-off row. (Fig. 155).

(2) Or, shaping cap at top by binding off 2 or 3 sts at the beginning of last 2 or 4 rows before final bind-off of cap (Fig. 156).

(1) DIRECTIONS: Bind off 5 sts at the beginning of next 2 rows (46 sts). DOUBLE DECREASE ROW: K 3 tog. at each end of row, every other row 3 times (34 sts).

REGULAR DECREASE ROW: K 2 tog. at each end of row every other row 10 times (14 sts). Bind off 14 sts.

(2) DIRECTIONS: Bind off 5 sts at beginning of next 2 rows (46 sts).

DECREASE ROW: K 2 tog at each end of every other row 11 times (24 sts).

Bind off 3 sts at the beginning of the next two rows and 2 sts at the beginning of the next two rows (14 sts). Bind off 14 sts.

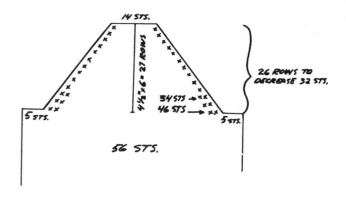

Fig. 156

TO CHART A COLLAR

If designing collars for sweaters or coats, width around neck in any pattern should be 14" to 16" finished, the exact length depending on size of garment and how far apart ends of collars are at fronts.

Any shape, size, pattern stitch or style of collar can be made, keeping neck edge to the correct measurement.

For double-faced coat collars, top side should be at least 1/2" deeper than facing, to allow more material for folding back from neck edge.

SHORT ROWS

Short rows are rows that are not completely knitted across every row. If instructions say, "Turn." and you have not reached the end of the row, this indicates a short row and you turn work around as if at the end of a row and place needles in the opposite hands.

After turn, the first stitch is slipped to make the smallest and smoothest connection for these extra rows. The turning points are usually staggered at even intervals across the knitting with complete rows in between. Turning points would not be lined up on top of each other without one or more complete rows between turning points.

These short rows are used in pieces to make a section deeper, yet not disturb depth of the rest of the piece, as in collar, pants, darts, borders and diagonal shapings as for shoulder shapings, pockets, etc.

TIGHTENING SLIP STITCH IN SHORT ROWS

Sometimes the turning stitch will look loose, particularly on Stockinette. In the piece of knitting to eliminate this loose stitch, work over to this slip stitch on next row. Insert needle through stitch in the row below and stitch on needle. Knit the two off as one stitch. It is a little difficult to get this picked up because it is tight but is excellent in eliminating the loose slip stitch. This is used in pieces of knitting like collars, pants, etc. but is not applicable to shoulder shaping.

SHAPING SHOULDERS IN SHORT ROWS

In this method of shaping shoulders stitches are not bound off but remain on needle and are bound off after shaping is done on back and fronts.

Instructions would read:

BACK: Bind off 8 sts at the beginning of next 6 rows.

Row 1: Knit across to last 8 sts. Bring yarn to front of work. Sl 1 st. Put yarn to back of work. Turn.

Row 2: Purl across row to last 8 sts. Put yarn to back of work. Sl 1 st. Bring yarn to front of work. Turn.

Row 3: Knit across to last 16 sts. Bring yarn to front of work. Sl 1 st. Put yarn to back of work. Turn.

Row 4: Purl across row to last 16 sts. Put yarn to back of work. Sl 1 st. Bring yarn to front of work. Turn.

Row 5: Knit across to last 24 sts. Bring yarn to front of work. Sl 1 st. Put yarn to back of work. Turn.

Row 6: Purl across row to last 24 sts. Put yarn to back of work. Sl 1 st. Bring yarn to front of work. Turn. Back of neck stitches are put on holder or bound off.

When shaping shoulders on fronts, left front would be worked as the purl rows and right front would be worked as the knit rows.

BINDING OFF SHORT-ROW SHOULDER SHAPINGS

(1) Weave or graft (Kitchener stitch) these shoulders together on right side of knitting.

(2) Or, on wrong side, bind off shoulders together as follows: Match fronts to back. Have points of needles for back and one front pointing in the same direction.

Insert needle through first stitch on front needle and first stitch on back needle. Knit these two stitches off as one. Knit another stitch off both needles in the same manner. Bind off one stitch. Continue in this manner across until all stitches have been bound off.

(3) Each piece can be bound off separately and sewed together.

CHANGING PATTERNS AND PIECES

One of the most frequent questions asked by knitters is how do I change a pattern or the size of a garment.

SUGGESTED ADJUSTMENTS HERE ARE BUILT ENTIRELY ON THE PREMISE THAT YOU ARE KNITTING TO GAUGE AND WITH GOOD TENSION.

Since the adjustments of patterns could be innumerable, the following are some ideas to solve the problems we have frequently in yarn shops. With this knowledge, you will be able to try, pick and choose those ideas that will be most successful in making adjustments in your knitting.

During the last few years, patterns have been designed not only for (new) Sizes 10, 12, 14 but also 16. The persons who have difficulty in securing patterns are those that wear sizes under and over these, such as, Sizes 6, 8, and 18 and over.

Just recently (new) Size 8 is being published for the young adults. These patterns, young, smart and up-to-date, are greeted with delight and are introducing many new young knitters to the pleasure of making their own garments and wearing lovely custom made knits at a very reasonable cost.

For the Size 18 and over, patterns are scarce. There are a few publications, some old and some new—but you do have to hunt and watch for the new designs.

Since you can always figure from the stitches and gauge in a pattern the finished size of the garment, you can compare the measurements to the garment you need. This will quickly show you which of the methods of changing size you will have to use to make garment fit well.

TO CHANGE SIZE

(1) Add or subtract stitches in width
(2) Raise or lower needle size
(3) Knit to a paper pattern
(4) Chart your own pattern

ADD OR SUBTRACT STITCHES IN WIDTH

I would add or subtract stitches in width, ONLY TO MAKE ONE SIZE DIFFERENCE, in pattern as printed and this is applicable only so long as it does not interfere with the style or pattern stitch, such as an Aran pattern.

EXAMPLE: Size 10 pattern would be used for Size 8 garment but subtract 1″ of stitches in back and 1″ of stitches in front, dividing the stitches evenly and substracting these from the shoulder sections. Shorten length of body and sleeves if needed but the usual adjustment is in width only for this size.

EXAMPLE: For Size 18, ONLY TO MAKE ONE SIZE DIFFERENCE, use Size 16 pattern but add 1″ of stitches in back and 1″ of stitches in front, dividing the stitches evenly and adding these to the shoulder areas. Lengthen the body and sleeves if needed. If person has extra heavy arms, increase by one-half the number of stitches bound off under the arm in both body and sleeves, which will not make sleeves larger around but will allow a little more room in the armhole.

RAISE OR LOWER NEEDLE SIZE

After stitch gauge and size of needles for body of garment have been determined, raising or lowering needles one size is the easiest manner of changing pattern ONE SIZE and a method which I have used many times. Its accurarcy can only be determined by measuring as pieces are worked.

Basically there is 2″ difference in the finished bust measurements in garments. See page 1 for table. Although this rule cannot be exact because of the difference in tension, yarn, needle sizes and pattern stitch, on Stockinette stitch, with needle sizes from 4 through 9, and sometimes 10, we can secure 2″ more in width by raising needles ONE SIZE and 2″ less by lowering needles ONE SIZE.

EXAMPLE: If you wish a Size 18, work for gauge on the Size 16 pattern and then RAISE ALL NEEDLES REQUIRED, ONE SIZE. Since there is no exact proportionate measurement possible with this rule, be careful when working with bulky yarns and measure frequently. The larger needles from 10-½ up, the faster you will get extra width.

EXAMPLE: If you wish a Size 8, work for gauge on the Size 10 pattern and LOWER ALL NEEDLES REQUIRED ONE SIZE. This will give you at least 2″ less in the bust measurements of garment.

USING DIFFERENT SIZED NEEDLES ON THE SAME YARN

Note that after just a little knitting experience, you have learned that different sized needles can be used on the same yarn. These sizes can vary from seven sizes for use on one basic yarn on the market today to three sizes on another, such as bulkies. Unless a novelty item, the needles and gauge given in the pattern are the preferred sizes for a particular yarn and pattern stitch for the average knitter.

You will have to use your own judgment as to whether the changing of needle size will work the yarn for its best results. If too tight and hard, the desirable softness and pliability of the knit is lost; if too loose, knit is "sleazy" and shape will not hold in wearing or washing. These factors seldom cause trouble except when going extremely away from the basic size needles for a particular yarn and stitch.

KNIT TO A PAPER PATTERN

If the pattern you need is more than one size over or under basic sizes, as a Size 6 or Size 20, I do not recommend adding or subtracting stitches or changing needle sizes but work from a paper pattern or chart your own size. If you cannot locate patterns for these extra sizes, the paper pattern method is a most convenient manner of working out this need.

Make a pattern from one of your own garments. It is a good idea to select a garment that has been worn several times, which fits well and comfortably. Using a strong wrapping paper, make paper pattern from this garment, to its measurments, in different pieces, as you would need when knitting a back, fronts, sleeves, etc. Take the yarn to be used, work a square 6″ swatch and measure for stitch gauge. Multiply gauge by the number of inches pattern measures across bottom edge of one piece. Cast on. Knit in pattern stitch to fit this paper pattern piece. Use yardstick or ruler and draw 1″ block squares on pattern pieces. This will show you very quickly how much shaping will need to be done in each inch. Mark on this paper pattern, any and all information as you work, as to size of needles, stitch gauge, number of stitches cast on, pattern stitch and shapings—this will give you a permanent record for future use.

To double check the correctness of the paper pattern, before beginning to knit your garment, cut out pieces of brown muslin or old sheeting, using your paper pattern. Baste pieces together and try on for fit. This will quickly show you what adjustments, if any, need to be made before knitting.

Guard against judging sizes of pieces by looks. MEASURE!

With the great variation in yarns, stitches, needles and materials, plus borders and trims, you can make any style knit garment for any occasion. This method requires a little more preparation, constant measurement and checking for size but can be done very easily with fine knitting results.

KNITTING TO PAPER SEWING PATTERNS

Purchase a sewing pattern of the item you wish to knit, being careful that size is not too big. Very simple patterns with few pieces should be selected.

This is worked in the same manner as making your own paper pattern. Knitting should be shaped so vertical rows are on the straight of the pattern. Because of the softness and stretch of the knitted fabric, slanted, draped or bias knitting is difficult to hold in shape and is not recommended.

After pattern has been adjusted to fit you, rule paper pieces off in 1" blocks, which will show you how much shaping needs to be done in each inch.

CHART YOUR OWN PATTERN

Method (4) is for professional designers and those knitters who like a challenge and wish to create an entire garment of their own design. Few knitters have the talent or the time for this and from the innumerable patterns available, can select a pattern similar to the one desired and adapt it to their needs. For the beginner in designing, chart a pattern and expect to make the garment twice, once to make a model and the second time to make corrections.

CHANGING BASIC PIECES

Since the need for and the possibilities of adjusting patterns is unending, this can be discussed only in general. Adapting these ideas will solve many a knitting problem and adjustment which occur constantly in yarn shops.

The following instances concerning sweaters presumes they are in Stockinette stitch with ribbed bottom edges and cuffs and knitted to gauge, although the same principles apply to other pattern stitches also.

SLEEVES TOO TIGHT

Usually this occurs because knitter is using an "old-fashioned" pattern that was designed with skinny, tight sleeves and a long sleeve cap. If sleeve is adjusted to contain more stitches at this spot, cap would have to be shortened and reshaped, which can be done by the trial and error method.

I seldom try to change sleeve caps and sizes of armholes. Where armhole is for set-in sleeves that are just too narrow across the upper arm, most knitters, rather than make changes or adjustments, select a better fitting sleeve from another pattern with the same stitch gauge and the same armhole shaping and length.

If knitting sleeves from top down as on page 74, additional stitches can be allowed for more width.

CHANGING ARMHOLES AND SLEEVES CAPS FOR UNDER AND OVER SIZES

If you need a Size 8, the Size 10 armhole will fit. Make your adjustment in number of stitches in front and back of garment to make the smaller size. Shorten pieces if necessary.

If you need a Size 18, you can wear the Size 16 armhole, adding

the number of stitches needed to the front and back of garment to make a larger size.

For all other under and over sizes, patterns must be secured in correct size or charted specifically to have correct proportions in shaping and fit.

CUFFS

People probably are more uncomfortable with badly fitting cuffs (and too long sleeves) than any other part of a garment. Changes can be made to make cuffs more narrow, wider, shorter or longer.

If your cuffs have a tendency to become loose after a few wearings or are always too big, make them smaller on the original knitting by subtracting 1" or more of stiches from the number to be cast on for cuff and increase this amount of stitches at top of ribbing or on first row of knitting.

TO MEASURE ACCURATELY FOR CUFF SIZE

I use a piece of the ribbing that has already been knitted, as at bottom of back and place this around wrist like a cuff. Count the stitches and use this number to cast on.

Since you must have the correct number of stitches pattern calls for when you reach the underarm, any stitches omitted in the cuff must be placed at the top of the ribbing, or in the first row of knitting, or added to the number of increases to be made at the underarm edges.

In good designing all increases on the underarm of a sleeve should be done several inches before you reach the armhole shaping. This will vary from 6" to 1-½", the average being about 3".

In working in extra increases, if they cannot all be worked in before this straight section is reached, space the increases closer together.

CHANGING SHAPE OF SLEEVES TO ARMHOLE

FOR MORE FULLNESS ABOVE CUFF, add at least 1" of stitches at top of ribbing and subtract these stitches from the number to be increased on the underarm edges and space underarm increases further apart.

FOR WIDER SLEEVES AT LOWER HALF OF SLEEVE, make increases evenly at regular intervals but close enough together to finish just above elbow. We have had more complaints from both men and women and altered more sleeves of this shape than any other kind. Be sure you want plenty of room at the elbow if you use this.

FOR A SLIM, TAPERED SLEEVE, spread all increases evenly, beginning 1" above and ending 2" to 3" below armhole shaping.

FOR GOLF OR FULL SLEEVES, make a very firm tight cuff and put three-fourths to four-fifths of the increases evenly spaced across top of ribbing at cuff and balance on edges.

CHANGING OR ALTERING SLEEVES CAPS THAT ARE TOO LONG

If you do not wish to reknit these, sew sleeve cap in, easing any excess under shoulder seam. This can be left in the garment or the excess material double stitched on sewing machine and cut off.

TO FIT AND REKNIT CAP OF SLEEVE

Fit and baste in sleeve cap, allowing any excess to fall to the inside. With a contrast color of sewing thread, run thread around top edge of sleeve cap at seam to mark shaping. Remove sleeve and knit the SECOND sleeve cap to the shape as outlined on first cap. Then remove basting and reknit FIRST sleeve cap to match second.

If sleeve caps are too long and shoulders are too wide, treat the knitting as fabric. Fit, baste, machine stitch and trim.

ADJUSTING SLEEVE CAPS THAT ARE TOO SHORT

Because of the variance in the row gauge of knitters, be careful of set-in sleeves that are written by rows. If you knit MORE rows per inch than gauge, cap will be SHORTER than needed. The shaping of the sleeve cap is probably correct but to make the extra length needed, it will be necessary to work a few more rows in the straight section before again shaping top of sleeve cap. To determine how many more rows are needed, fit sleeve and measure. Unravel the top of sleeve cap and add the number of rows needed. Shape top of sleeve cap. Baste and fit again before final sewing.

CHANGING LONG SLEEVES TO THREE QUARTER SLEEVES AND VICE VERSA

When designing sleeves, you will find styles large, small, short, long, loose, tight. Many are influenced by the size needle, pattern stitch or texture, kinds of yarn, style of garment and the individual's knitting tension. Since there can be no hard and fast rule, the following will give you a basic example.

TO CHANGE LONG SLEEVES TO THREE QUARTERS, which are 3" to 4-1/2" shorter, add 1" of stitches to number of cast-on stitches for cuff. Make increases closer together, always evenly spaced on edges, beginning 1" above cuff and ending 2" to 3" before underarm shaping.

EXAMPLE: CARDIGAN, SIZE 10
Gauge: 5 sts = 1", 6 rows = 1"
Length of long sleeve to underarm, 16-1/2"
Length of three quarter sleeve to underarm, 12" (Fig. 157)

Referring to long sleeve (Fig. 16), increases on edges have been done beginning 4-1/2" from beginning and ending at least 3" before underarm shaping. In this instance the five increases, 2" apart, were finished at 4-1/2" before underarm shaping.

Enlarge cuff in the three quarters sleeve by adding four stitches to the number to be cast on (44 sts), making ribbing 1-1/2" deep. In-

crease 4 sts, approximately 1", at top of cuff (48 sts). Spreading the remaining increases every 2" four times, shaping is finished at 3-1/2" before underarm shaping.

TO CHANGE THREE QUARTER SLEEVES TO LONG SLEEVES, do the opposite of the above by subtracting at least 1" of stitches from number of cast-on stitches for cuffs. The subtracted stitches will have to be added to the increases to be made. The spacing of the increases

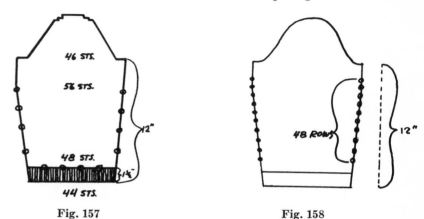

Fig. 157   Fig. 158

will depend upon the shape sleeve you desire, but still must be evenly spaced on edges, bginning 1" to 2" above cuffs and ending 2" to 3" from underarm shaping.

INCREASES SPACED BY ROWS

In this cardigan pattern there has been plenty of room to change and adjust. In some patterns you may have only 8" to make 10 increases under the arm. In this case, increases are spaced evenly by ROWS, instead of inches. You will therefore need to learn the number of rows you will have in which to work these increases.

EXAMPLE (Fig. 158): Here shaping will begin on the 4th or 6th row from top of cuff and end 2" or 3" below underarm shaping.

8 (inches for increases) x 6 (rows per 1") = 48 (total rows in which to increase).

48 (rows) divided by 10 (number of increases on one side) = 4-3/4 (row on which to make increase). We will use the closest number of rows 5, as the row on which to make increases on each edge. All increases would be finished in 50 rows.

Since a fifth row increase would necessitate alternating increasing on both right and wrong sides and since it would be difficult to keep count of the uneven row increasing, the same results can be obtained by making increases on the knit side only, alternating increases every 4th and every 6th row.

Should you at any time need to do increases every 3rd row, they can be done on the knit side, alternating increases every 2nd and 4th row for the same result.

HOW TO KNIT SLEEVES (NOT RAGLAN) FROM TOP DOWN

This is one of the questions most frequently asked. Some of the advantages of knitting sleeves from the top down are: They can be controlled for width and various lengths; if sufficient yarn was not purchased, sleeves can be shortened to use amount of yarn available; those sleeve caps picked up and worked down by circular knitting eliminate the sewing of underarm seams and the armhole seams have excellent elasticity for comfortable wearing.

SET-IN SLEEVES (separate pieces), WORKED FROM TOP DOWN

Use your regular sleeve pattern, reversing the order of the instructions and working from top down. It may be necessary on some sleeves, where you have an area which is worked even for several rows (Fig. 9F) to know your row gauge. The easiest way to learn the number of rows in a sleeve cap is to chart the stitches as per the pattern on graft paper or draw a rough outline of the sleeve shaping. Knowing the row gauge or the depth in inches, you can determine how many rows are worked in a sleeve cap.

This manner of knitting from top down can be done from any pattern since it does give you definite measurements and numbers of stitches.

IN REVERSING INSTRUCTIONS, YOU WILL BE CASTING ON AND INCREASING STITCHES RATHER THAN BINDING OFF AND DECREASING.

TO PICK UP AND KNIT SLEEVES FROM TOP DOWN

LET ME MAKE IT VERY CLEAR THAT IDEAS AND EXAMPLES ONLY ARE GIVEN IN THE FOLLOWING TWO METHODS. DEFINITE NUMBERS OF STITCHES ARE NOT AND CANNOT BE GIVEN BECAUSE OF THE UNENDING COMBINATIONS POSSIBLE WITH SIZES FROM 2 TO 44 AND AT LEAST 15 BASIC STITCH AND ROW GAUGES.

(1) TO PICK UP AND KNIT IN LONG SLEEVES

Sleeve cap in this method is shorter than most regular caps and picks up most of the sleeve stitches on the first row and is worked flat for the entire cap and sleeve. The following example is in sport weight yarn. Other yarns would be worked proportionately in number of stitches and rows.

EXAMPLE: Sport Yarn
1 pair each No. 4 and No. 2 needles
6-1/2 sts = 1"
Sizes 10, 12, 14, 16
Armholes measure: 8"-8"-8-1/2"-8-1/2"
Total number of stitches to be picked up,
84-90-94-100

DIRECTIONS:
Sew in shoulder seams. With right side of work facing you, and with No. 4 needles, pick up and knit 64-66-70-72 sts between last decrease on front and last decrease on back of armhole shaping.
*Turn and purl back, picking up 2 additional sts at end of row. Turn. K across, picking up 2 additional sts at end of row. Repeat between *'s until entire armhole is picked up (84-90-94-100 sts). Work even for....

(2) SHAPED CAP SLEEVE PICKED UP AROUND ARMHOLE AND KNITTED DOWN IN CIRCULAR KNITTING

These instructions are to give you the IDEA of how this is done. You will need to adapt and adjust this method to different sizes and different kinds of yarns. Keep a record of exactly what you do on each sleeve and each weight yarn.

This manner of doing sleeves allows much more elasticity in seams and less thickness in the underarm area.

Garments should be knitted from bottom up, preferably with the body in one piece and stitches for bind-off at underarm placed on stitch holders. However, garments can be knitted in pieces with stitches bound off under the arms.

TO WORK: Sew shoulder seams together and underarm seams, if body has been made in pieces.

Slipover sweaters may have shoulder seams woven but cardigan seams should always be sewed with back stitch.

EXAMPLE: Knitting Worsted
1 set Size 8 d.p. needles
Gauge: 5 sts = 1", 6 rows = 1"
Size 10 garment
Armholes measure 7-1/2"
Total number of stitches to be picked up, 56 sts.

KNITNOTE: INSERT NEEDLE ONE ROW DOWN IN MATERIAL TO PICK UP STITCHES.

Row 1: With knitting worsted and working across top of armhole on knit side, pick up and knit 5 to 6 sts on each side of shoulder seam over an area of about 2-1/2" to 3".

Row 2: Sl 1 purlwise, purl across row. Pick up and purl 3 sts at end of row inserting needle from knit to purl side of knitting. These three stitches will be picked up 3 out of 4 rows or 3 out of 5 rows. Do not pick up a stitch if it looks like you are going to leave a hole. Usually your needle will go under two horizontal threads twice and one horizontal thread once. Turn work.

Row 3: Sl 1 knitwise and knit across row. Pick up and knit 3 sts at end of row, inserting needle from knit to purl side of knitting. Turn.

Repeat Rows 2 and 3, keeping stitches picked up evenly along both sides of armhole edges until you have reached the beginning of the armhole shaping (the last decrease worked when knitting armhole from bottom up), ending with a KNIT row.

With knitting worsted for a Size 10 to 12 garment, this will be approximately 40 sts.

BEGIN CIRCULAR KNITTING AS FOLLOWS:

Take a d.p. needle, pick up in every tight nub (every other row) to stitch holder, pick up each stitch on stitch holders and pick up every tight nub on other side of armhole shaping. The number of stitches must come out even and if an extra stitch is needed, pick up at the center of the underarm seam.

If stitches are bound-off at underarm and seam is too thick, pick up front thread only across this section.

Place marker on needle at center of underarm seam.

Divide the stitches on three needles and knit around and around, continuing with your sleeve pattern making decreases on each side of marker.

GUSSET

If you have more stitches than pattern calls for, these are decreased at the underarm shaping, making a small V-shaped section called a gusset.

EXAMPLE: Should you have 10 sts too many, place markers on each side of the center 12 sts at underarm. ON EACH OF THE NEXT 5 ROUNDS, INSIDE THESE MARKERS, KNIT THE FIRST 2 STS TOG. AND THE LAST 2 STS TOG. This will eliminate the extra 10 sts as well as give more room under the arm.

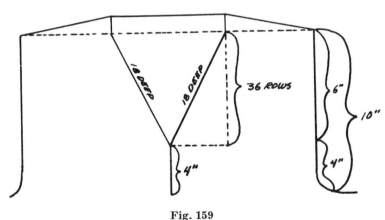

Fig. 159

CHANGING THE DEPTH OF A V-NECK

A regular V-neck shaping begins in the same row as first bound-off stitches at underarm.

Numerous times knitters wish to make a short V-neck from a long V or vice versa and do not know how to change pattern. This may sound difficult or complicated but it is really very easy to do and has been done many, many times. You can do it too.

It merely requires counting and this is done (1) by working from the finished back of the sweater or (2) by changing the pattern.

USING BACK OF SWEATER AS GUIDE IN MAKING A SHORT V-NECK

Because of the variance of row gauge of different knitters, I prefer to work from the knitted piece of back of sweater because I have found it to be the easiest and the most accurate way to determine the actual number of rows involved for that particular knitter.

You will need to learn (1) how many stitches are to be decreased on each side of V and (2) how often.

The number of stitches to be decreased is the same as the number of bound-off stitches across back of neck. For example, if back of neck has 36 stitches bound off, 18 stitches will be decreased on each side of neck.

Place a marker at center of row where you wish V to begin. Always remember that a regular neckband will fill in neck space at least one more inch. Depending on the size, this V should not be started higher than 3-1/2" to 4½" above beginning of armhole shaping, since we need sufficient rows to make all the necessary decreases for a well-shaped V.

Next, count the knitted rows from the marker to the first row of shoulder shaping or within 1" of bound-off stitches at back of neck. For easy and good fitting, decreases should not extend above this.

To learn how often to decrease, divide the number of rows you have counted by the number of decreases to be made. Therefore, 36 (rows for decreases) divided by 18 (decreases) equals 2 (number of the row on which decreases will be made). Instructions would read: "Decrease 1 st on each side of neck every 2nd row 18 times . . . ."

CHANGING FROM A REGULAR V-NECK PATTERN TO A SHORT V-NECK

Since most of these short V's are made in men's sweaters, a Size 40 man's regular V-neck sweater will be used as an example to be changed to a short V-neck.

In this example, Fig. 159, 36 sts are at back of neck, making 18 sts to be decreased on each side of V. Short V is started 4" above first bound-off row of underarm with 6" of rows left for shaping. Therefore, 6 (inches) multiplied by 6 (rows per inch) equals 36 (rows). The 36 (rows) divided by 18 (decreases on one side of neck) equals 2 (number of the row on which decrease will be made).

Most of the time these rows and decreases don't work out exactly even by numbers and the decreasing may be finished too soon, making a jog in the V shaping or may finish too close to top of neck.

EXAMPLE: If you have 36 (rows) divided by 15 (decreases) equals 2 (number of the row for decrease), plus an additional 6 rows left to work even, this would end the shaping 2" below bound-off stitches of back of neck. Decreases should be spread more toward the top for a better looking and better balanced V shape.

The following are two different distributions for this example which will spread the decreases as evenly as possible and still distribute them over the length needed to make a good V.

(1) Make 3 decreases every 4th row (12 rows) and balance of 12 decreases every 2nd row (24 rows), totaling 36 rows.

(2) Or, alternate decreases every 2nd and every 4th rows three times (18 rows) and every 2nd row 9 times (18 rows), totalling 36 rows.

RAGLAN SHAPINGS

ADJUSTING RAGLAN ARMHOLES

In knitting raglans, few persons knit exactly to gauge both by stitch and row. THEREFORE, IT IS IMPORTANT THAT YOU HAVE YOUR STITCH GAUGE CORRECT FIRST FOR THE WIDTH OF GARMENT. If your gauge makes your knitting FEWER rows per inch than gauge, your armhole seam will be LONGER because it will take more space to use up all the rows. If your gauge makes your knitting MORE rows per inch than gauge, your armhole will be SHORTER because you have knitted rows closer together and used them up quicker.

KNITNOTE: BE SURE TO WRITE DOWN ANY CHANGES YOU MAKE IN PATTERN INSTRUCTIONS. IF YOU ADJUST THE RAGLAN ARMHOLES ON THE BACK, YOU MUST MAKE THE SAME ADJUSTMENTS ON FRONTS AND SLEEVE EDGES. RAGLAN SEAMS SHOULD MATCH STITCH FOR STITCH AND ROW FOR ROW.

ADJUSTING TOO LONG RAGLAN SHAPING

Determine the actual length of armhole according to your row gauge and compare to pattern armhole gauge. If your raglan armhole is 1" longer than pattern's, it certainly will not look different, will be quite satisfactory and comfortable but will have made garment 1" longer.

However, if 2" or more longer, (1) probably garment is too large all over. You could drop needles down one size, which will make entire garment proportionately smaller all over.

(2) Some men's patterns are designed to have long raglan seams which can become too long when knitted too loosely. This is a tension problem which you must solve. Perhaps the pattern size was too large and a smaller size should have been selected.

Or, (3) raglans can be shortened as a last resort, if body size is correct width, by making double decreases a few times to use up stitches quicker. The double decreases are made at the beginning of the shaping at underarm and each double decrease will shorten raglan by two extra rows. A double decrease is made by K 3 tog. or Sl 1, K 2 tog., PSSO. I would not use more than three or four of these in one raglan shaping.

ADJUSTING TOO SHORT RAGLAN ARMHOLES

Raglan armholes are usually too short because knitter is a tight knitter and uses up the rows too quickly, making raglan armhole not only too short but too small. Length of raglan edge should never be less than 10-1/2" for Size 10 pattern. A quick check of the length of armhole seam will allow you to figure how many additional rows are needed for proper length.

Sometimes patterns are designed badly and although the width of the garment is correct, the raglan armholes are just too short in depth and need more rows. Like a lot of knitters, I too learned the hard way. I blithely knitted a sweater, finished and blocked it—never checking the measurement of the armholes along the raglan edge or the depth vertically. I was quite surprised that I couldn't get the sleeves on. Raglan seams were only 9" long on the edge. I chalked that sweater up to experience, unraveled the yarn and have yet to reknit it. Since that experience, I always check the finished length of armhole and if it is not long enough, see that the additional rows needed are added.

EDGES

Too many knitters worry unnecessarily about the edges of their knitting being loose, uneven, curling, different lengths on the sides of the same piece, etc. Read Manual, page 33 for basic information.

Another example of a too short armhole is: Recently I had a knitter who brought in pieces of a raglan sweater to be sewed together. Because she liked the "looks of it better", the end stitches had been pulled so tight that edges were knotted, seams would not stretch at all, and the armholes were too short.

Try always to look ahead for the desired results in your knitting but don't over-compensate by working too tight or too loose. Here again, let the yarn work itself.

Do not worry about loose or uneven edges that are to be sewed into a seam. Difference in length of edges can be eased in to fit and a good back stitch seam will give it body.

If border edges of piece are loose, try some of the following: Slip first stitch at the beginning of each row; crochet edges with slip stitch or single crochet; face with ribbon or other materials; use smaller needles on edges only; keep needle points closer together while knitting end stitches. For extreme looseness, work off very tip of needle which will make stitches smaller but don't overdo this.

Vertical edges on borders can be reinforced by picking up a separate strand of yarn and KNITTING THE EDGE STITCH ONLY WITH DOUBLE STRANDS OF YARN.

Silk thread knitted with the yarn for the first few rows at bottom edges of sweater, cuffs and at top of ribbing on neck edges will help keep knitting from stretching and in shape.

TO MAKE RAGLAN ARMHOLES LONGER

Work three rows of pattern between decreases (decrease every 4th row) instead of one row of pattern (decrease every 2nd row), until all the extra length needed has been worked in.

Three rare exceptions are:

1. On the fronts of a cardigan to help shape neck, sometimes the tops of the front armhole will slant off and finish before the top of the adjacent raglan sleeve seam.

2. There also are knits where on the front pieces decreases are every 4th row for about 3 times with the balance decreased every 2nd row. The

back decreases were all done every 2nd row. This is either to make the pattern work, give more length or to allow a piece to remain wider for a longer time.

3. A rare pattern has a longer front edge on the armhole than on back, in which case you will have a right armhole sleeve and a left armhole sleeve. These are used more in set-in sleeve patterns than in raglans.

TO MEASURE RAGLAN PIECES ALREADY KNITTED

Since few knitters check out patterns before knitting and if you have already knitted the back of a garment, you may suddenly have that old instinctive feeling that something is not right. Again determine what size the armhole is and what it should be.

Count up the number of rows used to make raglan shaping and divide by the row gauge. Result is inches in depth. Measure your knitted pieces straight up from the first point of shaping. The difference in depth between your raglan and the pattern raglan is what needs to be adjusted.

Decide what needs to be done and then unravel to armhole shaping, use new yarn and knit again. Frequently you can get by by using a too long raglan seam but a too short seam will probably have to be redone.

Another way of checking is to remember that the slanted outside edge of a raglan should never be less than 10-1/2" beginning with a Size 10 sweater, will vary in length with different designs and can be as much as 16" to 17" on men's sweaters.

Many times knitters think the raglan pieces are going to be too big and long for men's sweaters but when sewed together, they fit well.

So many knitters say the pieces "look" too big or too small. When asked, "Did you measure it?" "Well,—no." You are asking for trouble if you change the pattern, needles, tension or size but never measure. DON'T GO BY "LOOKS"! CHECK PATTERN AND MEASURE.

TO KEEP A RAGLAN SWEATER FROM "HIKING UP" IN BACK

You can do either of the following to help this.

(1) If knitting from the top down, sweater would be started with about two-thirds of the original number of stitches to be cast on and the balance cast on in sections as you work back and forth in short rows. This will keep the front at the correct place for wearing and build up the back of neck at least 1" which eliminates the usual "hiking."

(2) Or, work four to six short rows across back, level with the beginning of armhole shaping. These can be worked like basic short rows close to edges or by picking up bound-off stitches at underarm.

TO MAKE SMALL CAP AT SHOULDER ON SLEEVELESS SHELLS

Many adult women prefer a small cap to sleeveless shells.

To change a basic shell pattern, work to the place for underarm shaping. Place marker. Do not make underarm shaping but work even until the armhole measures 1/2" to 1" less than pattern indicates. Divide stitches to

be bound off on shoulders into five or six sections and bind off shoulders.

If even more cap is wanted, at marker cast on 1" of stitches and work in same manner, binding off about 1" of stitches at a time on the shoulders.

CASTING ON AT END OF ROWS

This can be done using Method No. 1, 2 or 3 (see Manual pages 12 and 50-51). If, for example, you are working in Stockinette and instructions read, "Cast on 8 sts at the beginning of the next 2 rows.", instructions really mean that cast-on stitches will be put on needle at the end of row using Methods 1 and 3 BEFORE turning to work next row and using Method 2, AFTER turning row.

Using Method No. 1, knit across row. Pick up end of yarn and cast on 8 sts knitwise. Turn. Purl across row. Pick up end of yarn and cast on 8 sts purlwise.

Using Method No. 2, knit across row. Turn work and knit on 8 sts. Purl across row. Turn. Knit on 8 sts.

Using Method No. 3, knit across row. Take your free needle and with another piece of yarn, cast on 8 sts purlwise. With needle containing knitting, knit across these 8 stitches completing row. Turn. Purl across row. Take free needle and with another piece of yarn, cast on 8 sts knitwise. Purl across these 8 stitches completing row.

IF CAST-ON STITCHES TOO TIGHT

Try casting on over two needles held together. Or, use size needle for body of garment for cast-on row only, changing to smaller needle for knitting ribbing.

IF CAST-ON STITCHES TOO LOOSE

Use smaller needles. Or, knit in back of stitch on first cast-on row, which twists stitches and makes firmer, tighter edges.

TO MAKE OPENING IN BACK OF KNIT

If you wish to make an opening in a garment for a zipper or buttons at the back of neck, the opening should begin about 4" before first shoulder shaping. This will allow sufficient length for a 5" zipper.

To knit, work across one-half of the back and join another ball of yarn to work the other half. Work each side with its own ball of yarn across every row. Continue as per instructions.

To finish: Crochet edges and finish with zipper or crochet small loops for buttonholes and sew on small buttons.

TO MAKE SHOULDERS MORE NARROW

If in a pattern stitch that cannot be interrupted with decreases as in making darts, use smaller size needles, beginning when about one-third of armhole depth has been worked. Work this on back and fronts.

LENGTH OF ARMHOLES IN SHELLS

Many shell patterns are much too long in armhole depth, are unattractive to the eye when worn and spoiled if they have to be pulled up or in too much to fit when finishing.

If sizes are 10 to 12 and armholes are more than 6″ in depth or sizes 14 and 16 are more than 6½″, change the pattern and put the extra length from armhole into underarm measurement. This does not change the original total length of the shell, but allows better fitting and a more attractive shell.

On sizes 10 and 12, if measurements are 12″ to underarm and 7″ in armhole, change to 13-½″ to underarm and 6″ in armhole.

On sizes 14 and 16, if measurements are 12″ and 7-½″, change to 13″ to underarm and 6-½″ in armhole.

If crocheting, edges can be worked as follows: One row sc; or 2 rows sc; or 1 row sc and 2nd row, sc in BACK LOOP ONLY; or 1 row of dc. This trim can remain on the outside or be turned under and sewed down as a facing.

ALTERATIONS

BY HAND

Altering means shortening, lengthening, adjusting, reweaving pieces together, reknitting such as facings and separating pieces of knitting and sewing by machine stitching if necessary.

SEPARATING A KNITTING PIECE

Since knitting can not be unravelled from the bottom (unless knitted from the top down), we separate the knitting horizontally across a row by snipping one thread of the yarn and with a crochet hook, undo stitch by stitch across the row (Fig. 160). Although you can start anywhere on the row, I usually start in the middle, first working in one direction and then the other. Undo a few stitches and then cut off the thread. But when you get toward the edges, do not cut thread too short for one side of the row will have an end which should be long enough to tie or weave in later.

Some people take the cut thread and pull it as you would in pulling a thread in a fabric but I find it quicker to take out stitch by stitch. This does not mat, fray or disturb the yarn and keeps you from getting into a real mess if it doesn't pull easily.

Most alterations are too long sweaters, coats, dresses and sleeves. Once in a long time we have a garment that is too short and additional length is needed. With an understanding of how to alter, you will be able to use your knowledge to solve many and varied problems.

Fig. 160

Most of these problems can be discovered and corrected before the garment is finished, although after wearing a few times, they may drop and become too long. With the proper "know-how", you can easily fix it.

TO SHORTEN SWEATERS, DRESSES, COATS AND SLEEVES

SWEATERS

The success of correcting this depends entirely on how the front of the garment is made.

To shorten a pullover is a cinch because all you have to do is open up side seams to begin work or if done circularly, undo one row entirely around garment and continue with alterations.

However, if a cardigan, the borders, buttonholes, how they are spaced, ribbon facing, etc.—all are factors to consider in how much and where to shorten sweater.

First, decide how much the garment is to be shortened. Will it have ribbing knitted on after being shortened, a crocheted edge or facings? If to be ribbed, mark the garment at a spot where ribbing will be picked up and KNITTED DOWNWARD or grafted to body. If edge is to be crocheted or faced, the very bottom edge of sweater should be marked. If edges are faced with ribbon, it can always be pieced on the front edge, if necessary, and a new buttonhole made.

If you have additional new yarn, work with this. If not, pieces of knitting removed will have to be unraveled and "de-kinked" before reknitting. (See Manual page 54).

RIBBING AT BOTTOM EDGE

Separate knitting at the point ribbing will be worked or attached. Either (1) pick up loops on needle, rib down for length desired and bind off in pattern or (2) if you are adept at grafting (Kitchener stitch), separate knitting in SECOND row above top of ribbing border, separate length of piece to be shortened on body of sweater and graft ribbing back onto top piece of knitting. It is a little easier to graft if you have the one row of knit stitch on top of ribbing, although the rib stitch pattern can be grafted without too much trouble.

FACINGS

If facing goes across entire bottom of piece, undo sewing of facing. Separate knitting at what is to be bottom edge of knitting. Pick up loops on knitting needle and make a hem line by purling one row on right side of knitting or knitting one row on wrong side. Continue for depth of facing in Stockinette stitch. Fold facing back and overcast to body.

DRESSES

I recently shortened a blue dress that had a white 2" Stockinette stitch border with matching hem facing. I undid the sewing of facing, opened up the side seams about 8", removed 2" of knitting ABOVE the border on back and front of dress and grafted the white border back on bottom edges of pieces and sewed side seams and facing on hem.

My daughter was skeptical that it could be done or even that it could be grafted, particularly since it was a contrast color. After it was finished, I think one of the nicest compliments I have ever received was my daughter's comment, "Mother, you can do anything!" Even though that isn't true, it made me feel good.

People say, "How did you learn to do this?" There are problems but if you know the basic knitting and altering techniques, you can not only knit well but can use your knowledge to alter and correct too. Don't be afraid to try anything with your knitting.

SKIRTS

Skirts can be shortened by separating the knitted piece ONLY if the knitting has been done back and forth or around and around. Vertical machine-made knits, usually ribbed, are altered entirely by machine stitching.

In shortening any skirt, if too long, take off excess at the bottom and single crochet around edge. If hand-knitted, a pattern stitch border can be reknitted onto the bottom. In this case, shorten to length desired PLUS the depth of any border. Pick up loops on needle and knit.

If skirt is too long and too tight, take off at waist to allow more width through hip line. Finish top with one row single crochet, beading or elastic band. In using beading, make additional allowance in shortening.

If skirts are in pieces, seams must be opened up to allow plenty of room to work and to allow finishing evenly on both sides. I have seen machine-made garments that after separating knitting would be 4" shorter or 4" longer at one corner of a seam. You will have to decide which seam

you are going to use as the finished length and continue to open up the second side seam until material is released and can be fitted to match. Just be cautious before beginning separation of knitting. It is better to separate a piece too long than too short. If too long, you can always shorten a little more.

Knitting yarn back on machine-made garments is usually difficult because (1) it is almost impossible to get the kinks out of the yarn and (2) usually the yarn is cut at each end of the row, making so many, many knots in the knitting, it is hardly worth the trouble.

In crocheting an edge on the bottom, you will usually use three or four rows of this yarn, which creates no particular problem in finishing ends.

Shortening a circular skirt is very easy. Snip yarn at length desired, separate knitting and finish with a row of single crochet or make allowance for a knitted border, pick up loops and knit.

COATS

Coats are shortened in the same manner as for sweaters.

To shorten a garment with a double facing front border and facings on hem, which require a tailored corner, a little more knowledge is needed.

Many coats have these facings on the bottom and front edges and should be shortened BEFORE assembling but they can be shortened after assembling also.

TO WORK: Undo hem facings. Side seams and front border facings should be opened up for about 10" to allow room to work. Turn up to length desired (not counting hem facing). Snip and separate piece. Beginning at front facing edge, bind off all stitches required for double facings, turning edge and front border. Make hemline across balance of row. Work facing in pattern until correct depth. Bind off easy. Take the same number of rows off each piece of garment unless pieces are not the same length. Resew side seams and facings.

I have seen coats where the fronts and back were three different lengths. This is often caused by not pinning seams together evenly before sewing. If one seam is longer than the other, undo more of it, even to armhole if necessary until it can be matched and sewed evenly.

Frequently where tension was not sufficient to hold in shape, particularly on Stockinette stitch, the back of a coat after frequent wear will "sit out" and have a tendency to drop. Length can be taken off one piece only to make an alteration. A common error in knitting is to have two fronts of different lengths. Fronts will usually remain the same or seem a little shorter. This is caused by the front border edges being reinforced when coat is lined which keeps the fronts in shape.

With the fashion of shorter and shorter garments recently, our own knitted coats and linings have been shortened every year for three years now.

SHORTENING SLEEVES

Many times I have had knitters call and say the sweaters they had just finished were too large and, of course, they were quite upset. If possible, the owner of the garment was asked to come in and let me see the fit of the garment. Nine times out of ten, the sleeves were too long. We fixed the sleeves and that solved practically all of the problems. If the sleeves are a comfortable length, sweaters can actually be too large and still be used satisfactorily.

Shortening sleeves is done the same as shortening the bottom of sweaters, except if you have more stitches in the sleeve than you should in the cuff, decrease evenly across first row of ribbing to the correct number of stitches. Rib cuff to length desired and bind off in pattern.

TO GRAFT CUFFS ON

I often graft the ribbed cuffs back on to the shortened sleeves.

TO WORK: Lift top edge of ribbing of cuff up on sleeve and mark where knitting is to be separated. At top of ribbed cuff, snip and separate knitted fabric. Put loose stitches on needle for grafting (page 25). If there are more stitches on the sleeve section than on the top of cuff section, decrease evenly across as you graft pieces together by picking up two stitches as one on the sleeve. This will work fine.

HOW TO MAKE CUFFS SMALLER

Many times after some wear in a garment, cuffs stretch and get bigger and looser. It is very easy to fix these.

To measure, hold cuff around wrist to size desired. Count the number of stitches cuff will contain. Open up underarm seam and separate yarn at top of cuff.

Use new yarn for knitting, if possible. If new yarn is not available, unravel and prepare yarn for reknitting. Using proper size needles for the ribbing, pick up loops across bottom of sleeve. Count the loops. You will probably have more loops on needle than you wish in cuff. The extra stitches are to be decreased evenly across the first row, working in either knit or purl stitch. Continue in pattern until length desired and bind off.

KNITTING ON ADDITIONAL LENGTH

Knitted pieces in any pattern stitch can be separated horizontally at any place in the knitting. Of course, the more complicated the pattern stitch, the more careful you must be in snipping the yarn at a correct starting place and in undoing the stitches. Most of the basic pattern stitches used for garments can be separated easily at bottom of piece so loops can be picked up.

It is difficult to pick up Stockinette stitch and knit down without a horizontal line showing across knitting where stitches are picked up. Sometimes the vertical line of the knitting is interrupted since the loops you pick up are really one-half stitch to the side from those in the first piece of knitting.

Although we have been able to lengthen in Stockinette stitch without interrupting the pattern, the best way to eliminate any markings is to knit a band in another pattern stitch, contrast color, or stripes, etc. This will make a break between the two directions of knitting and act as an insertion or trim. Bottom edge can be finished with original pattern stitch, a crocheted edge, hem or in any manner which will harmonize with the style and trim on garment.

SOLVING ONE KNITTER'S PROBLEM

This is an excellent example of adapting basic knitting knowledge to solving a problem.

A young woman brought in a V-neck sweater to have a neckband knitted. On one side of the neck the decreases were not made at the right times and the shape ended up as Fig. 161. It looked as if this extra section of knitting would surely show even if the neckband was put on correctly.

It was decided to work neckband as it should be and if necessary, double stitch the extra piece and cut it off. My method of picking up stitches was used except on the dotted line.

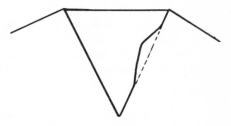

Fig. 161

To pick up three out of four rows across the knitted fabric would not look good. Therefore, I picked up one-half of a thread of one stitch in each row along the dotted line. On the next round, the picked up stitches on the dotted line only were decreased one stitch in each group of four to secure three out of four rows for vertical edges.

This neckband was worked as follows:

PREPARATION ROUND: Pick up stitches across back of neck. Pick up nubs around edges to the dotted line. On OUTSIDE of garment pick up along dotted line one-half of a stitch (one thread) in every row (Fig. 123). Pick up nubs for balance of round.

KNITTING AND INCREASING ROUND (Plus decreasing section

on this garment only): On right side of garment, *knit two nubs and pick up a stitch (Method No. 3 inc), repeat between *'s TO THE DOTTED LINE.

*K 2, K 2 tog., repeat between *'s to end of the dotted line.

*Knit two nubs and pick up a stitch (Method No. 3 increase) on edges, repeat between *'s to back of neck. Knit across back of neck. The correct number of stitches for this neckband are now on needle.

FIRST ROW OF PATTERN STITCH: Work in pattern mitering at V . . . ."

This procedure worked perfectly on this piece and, believe it or not, the 1" ribbing completely covered the extra piece and it layed so very nice and flat under the neckband, it was not necessary even to tack it down.

BY MACHINE ON HAND OR READY-TO-WEAR KNITS

I have had only one or two knitted garments that couldn't be fixed in some manner and these were ready-to-wear and not hand knits.

Sewing knits on the machine is done only as a last resort, for special reasons, as for buttonholes and alterations.

TO ALTER BY MACHINE: USE STRAIGHT MACHINE STITCH. USE ZIG-ZAG ATTACHMENT *ONLY* ON BUTTONHOLES. TO DOUBLE STITCH, MAKE TWO ROWS OF CONTINUOUS STRAIGHT STITCHING ONE ON TOP OF THE OTHER. AFTER ALTERING, TRIM EXCESS MATERIAL AT SEAMS, LEAVING A ¼" TO ⅜" SEAM.

I have never had one of these seams come open. This is a little frightening to do the first time but it can be done quite well and satisfactorily. Never get in a hurry when altering knits. Just be sure you have the correct fit before final stitching and cutting because once stitched and trimmed, there can be no changing.

ALTERING GARMENTS

MAKING A PULLOVER INTO A CARDIGAN

Mark at top front center of neck. Sometimes center of neck is not in the same vertical line as center of bottom edge and any unevenness of front pieces will show less if alteration is made in line with front center of neck.

Keeping in the same line between two stitches, baste from top center to bottom of sweater. Double machine stitch one stitch in from each side of this basting. Remove basting thread and cut front between the two rows of stitching.

Ribbon or trim can be put on inside or outside of these edges. On machine-made sweaters I put the ribbon on the outside as a trim. Turn edges of sweater to outside; fit, turn under ribbon and pin. Baste in place. Machine stitch once around four edges of ribbon and make buttonholes on the ribbon side. Should the pullover be too tight to wear buttoned,

omit buttonholes and wear as a chanel jacket. If ribbon is to be put on as facing, turn under raw edges and work as on page 45.

IF GARMENT IS TOO WIDE UNDER THE SLEEVES AND UNDERARMS

Turn wrong side out, fit on person who is to wear garment and baste to proper size along seams, double stitch seams and cut off excess. If this is a very fine garment or if the raw edges will often show in use, as on a cardigan, cover seams with silk seam binding, sewing by hand.

IF SHOULDERS HANG DOWN TOO LONG

Take out sleeves. Turn pieces wrong side out, fit on person who is to wear garment. Baste. Keep fitting until right. Double machine stitch and cut off excess.

IF SLEEVES ARE TOO LONG

Lift cuff up and pin to correct length on sleeves. Baste. Double stitch and cut off excess.

IF MAKING SHORT SLEEVES OUT OF LONG SLEEVES

1. Often the elbows wear through on a garment which could still be worn if short-sleeved. However, this bottom cuff must be large enough to go around arm comfortably.

To allow easier fitting, cut cuff off at about 1" above top of ribbing, pin cuff at top of sleeve at desired place, fit, double stitch and cut off excess. Any extra fullness can be eased in in the basting. If too much fullness at underarm of sleeve, alter before putting on cuff.

2. Or, you can turn up bottom of sleeve and make a 1" hem, providing the bottom of sleeve is not too large or loose. Here is a place sleeve probably should be shaped to fit and machine stitched before bottom edge is finished.

IF SLEEVES ARE TOO LONG AND TOO WIDE

Usually the cuff is also too wide in this instance, so alter cuff first as above and then alter underarm seam.

IF ENTIRE GARMENT IS TOO LARGE

If neck would be too large after rest of garment has been altered, entire garment should be reknitted or given to someone who can wear it.

IF PULLOVER TOO TIGHT AROUND NECK

Make a center back opening for zipper by basting along length desired. Double stitch around opening. Remove basting and single crochet over edges. Sew in Zipper as on page 46.

FOR GARMENT WHERE NECK ONLY FITS

If neck fits, but shoulders are too long and sleeves and body too wide, undo all seams. Handle pieces like fabric. Fit, baste, refit, double stitch and trim excess.

I know one woman who pays absolutely no attention to gauge, size of pieces, or pattern in general. She says, "I can't worry about it! I just stitch it up on the machine to fit me afterwards." That's not my cup of tea! It certainly is not worthy of being called a handknit or custom garment if made in this manner.

MACHINE-STITCHED SWEATERS

There are some European and Scandinavian sweaters that are designed to be machine stitched in finishing and are knitted in three circular tubes of knitting—one for the body and one each for the sleeves. Length and place for sleeves is marked in body, outlined with machine stitching and cut, as for altering. Pieces are then assembled and machine stitched together.

COLOR KNITTING

COLOR KNITTING is using two or more colors in a knitted piece.

KNITTING IN THE COLOR can be done in stripes, spots, alternating colors in the same rows, as in Fair Isle or slip stitch patterns, combinations of spot and Fair Isle, design knitting, as painting with yarn in pictures, or designs utilizing knit and purl stitches to make color patterns and variations.

COLORS APPLIED AFTER KNITTING, which are usually considered trimmings, can be done by duplicate stitch, crocheting, embroidery or crewel work.

The ultimate aim of all knitters when working in colors is to change smoothly from one color of yarn to another between any kind and any number of stitches in the same row without leaving holes between stitches, retaining the stitch gauge and natural elasticity of the pieces.

With few exceptions, materials should be of the same kind and ply.

Fig. 162

KNITTING IN COLORS

Most of the color knitting in the United States is worked:
  With bobbins for spot knitting
  Alternating colors in the same row
    Knitting in colors
    Slip stitch patterns
  In combinations of bobbin and alternating colors in same row
  In designs with yarn or stitches
  With balls of yarn for stripes

COLOR APPLIED AFTER PIECE IS WORKED

Manner to obtain trim or to finish designs is:
  In duplicate stitch with yarn and sewing needle
  By crocheting yarn with a hook
  Embroidering with yarn

BOBBIN KNITTING

In bobbin knitting, you do not carry yarns across back of work but colors are changed as the pattern changes and yarns must be overlapped or twisted in such a manner that no hole appears between stitches.

Knitting with bobbins is sometimes called "geometric" knitting, as used for Argyle sock designs (Fig. 162), which are built into diamonds, with or without intersecting accent lines and Tartan designs (Fig. 163), which have straight edged designs, both horizontal and vertical. Bobbin knitting would knit these vertical lines in but sometimes only the stripes are knitted horizontally and the vertical lines are put on after with duplicate or chain stitch.

KNITNOTE: BOBBIN KNITTING IS BASICALLY WORKED IN STOCKINETTE STITCH, BACK AND FORTH IN ROWS. YOU CANNOT WORK AROUND AND AROUND, AS IN CIRCULAR KNITTING FOR AFTER ONE ROUND, COLORS WOULD BE IN THE OPPOSITE END OF COLOR SECTIONS WHEN NEEDED TO WORK.

A separate bobbin is used for each change of color in a row, except where there is one bobbin for each diamond, the colors are twisted and worked back and forth under any intersecting lines (Fig. 162).

BOBBINS

WHAT ARE BOBBINS? They are holders for small quantities of yarn. They can be made of plastic, wood, cardboard or any suitable material, cut with a slot for fastening the yarn (Fig. 164). Bobbins secured at yarn and art needlework departments are very convenient and easy to use but you can make your own if you wish.

SIZES? At present bobbins come in two sizes, the smaller called the sock or Argyle bobbins and the larger for use with bulky and gigantic yarns.

Fig. 164

TO HOLD HOW MUCH YARN? The bobbin is to hold the amount of yarn needed to work one spot or section of a design, as a diamond in an Argyle sock pattern. Allowing 1″ of yarn per stitch is a rough estimate of the amount you will need. If you run out of yarn on a bobbin, wrap

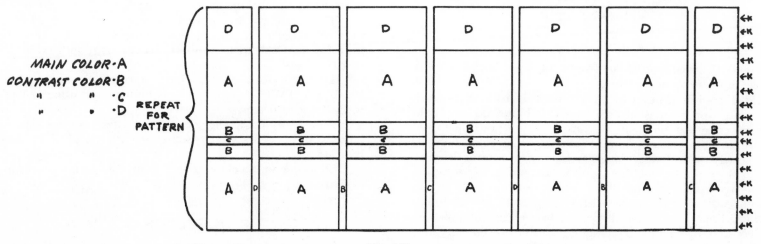

MAIN COLOR·A
CONTRAST COLOR·B
  "   " ·C
  "   " ·D
REPEAT FOR PATTERN

Fig. 163

again and join in new yarn at point where colors change or where joining will not be obvious. If you allow four times the width in a row of any color section, you will have plenty of yarn.

TO PREPARE BOBBINS: Yarn is wrapped several times horizontally around the bobbin and fastened in the slot. This is repeated until sufficient yarn is wrapped or bobbin is full. In preparing your first bobbins, try wrapping around about three times to once in the slot. This will allow a length of yarn that is not too long or too short until you can learn whether you should wrap bobbin three, four or more times to

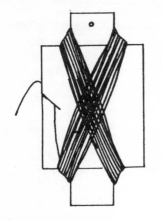

Fig. 165

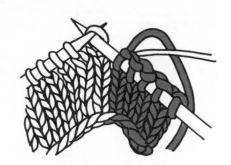

Fig. 166

Fig. 167

one fastening. You will need sufficient length of yarn to place over fingers, hold and work the necessary stitches.

Do not overload bobbin. They can be a nuisance, difficult to work with if too full and won't unfasten easily. (If bobbins do not hold enough yarn for its color section, balls of yarn can be substituted.)

Guard against freeing too much yarn at one time since bobbins will tangle more easily with longer lengths than with shorter lengths. If they tangle, hold work up, let bobbins swing in air and gently separate. They will easily fall free from each other.

If you should be working with a very stiff, springy or bouncy material, like some synthetics, linens and "round" yarns, better control over the material can be secured by making rectangular cardboard bobbins and wrapping in a figure eight across opposite corners (Fig. 165).

BASIC RULE IN CHANGING COLORS WITH BOBBINS

DROP "OLD" COLOR ON WHICHEVER SIDE THE STITCH ENDS, AS KNITS AT BACK OF WORK, PURLS ON FRONT OF WORK (Figs. 166 and 167).

WITH RIGHT HAND, REACH *UNDER* "OLD" COLOR FOR "NEW" COLOR.

AFTER NEXT STITCH IS KNITTED, THIS MAKES A LOOP IN THE YARNS WHICH TWISTS THE OLD AND NEW COLOR WITHOUT LEAVING A HOLE. This is the "twist" which many instructions refer to in color knitting patterns.

EXCEPTION WHEN CHANGING COLORS ON DIAGONAL DESIGNS

ON KNIT ROW: In moving diagonal design to RIGHT, first lay "old" color from right to left along loops of left needle. Pick up "new" color and knit. As you knit stitch, note "old" color lays on TOP of "new" color. At this point on next row, twisting of purl stitch is not necessary since new color lays in such a manner that it automatically will be twisted.

ON PURL ROW: In moving diagonal design to right, first lay "old" color from right to left along loops on left needle. Pick up "new" color and purl. As you purl stitch, note "old" color lays on TOP of "new" color. At this point on the next row, twisting of knit stitch is not necessary since new color lays in such a manner that it automatically will be twisted.

CHART

Designs for bobbin knitting are worked from a chart.

A color chart shows you each stitch of the knitted piece as a square in sections indicating what color each stitch should be.

The chart can be printed in black and white with colors indicated in a color key or legend printed along with chart (Fig. 177) or printed **in color marked with symbols, letters or numbers in the squares for** specific colors.

To begin Row 1 of a chart, start at the lower right hand corner. Work KNITWISE across row, fastening and using colors in stitches as each square indicates.

Row 2 begins at the left side of chart on the second row up from bottom and is worked across the row PURLWISE in the colors squares indicate.

Continue in Stockinette stitch in this manner working row by row of chart.

DIRECTION OF DESIGN

If you are knitting a design to be used from the bottom up, as for a band on a dress or sweater, it will appear as on the chart, the first row being the bottom of the design.

If you are knitting a design to be used from the top down, as for socks, the Row 1 of chart will be at the top of the finished item and to see how this design will look when finished, turn up-side-down.

WORKING THE FIRST TWO ROWS OF AN ARGYLE COLOR CHART
(Fig. 162)

When ready for the color knitting, the ribbing of the sock would be finished and the one bobbin for each color change wrapped and ready to use. The chart with diagonal lines shows that you will need 10 bobbins, nine used on Row 1 and the 10th will interchange later for one of the other bobbins when diamonds alternate color. Although I tie the yarn for Argyles in the first stitch of color only, many knitters will feel more secure if each color can be fastened by looping the new color one time around old color (Manual page 34). If you fasten the first color change only, pick up and knit each new color without fastening and when ready to finish sock, ends will be pulled up to fit knitting, fastened and woven in.

Knit Row 1 according to chart, joining in new color bobbins as chart indicated. On Row 2, purl across each stitch following the basic rule of picking up the new color. THERE MUST BE NO HOLES BETWEEN COLORS. It is not necessary or advisable to pull these stitches between colors too tight. Work with a regular tension. The weight of the bobbins sometimes is helpful in keeping the work even between color changes.

FAIR ISLE KNITTING

The balance of our color knitting here will be designs that mix two or more colors in the same rows with the yarn not being used carried or "stranded" across wrong side of knitting.

In this country we are accustomed to calling all methods of this kind of knitting, "Fair Isle" knitting, but technically this is incorrect.

A brief summary of some of the designs indicates the source of the patterns, traditions of peoples and geographical location are all contributing factors in the emergence of distinguishing characteristics retained for many years in these designs.

FAIR ISLE: Probably these designs were learned or copied from the Spanish survivors of the Armada. The designs are religious in origin and the symbol of the cross appears frequently.

Two colors only are worked in two successive rows. Background colors are neutrals—white, cream, grey and brown—with bright pattern colors which change in regular sequence. Often a wide pattern with several colors is alternated with a narrow pattern of two or three colors. This is usually knitted in fine or 3 ply yarn at 8-1/2 to 9-1/2 stitches per inch.

FAROE ISLE KNITTING: The Faroe Isles are famous for their knitted coats which are designed with bold geometric figures, each in a different color, on white backgrounds. Ribbings are bright in multiples of one, two or three stitches to a rib followed by borders of bright colors and scattered alternating single stitch patterns, called "seedings". Yoke and sleeve caps match in design giving a yoke effect and are in very bright colors with front borders in ribbing. Neckbands are ribbed, folded and sewed down for a double thickness and buttons are in peasant style—metal and wood—often painted to match colors and designs in coats.

FLORENTINE OR JACQUARD KNITTING: Floral, animal and insect designs are inserted in an all-over pattern with small sections of designs using separate short lengths of yarn. Florentine is a very luxurious knitting, often referred to as "brocaded" knitting. Parts of the designs are knitted in silk, trimmed by embroidering with stem and chain stitch in gold or silver.

Jacquard knitting is very similar to Florentine being worked in the same manner and with short lengths of yarn, but usually with the same kind of yarn throughout, and with any arrangement or design desired.

EUROPEAN AND SCANDINAVIAN KNITTING: Here motifs, figures of people and animals, natural settings or scenes with motif or seeding borders are used. Many of these patterns and charts are based on old embroidery designs. Patterns are made in heavy yarn in navy, dark brown or green with light patterns of white and natural as well as dark seedings, motifs and borders in dark colors on light. Bright red, yellow and blues are popular too.

Many of these garments are worked with no shaping in the armholes but with gussets sometimes inserted under the arms. Necks are finished in crew and turtle styles.

SHETLAND KNITTING: This has two distinctive designs. Bands of dark to light colors on contrast shades of light to dark and all-over patterns with numerous color changes in a definite sequence.

COLOR KNITTING WITH STRANDED YARN

For convenience of discussion, stranded color knitting will be called Fair Isle knitting.

In color knitting stitches should lay firmly together, have a nice "sponginess" but not spread apart in the normal wear of garment to show colors carried underneath.

The success of good color knitting depends upon good designing as well as good knitting. Many good knitters have been unsuccessful and unhappy with Fair Isle knitting. They are unaware that this was not all caused by their efforts but because some patterns presented to the public were gauged too loosely, garment was designed to go abruptly from plain knitting to bands of two or more colors across sections of body, as at chest, where the greatest elasticity for fit is needed, and materials, such as synthetics, did not have the property to bounce back into shape like wool.

Unfortunately, the attitude of some companies is geared to the pressures of today and everything is made on the very largest needles possible to knit quick, quick, quick! You would be surprised the number of people who want to knit on Size 10 needles to get fine knitting, as 8 sts to 1″, which is worked on a Size 2 needle. This just can't be done.

Personally, I am very careful in selecting the material and pattern for Fair Isle knitting. I know if a pattern using knitting worsted yarn calls for a No. 10 or No. 10-½ knitting needle, instead of a 6, 7 or 8 needle, it is going to be fairly loose knitting and more difficult to strand the yarn satisfactorily, to allow good blocking, good maintenance and reasonable wear in the garment. You will find that most patterns that come from Europe and surrounding countries will be gauged tight enough, for they usually knit much tighter than we do, mainly for warmer garments.

To be satisfactory, Fair Isle knitting should be designed to a rather tight gauge. If done on too large a needle for the weight of yarn, it is difficult to carry other colors loosely enough and it is most unsatisfactory if this kind of design has to be blocked out and the undercolor threads show through. To the contrary, if done on too small a needle or yarn too thick, the knitting will become very heavy and hard.

Tension on these yarns is important. Yarn being carried must be allowed to lay loosely enough on back of knitting to make smooth, even stitches for the entire pattern with the same elasticity as regular knitting. If yarn is carried too tightly, the garment will not be large enough and stitches will be uneven.

If the garment has an over-all design and your stranding is on the tight side, you may need to select a larger size garment to give the necessary width for fitting.

Stranding of color is a most difficult thing to adjust, particularly if you have large sections of plain knitting alternating with Fair Isle knitting. Usually the Fair Isle knitting is done too tightly. The stranding yarns at the back should "puff up" but not be big, loose loops. I think it is well worth your time before starting a garment, to make the effort to practice stranding until you get satisfactory swatches.

Usually if stranding is tight, stitches worked are smaller. In these cases we have tried using a larger needle on the color section when going from plain knitting to a two or more color pattern, as across the chest of a sweater. This will help to keep the same stitch gauge between the two sections but as to the exact size of needle you would use, that will depend entirely on your individual knitting. This idea many help this kind of situation but will not necessarily solve the problem of carrying the colors too tightly.

INSTRUCTIONS FOR FAIR ISLE PATTERNS

Fair Isle color changes are basically in any combination of one to five stitches.

Fair Isle instructions can be worked from a chart or can be written out, for example like this: Using colors called A and B and knitting across row, K 1A, 1B, 1A, 3B, 1A, 5A, 1B, etc.

REPEAT SECTIONS IN A CHART

TO WORK FLAT COLOR KNITTING: Since it is unnecessary and impractical to print over and over the design, charts are marked for "repeats" (Fig. 177). These are worked the same as charts for bobbins, beginning at lower right hand corner and working across the stitches marked as containing the repeat. This group of stitches is repeated over and over, always beginning at the right hand side of repeated section until extra stitch or stitches necessary to complete the chart remain. Work the remaining stitch or stitches and row is completed.

On the next row, begin at the left side on second row from bottom, PURL TO THE REPEAT SECTION, WORK REPEAT SECTION ACROSS ROW, ALWAYS BEGINNING AT THE FIRST STITCH (LEFT SIDE) OF THE REPEAT, NOT THE FIRST STITCH OF CHART. Continue in this manner alternating knit and purl rows.

TO WORK CIRCULAR COLOR KNITTING: USE THE REPEAT SECTION *ONLY*, SINCE DESIGN MUST COME OUT EVEN.

CHANGING COLORS IN FAIR ISLE
WORKING WITH YARN IN ONE HAND

This manner of working is the same as for bobbins, where the old color is dropped and you reach under with the right hand for the new color, all colors being dropped, picked up and worked with the same hand, as the right hand for English knitting.

Of course, at the end of the row, there are going to be many twists with the two yarns. If you wish, on the next row reverse the manner of picking up the old color—reach OVER the old color—and the yarns will untwist themselves. Otherwise, they will frequently have to be untwisted.

Be careful when you are working with colors like red, white and blue that the yarns do not twist and rub each other, for the light colors quickly can pick up any "fuzz" or extra dye from the other colors. A good way to keep the yarn separate is to use regular brown grocery bags, one for each color. They will sit squarely on the floor, not tip easily and make separating the colors quick work.

WORKING WITH YARNS IN TWO HANDS

The easiest manner of working two colors in one row is to use both hands to knit threading one color on left hand and knitting Continental style and the other color on the right hand knitting in English fashion. This automatically twists and strands the yarns eliminating the picking up and twisting of colors.

It is wise to teach yourself to work both English and Continental fashions of knitting (Manual, pages 16 and 48). Since I use the English method and am righthanded, the color used the most is placed in my right hand and the other color in the left.

In using both hands and flat knitting (back and forth), the purl stitch is sometimes difficult for knitters to do. The loops must be worked to lay in the same direction on the needle with both fashions of knitting. It is well to practice your design before beginning, to get the right tension, rhythm, even stitches, the feel of the pattern and to be SURE that all loops, particularly the purls, lay on needle in the same direction.

CHANGING COLORS WHEN THREE OR MORE COLORS ARE IN A ROW

If more than two colors are used, drop one of the yarns from either hand and put in the extra colors as per pattern. Three or more colors in the same row makes it a little more complicated and you will have to judge and decide, depending upon how many times a color is used in the row, whether to carry these extra colors across the row, or to use short lengths where needed, or possibly put these stitches on with duplicate stitch after the knitting has been finished.

STRANDING YARN

TO WHAT LENGTH SHOULD A YARN BE STRANDED?

Although there is frequently a difference of opinion on this, I believe most knitters work better when stranding is not longer than five stitches. Where one color strand is to be longer than five stitches, we "catch" this strand at intervals. Basically, this is done every third or fourth stitch. If you have seven stitches of one stranding, catch the color on the fourth stitch; if you have nine stitches, catch on the fifth or catch on both the fourth and seventh stitches. If most of the pattern has very close changes of color, I would try to catch strand at about the same intervals as pattern. However, catching color every second stitch is too close, mainly because garment becomes too thick and unless tension is worked perfectly, knitting material gets pretty hard and stiff.

There is a manner of knitting called "woven stitch" for a particular type of knitted fabric. Although we will use some of the principles in catching strands, this particular manner of knitting does not apply here.

The objection to "catching" stranding yarns is that they disturb the outside finish of the knitting and colors show through. I have found that most of the time catching and stranding works fine with no bad results.

You will find dark colors difficult to strand under white and very light colors, for they have tendency to make "shadows" or darken the shade of the light color. It is easier to strand light colors behind dark colors but extreme contrasts can create problems any time in color knitting.

A few times, as previously discussed, on patterns that were not well designed in material and gauge, the results were not satisfactory. It would be wise to make a swatch with correct gauge and block it to see the results of that particular pattern.

WHEN STRANDING YARN

IF TOO TIGHT: Of all the words I have heard or read to date, I believe the word "floating" best describes stranding yarn. This would indicate the stranding would be light, laying freely and easily on top

of other knitting stitches at back of work and under the needle.

It also might be helpful, before you work stitches with a new color, that on the right needle you spread apart the first few stitches down and away from the point. This will lengthen the piece being stranded and help to eliminate too tight stranding. A little practice will show you how far and how much to spread these stitches to adjust your stranding for good results.

IF TOO LOOSE: Keep stitches a little closer together, catch stranding yarn oftener or tighten tension a little.

Usually if stranding is too loose, yarn has been stranded across too many stitches without being caught. I have seen some that stranded over one-third across a sweater without stranding being "caught". These long strands would be very annoying in putting on and taking off garment and obviously make it much easier to fray, snag and pull these loose loops of yarn.

"CATCHING" STRANDED YARNS WHEN KNITTING WITH TWO HANDS
HOW TO "CATCH" STRANDED YARN CARRIED ON LEFT HAND

KNIT ROW: Insert needle in next stitch.
Lay thread to be caught from right to left over top of needle already inserted.
Work a knit stitch, bringing through only the color from right hand. Continue in pattern.
PURL ROW: INSERT NEEDLE IN NEXT STITCH.
Lay thread to be caught from right to left over top of needle already inserted.
Work a purl stitch bringing through only color from right hand. Continue in pattern.

HOW TO "CATCH" STRANDED YARN CARRIED ON RIGHT HAND

KNIT ROW: Insert right needle into next stitch.
Wrap right hand yarn around right needle like regular knit stitch.
Wrap left hand yarn counterclockwise from under and over top of needle.
Take right hand yarn clockwise under and around end of needle to back.
Pull through left hand color for stitch. Continue in pattern.
PURL ROW: Insert needle to purl.
Wrap yarn in right hand counterclockwise under around and to back of right needle.
Place yarn in left hand from right to left over top of needle.
Pass yarn in right hand from back to front under point of needle.
Push out and pull off left hand color for stitch. Continue in pattern.

SLIP STITCH PATTERNS

These patterns have little difference in appearance than Fair Isle knitting and with the elimination of stranding yarns, slip stitch work is preferred by many knitters since it is quicker and easier to do.

These patterns are usually worked in Stockinette stitch, alternating knit rows or purl rows with slip stitches. Lovely and unlimited designs emerge with the color changes and slip stitches worked either on wrong or right side of knitting. Not more than one or two stitches are slipped at one time.

The same colors are usually used for two rows. Although only two colors are frequently used, three or four seem to be more satisfying and allows much more variation in pattern.

Be very neat with the knitting and slipping. Although the finished knitted fabric has a more rough or "puffy" surface than regular flat knitting, if slip stitches are worked with a regular tension, not too tight or too loose, these patterns will finish and block very well.

COMBINATION OF BOBBIN AND FAIR ISLE KNITTING IN THE SAME ROW

The aim in combining these two methods of color knitting is to eliminate breaking off and tying in of yarns as much as possible and to strand and catch yarns to the places needed.

If there is any probability of holes appearing between sections of Fair Isle and sections of solid colors, always twist or overlap yarns, as in bobbin knitting, not only to eliminate possible holes but to sharply define the change in colors.

As an example: In working Fig. 168, Fair Isle knitting would be used in this design where colors stranded over two, three, four or five stitches and bobbins, or separate balls of yarn, used for large areas of single colors. Where one color ends several stitches from the place next needed, either regularly "catch" the stranded yarn across to the place needed or break off and retie.

TO WORK: After this design has been knitted to the top of the legs of the animal (A), three bobbins would be used for the solid X-color sections—one for the body of the animal and one for each star (B and C). For the background, one for right half of picture and one for left half. When you have finished half-way up on the antlers design (D), resume Fair Isle knitting only.

Fig. 168

CHRISTMAS STOCKINGS

A good item to make to learn combining these two methods is a Christmas stocking. If you wish to place a name on the stocking, the letters can be knitted in as you go or made in duplicate stitch after stocking is finished.

Since this kind of stocking is not worn, you can break off and join yarns as often as you wish. However, if you do not like so many knots in your work, you must look and plan ahead to be sure colors needed are ready and at the correct spots for working. Fig. 169 is an excellent example for you to knit to learn this needed preparation of colors.

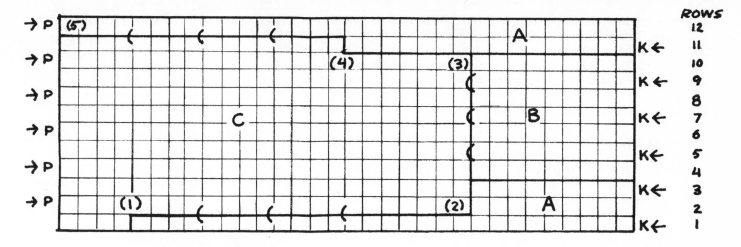

COLOR A-GREEN
COLOR B-RED
COLOR C-WHITE
SIGN (- WHERE TO "CATCH" STRANDS OF YARN

Fig. 169

1. Color A on Row 1 ended far from the needed place on next row (2). As you work Row 2, strand and catch Color A regularly to (2). Continue in pattern and work through Row 4.

2. Since Color A is not needed until several rows about at (3), yarn can be caught on Rows 5, 7 and 9 as follows: As you work across these rows, twist Color A once around Color B or C. This will catch Color A and carry it up easily to point (3). This is the same principle as we use when carrying yarns along the sides of stripes. Or break off A and tie in again when needed.

3. As you knit Row 11, catch Color A from (4) to (5) in preparation for Row 12.

Since you have now learned the rudiments of carrying yarns back and forth and up on pieces of knitting, you will find many places to use this knowledge as in a Norwegian yoked sweater. You can work your own design into the yoke, being sure on a cardigan that the same pattern matches on each side of the front and on a pullover that the pattern is centered at front and works out to an even multiple each time a new pattern is introduced. There are several patterns on the market. Use one as a guide, being sure that the decreases are made at the intervals and as many times as per instructions. This takes some figuring but is rather fun to do.

KNITNOTE: ALWAYS KEEP CHECKING ON THE RIGHT SIDE OF KNITTING TO SEE THAT STRANDING AND CATCHING DOES NOT SHOW COLORS THROUGH.

COLORED STRIPES
CARRYING OR NOT CARRYING YARN ALONG WITH KNITTING

The question most asked about working in stripes is, "How do I know when to carry the different colored yarns up one side of the knitting and when to break them off? When do I tie them in again?"

This is a matter of judgment. If you have regular stripes of two or more colors and the distance between two stripes of the same color is not more than eight rows, I would probably carry the yarn along the side. If a stripe and the next stripe of the same color is far apart, break off yarn, leaving a sufficient end to sew this color's seam.

You can combine carrying and breaking off yarn. If some of the same colors are close, carry that color yarn but break off same colors that are far apart.

If numerous colored stripes are used, I would not carry more than three yarns up the sides because more would be undesirable and make too much thickness at the seams.

Most striped patterns use an even number of rows so all joinings of colors on a flat piece of knitting will be made at the same side. When you are ready to sew a front and back together, note there will be ends of yarn on BOTH side seams of garment.

INTERTWINING OR TWISTING YARNS CARRIED UP SIDE SEAM

When you are changing to a new color, with your right hand, reach under "old" color or colors and pick up the "new" color you will knit with. Each time you come to the "old" color or colors, repeat this whether the yarn you knit with changes or not. You may work several rows of one color but still intertwine yarns every 2nd row, which will eliminate long loose loops. Some knitters prefer to carry these colors every fourth instead of every 2nd row.

KNITNOTE: Be sure that twisted yarns are carried loosely along edges which should have the same length and elasticity as a regular edge.

SEWING AND WEAVING ENDS OF YARN FROM STRIPES

WHERE DO YOU WEAVE? All ends are woven into seams after they are sewed. I NEVER WEAVE ENDS HORIZONTALLY INTO THE KNITTED PIECE. Exception: If working circularly, where there are no seams, weave color ends into matching color.

LENGTH OF YARN? When breaking off yarn, always leave at least a 5" end that can be threaded into a yarn sewing needle for weaving or sufficient yarn to sew entire stripe of that particular color.

To weave in ends, see page 22.

WHAT COLOR YARN TO SEW STRIPES?

If colored stripes are wide enough, sew stripe with its own color. If you have an end on this stripe of the same color and length is sufficient, sew with it. Otherwise, use a new piece of the same color.

If stripes are too narrow to be sewed with each matching color, choose a color for sewing seams that will show the least or be the least objectionable should the yarn show through to outside of garment. This you will have to try before choosing a final sewing color.

CHANGING COLORS IN STRIPES WHEN RIBBING

When working in ribbing and changing from one row of one color to the next row in a second color, the purl stitches will show both colors, having a two-tone or "tweedy" look, which is acceptable and must be used where both sides of knitting are seen, as for a striped ribbed scarf.

Usually an immediate clean-cut change from one color to another, without any mixtures, is desired. This is particularly needed when working with two or three colors in ribbed border sections as for tennis pullover and cardigan sweaters.

TO ELIMINATE MIXED COLORED PURL NUBS

1. Mark the side of the knitting that will be the right side of garment.
2. WHEN CHANGING COLORS, THE FIRST ROW OF A NEW COLOR MUST BE MADE BY KNITTING THE ENTIRE ROW ON THE RIGHT SIDE OF PIECE OR PURLING THE ENTIRE ROW ON THE WRONG SIDE OF PIECE.

This puts the mixed colored purl nubs ALL on the wrong side. On the next row, resume ribbing pattern. It is a little amazing that this one knit row or one purl row does not seem to interrupt the pattern stitch.

WEAVING ENDS IN RIBBING

Weaving ends into ribbing is very easy but we have two problems here: (1) Weaving ends of two different colors and (2) the other of keeping ends fastened or from "popping out" after weaving.

TO WORK: Thread end of yarn into sewing needle, weave back and forth under consecutive knit stitches in one knit rib for three or four times (Fig. 170).

Do not cut yarn here but turn and work back two or three times under the same rib and stitches. (Fig. 171).

Pull yarn out a little, cut on the slant and pull knitting slightly until end disappears.

Fig. 170

Fig. 171

DUPLICATE STITCH (Swiss Darning)

This stitch is an embroidery stitch and does exactly as it says, duplicates a stitch already made. The duplicate stitch is used on Stockinette stitch to decorate and trim with contrasting colors.

In color knitting, if you have only a few scattered stitches of one color, rather than stranding this color yarn over large areas, work these few stitches in duplicate stitch after knitting has been finished.

I have used this stitch often to reinforce a split stitch or thin spots in knits, as at the elbows.

The basic duplicate stitch is worked over one stitch at a time, one row high. Frequently, pattern designs are worked over one stitch, two rows high, sometimes called a double duplicate stitch.

Weight of yarn must be the same or slightly heavier than that in knitted piece.

Although duplicate stitch can be worked from any direction, it is easier and you can do better work if done from the bottom up.

TO WORK: Thread yarn into blunt end needle.

1. From wrong side, insert needle and bring up through center of stitch BELOW first stitch to be duplicated.

2. As in Fig. 172, follow up right side of stitch and insert needle horizontally from right to left under both threads of the next stitch ABOVE one being duplicated.

3. Before you insert needle down through same spot as stitch was started, decide where next duplicate stitch will go so you may finish this stitch and bring needle up in correct place to begin next stitch. (Fig. 173).

Since the purpose of this stitch is to duplicate or cover what has been done previously, do not pull yarn too tight, but allow it to cover well and lay smoothly. (Fig. 174)

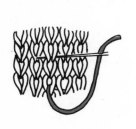  

| Fig. 172 | Fig. 173 | Fig. 174 |

EMBROIDERING WITH YARN

I prefer to put trimming on top of knitted fabric, so it can be removed and changed if and when I get tired of it.

Embroidering can be done with yarn in Crewel designs, in free hand design, with embroidery on Penelope cloth (removing threads when finished), worked over tissue paper (but it takes forever to get all the pieces of paper out later) or worked on organdy or a similar material and appliqued to garment.

Embroidering with yarn is a great asset to knits and can make your knit "one of a kind."

KNITTING WITH BEADS

There is Bead Knitting and Beaded Knitting.

Bead knitting, sometimes called "purse" knitting is seldom used today. It is knitted using a twisted Stockinette stitch with a bead every stitch and every row. Designs are very intricate and beautiful and are all planned and beads strung in order for knitting before beginning to work.

The bead designs used today are called Beaded patterns and are knit in the garment as decorative designs and trims. Unless a very simple pattern, these are worked from a chart. Beads are counted and strung on yarn before knitting. The last bead strung is the first bead knitted. Yarn can be broken to string additional beads if you should run out or if beads are too heavy to string all at one time.

Beads can be knitted in on the purl side or the knit side of a garment.

TO WORK WITH PURL SIDE AS RIGHT SIDE, knit in pattern to spot for a bead; slide bead in place BETWEEN stitches and continue in pattern.

TO WORK WITH KNIT SIDE AS RIGHT SIDE, knit up to place for bead; bring yarn to front of work, slide bead in place, sl 1 st; put yarn to back of work and continue.

PATTERNS

Each item and pattern was selected and designed for a specific purpose —to teach finishing, an intricate stitch, color knitting, to fill the many requests for items to use up small quantities of yarn, for stoles and for more baby blankets.

Some pattern stitches are easy, some are difficult. Do not limit pattern stitches to these designs but use them in other knitted items. Use the multiple of stitches and make larger or smaller items.

Figs. 105 and 106, for Cardigan sweater pattern, see page 5. To chart a knitted skirt, see page 68. Matching and coordinated woolen fabrics are used to show some of the lovely costumes that can be yours.

PINK STOLE (Fig. 107)
18" x 48" (without fringe)

Fig. 175

5 - 2 oz. skeins
1 pair No. 6 and No. 8 needles
Gauge: 5-½ sts = 1"
KNITNOTE: Use row counter (Fig. 175) for this three row pattern.
PATTERN: Uneven number of stitches.
Row 1: K 1, *YO, with yarn at back of needle Sl 1, K 2 tog., repeat between *'s across row, ending with K 1.
Row 2: K 1, *YO, with yarn at back of needle Sl 1, K 2 tog. (the YO and next st), repeat between *'s across row, ending with a K 1.
Row 3: K 1, *K 1, twist next 2 sts as follows: Skip 1 st, K the YO st of previous row and leave on needle; knit the skipped stitch and pull off both stitches (twist made); repeat between *'s, ending K 1.
Repeat these 3 rows for pattern.

DIRECTIONS: With No. 6 needles, cast on 99 sts.
Knit 4 rows (Garter stitch).
Work in pattern until stole measures 47" or desired length.
Knit 4 rows.
Bind off.
Work 1 row of single crochet BACKWARDS along side edges.
Trim with knitted uncut fringe.

KNITTED UNCUT FRINGE
DIRECTIONS: With No. 8 needles and using double strands of yarn for fringe, cast on 10 sts.
Row 1: *YO (purlwise), P 2 tog., repeat between *'s across row.
Repeat Row 1 every row until about 1" less than width of stole, ending with knitting in left hand and cast-on end of yarn at bottom left corner.
Slip 6 sts off needle (or as many stitches as you wish fringe to be long) and pull out yarn. Bind off remaining 4 sts.
With fingers, unravel loose stitches across piece.
Pin and sew to stole. Weave in ends. Block.

QUILTED BABY BLANKET (Fig. 109)
36" x 40"

Knitting Worsted
Color A - 2 - 4 oz. skeins White
Color B - 3 - 4 oz. skeins Blue
1 pair No. 10 needles
1 crochet hook Size 6
Gauge: 4-½ sts = 1"
PATTERN: (Multiple of 6 plus 3)
Row 1 (wrong side): With A, K 1, P 1, *Sl 5 wyib, P 1; repeat between *'s, ending K 1.
Row 2: With B, knit.
Row 3: With B, K 1, purl to last st, K 1.
Row 4: With A, K 1, Sl 3 wyib, *insert needle under the loose strand of Row 1 and knit the next st bringing st out under strand to catch strand behind st; Sl 5 wyib; repeat between *'s to last 5 sts, ending knit next st under loose strand, Sl 3 wyib, K 1.
Row 5: With A, K 1, Sl 3 wyib, *P1, Sl 5 wyib; repeat between *'s to last 5 sts, ending P 1, Sl 3 wyib, K 1.
Rows 6 and 7: With B, repeat Rows 2 and 3.
Row 8: With A, K 1, * knit next st under loose strand of Row 5, Sl 5 wyib; repeat between *'s to last 2 sts, ending knit next st under loose strand, K 1.
Repeat Rows 1 through 8 for pattern.
DIRECTIONS: Cast on 159 sts.
Work in 8-row pattern until blanket measures 40", ending with Row 4.
P 1 row with Color A. Bind off with Color A.
FINISHING:
ROUND 1: With crochet hook and Color A, sc around blanket making 3 sc in each corner. Join with sl st.
ROUND 2: *Ch 3, dc in same st at bottom of ch-3, skp 2 sc, 1 sc in next st.
Repeat between *'s around. Join with sl st. Weave in ends. Block.

RED, WHITE AND BLUE SCARF (Fig. 108)
(DOUBLE KNITTING)
10" x 60" (without fringe)

KNITTING WORSTED, 1 - 4 oz. skein of each of following:
Color A - Red
Color B - White
Color C - Blue
1 pair No. 10-½ needles
Gauge: 3-½ sts = 1"
DIRECTIONS: Using Color A, cast on 36 sts.

Next row, increase 1 st in each st across row (72 sts).
PATTERN ROW: *K 1, bring yarn forward to front of work, Sl 1 (purlwise), yarn back between needles, repeat between *'s across row. Repeat this row until 3-½", ending with an even number of rows. Continue in pattern stitch, working 3-½" stripes as per color chart (Fig. 176).

DECREASE ROW: K 2 tog. across row (36 sts).
Bind off. Weave in ends.
Trim with fringe.

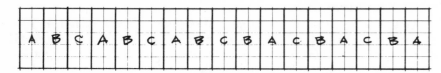

Fig. 176

FAIR ISLE SCARF (Fig. 112)

9" x 42" (without fringe)

Knitting Worsted

Main Color	4 - 4 oz. skeins
Color A	1 - 2 oz. skein
Color B	1 - 2 oz. skein
Color C	1 - 2 oz. skein

1 No. 8 - 24" circular needle or 1 set No. 8 - 10" d. p. needles
Gauge: 5 sts = 1"

DIRECTIONS: With MC, cast on 88 sts.
Join and always knitting around and around, work until 2" from beginning.
Using chart (Fig. 177), work through entire pattern one time, using the repeat of 8 sts only.
With MC work until piece measures 37" from beginning or desired length of scarf less 5".
Repeat pattern of chart one time.
With MC work 2" and bind off.

FINISHING:
Fold piece flat and overcast ends with yarn.
Block keeping vertical lines of knitting even at edges.
Using two strands of yarn make fringe through both thicknesses at each end.
[Trim as pictured is made with square knots (Macramé) using 20" lengths of yarn.]

COLOR KEY

MAIN COLOR □ - WINTER WHITE
COLOR A X - MARINE GREEN
COLOR B V - BURNT ORANGE
COLOR C ● - BREW BROWN HEATHER

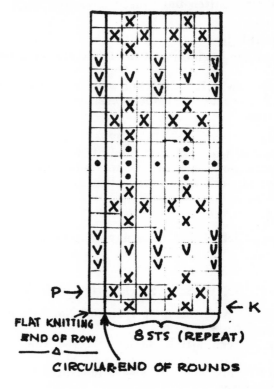

Fig. 177

CHANEL JACKET (Fig. 114)

	SIZES	10	12	14
KNITTING WORSTED - 4 oz. skeins		4	4	5
Blocked Measurements		36"	38"	40"

1 pair No. 10 needles
GAUGE: 9 sts = 2", 6 rows = 1"

BACK: Cast on 81-85-89 sts.
Work in Stockinette stitch until piece measures 13-½", ending with a P row.

SHAPE ARMHOLES:
Bind off 4 sts at the beginning of the next 2 rows.
Row 1 (Decrease row): K 2, Sl 1 knitwise, K 1, PSSO, K to last 4 sts,

K 2 tog (or make matching Sl st decrease-Manual P 47), K 2.
Row 2: Purl.
Repeat these 2 rows until 25-27-29 sts remain. Bind off.

LEFT FRONT:
Cast on 41-43-45 sts.
Work in Stockinette stitch until piece measures 13-½", ending with a P row.

SHAPE ARMHOLES:
Bind off 4 sts at the beginning of next row and knit balance of row.
Row 1: Purl.
Row 2 (Decrease row): K 2, Sl 1 knitwise, K 1, PSSO, K across row.
Repeat these 2 rows until armhole measurs 5-½", ending at neck edge with a K row.

SHAPE NECK:
At the beginning of the next row, bind off 6-7-8 sts, P across row.
Continue to make decreases at armhole edge and AT THE SAME TIME, dec. 1 st at neck edge every other row 5 times. Bind off remaining sts.

RIGHT FRONT:
Work the same as left front, reversing shaping of armhole and neck edge.

SLEEVES:
Cast on 43-43-45 sts. Work in Stockinette stitch for 1".

INCREASE ROW: K 2, inc. 1 st (Method No. 3), K to last 2 sts, inc. 1 st (Method No. 3), K 2.
Continuing in pattern stitch, make increase row every 1", 8-9-9 times MORE.
Work even on 61-63-65 sts until sleeve measures 12-½", 13", 13-½", ending with a purl row.
SHAPE ARMHOLES: Bind off 4 sts at the beginning of the next 2 rows.
Row 1 (Decrease row): K 2, Sl 1 knitwise, K 1, PSSO, K to last 4 sts, K 2 tog (or make matching Sl st decrease), K 2.
Row 2: Purl.
Repeat these 2 rows until 7 sts remain. Bind off.

FINISHING: Block pieces to size. Sew sleeves to fronts and back. Sew underarm and sleeve seams.
EDGING:
Work 1 row sc around all edges. For trimming ideas, see Fig. 116.

TRIMS (Fig. 116)

Your individual accessories or trims are what will make your knits smart, outstanding and valuable.

Trims can be purchased by the yard, as were the colored wool flower strips. Each piece shown is enough to trim the top pocket edge of two pockets.

Often matching or coordinated yardage is used to trim sweaters and jackets. Shown here at left is a bias strip to be sewed flat down the fronts or use a more narrow piece as piping around edges. The pockets are lined and need only to be sewed to garment. Buttons are molds covered with the matching fabric.

Directions for making the crocheted buttons in the center of picture are on page 30.

At lower left the white trims (Macramé) were knotted of nylon cord and the natural colored piece was made of string. Instruction books for learning Macramé are available at public libraries and local book stores. After learning two basic stitches and a few patterns, you are able to duplicate any pattern.

The crochet patterns, from right to left are picot, slant-shell filet, cluster, solid shell and open shell and at lower right, backward single crochet and crocheted fringe. These are basic patterns for anyone who crochets.

Keep your trims simple and to a minimum. Only an accent at the collar, cuffs, fronts or edges is needed to make a knit "all your own."

COAT (Fig. 113)

SIZES	10	12	14	16
Knitting Worsted - 4 oz. skeins	8	8	9	9
Blocked Measurements	39-½"	41-½"	43-½"	45-½"

GAUGE: 5 sts = 1"
        6 rows = 1"
1 pair No. 7 needles or size needed to get gauge

BACK: With No. 7 needles, cast on easy 80-84-90-94 sts. Beginning with a purl row, work in Stockinette stitch for 1-¾", ending with a purl row.
INCREASE ROW: Increase 20 sts evenly across row, using Method No. 3 (100-104-110-114 sts). On wrong side, knit one row for hemline. Beginning with a knit row, continue in Stockinette stitch until 25" or desired length to armhole above hemline, ending with a purl row.

ARMHOLE SHAPING: Bind off 7-7-8-8 sts at the beginning of the next 2 rows.
Row 1: K 2, Sl 1 knitwise, K 1, PSSO, K across to the last 4 sts; make a matching decrease as follows: K 1, slip purlwise this stitch back to left needle, lift second stitch on left needle over first stitch and off end of needle; slip first stitch on left needle purlwise back to right needle. Decrease completed. K2.
Row 2: Purl.

Repeat these last two rows 30-32-33-33 times (24-24-26-30 sts). Bind off.

LEFT FRONT: Cast on 38-41-43-46 sts. Beginning with a purl row, work in Stockinette stitch for 1-¾", ending with a purl row.

INCREASE ROW: Knit, increasing 10 sts evenly across row, using Method No. 3 (48-51-53-56 sts).

BORDER AND FACING: Cast on knitwise 25 sts.

HEMLINE ROW: Purl 25 sts, K across balance of row (73-76-78-81 sts).

Row 1: K 47-50-52-55, P 1, K 12, Sl 1 (purlwise), K 12.
Row 2: P 25, K 1, P 47-50-52-55.

Repeat these two rows until 25" from hemline, ending with Row 2.

ARMHOLE SHAPING: Bind off 7-7-8-8 sts. Work balance of row in established pattern.

Next row: Purl

Row 1 (decrease): K 2, Sl 1 knitwise, K 1, PSSO, K to last 26 sts, P 1, K 12, Sl 1, K 12.

Row 2: P 25, K 1, purl balance of row.

Repeat these two rows until 44 sts remain, ending with Row 1.

NECK SHAPING: Continuing in established pattern and making armhole decreases every 2nd row, AT THE SAME TIME bind off at neck edge 28-29-29-30 sts one time, 1 st every other row 5 times. Continue armhole decreases until 2 sts remain. Bind off.

Mark for 4 buttonholes 5" apart, placing first one ¾" from top edge of front border.

RIGHT FRONT: Cast on 38-41-43-46 sts. Beginning with a purl row, work in Stockinette stitch for 1-¾", ending with a purl row.

INCREASE ROW: Knit, increasing 10 sts evenly across row, using Method No. 3 (48-51-53-56 sts).

BORDER AND FACING: K 48-51-53-56 sts. Cast on purlwise 25 sts (73-76-78-81 sts).

Row 1: K 12, Sl 1, K 12, P 1, K 47-50-52-55.
Row 2: P 47-50-52-55, K 1, purl balance of row.

Repeat these 2 rows until same length as back to armhole, ending with Row 1 and AT THE SAME TIME making double buttonholes opposite markers in left front, as follows:

DOUBLE BUTTONHOLES: K 4, bind off 4 sts, K 4, Sl 1, K 4, bind off 4 sts, K 4, P 1, continue in pattern across row.

Next row: Working in pattern, cast on 4 sts over each of the two bound-off spaces of previous row.

ARMHOLE SHAPING: Bind off 7-7-8-8 sts. Work balance of row in established pattern.

Row 1 (decrease): Work in established pattern to last 4 sts. Make a matching PSSO decrease as on left back armhole, K 2.

Row 2: Purl to last 26 sts, K 1, P 25.

Repeat these two rows until 44 sts remain, ending with Row 2.

NECK SHAPING: Continue in established pattern and make armhole decreases every 2nd row and AT THE SAME TIME bind off at neck edge 28-29-29-30 sts one time and one stitch every other row 5 times. Continue armhole decrease until 2 sts remain. Bind off.

LEFT SLEEVE: Cast on 52-52-56-56 sts. Beginning with a purl row, work in Stockinette stitch for 1-½", ending with a purl row.

INCREASE ROW: Inc. 13 sts evenly across row, using Method No. 3 (65-65-69-69 sts).

On wrong side, knit one row for hemline. Beginning with a K row, work in Stockinette stitch until piece measures 4" from beginning, ending with a purl row. Increase 1 st each end of row and every 1" thereafter until 8 increases have been made (81-81-85-85 sts). Work even until piece measures 15" from hemline.

ARMHOLE SHAPING: Bind off 7 sts at the beginning of the next 2 rows.

Work matching PSSO decreases as on back armholes, alternating decreases every 4th and every 6th rows 3 times (30 rows), then every 2nd row until 21 sts remain, ending with a K row.

CAP SHAPING: Bind off 3 sts. Purl across balance of row.

Next row: K 2, dec. 1 st as before, K across row.

Repeat these two rows 2 times MORE. Bind off.

RIGHT SLEEVE: Work as for left sleeve to cap shaping, ending with a PURL row. Work as for left cap, reversing shaping and binding off the 3 sts on the RIGHT side of sleeve.

The bind-offs are the FRONT edges of the sleeves.

POCKETS (Optional): Make 2.

Cast on 31 sts. Work in Stockinette stitch until 6-½", ending with a K row. K 1 row on wrong side for hemline. Beginning with a K row, decrease 5 sts evenly across row (26 sts). Continue in pattern until 1" from hemline. Bind off easy.

COLLAR (Double faced):

Cast on 72 sts. Work in Stockinette stitch for 1", ending with a purl row.

FIRST INCREASE ROW: *K 8, inc. 1 st Method No. 3, repeat between *'s, ending K 8 (80 sts).

Work 3 rows in Stockinette.

SECOND INCREASE ROW: *K 9, inc. 1 st Method No. 3, repeat between *'s, ending K 8 (88 sts).

Work 3 rows in Stockinette.

THIRD INCREASE ROW: *K 10, inc. 1 st Method No. 3, repeat between *'s, ending with K 8 (96 sts).

Work even until piece measures 4", ending with a purl row.

HEMLINE: P 1 row.

Beginning with a purl row, work 8 rows in Stockinette stitch, ending with a purl row.

FIRST DECREASE ROW: *K 9, K 2 tog., repeat between *'s, ending K 8 (88 sts).
Work 5 rows in Stockinette.
SECOND DECREASE ROW: *K 8, K 2 tog.; repeat between *'s, ending K 8 (80 sts).
Work 5 rows in Stockinette.
THIRD DECREASE ROW: *K 7, K 2 tog.; repeat between *'s, ending K 8 (72 sts).
Work 1" even. Bind off.

FINISHING COAT UNLINED:
Block each piece to size.
Sew sleeve caps to armholes of fronts and back.
Sew underarm and sleeve seams.
Turn back and sew hemline of coat and sleeves and front facings on all edges.
Pin the cast on row of collar over the neck edges of coat with ends of collar slightly overlapping edges of double facing. Overcast. Pin top side of collar over neck edges evenly around and overcast.
Finish buttonholes and sew on buttons.
Steam seams if needed.

FINISHING COAT LINED:
Block pieces and cut paper patterns of each piece allowing for seams, pleats, hems, etc.
Assemble the same as above except do not sew hems on sleeves or inside edge of double facing until front borders have been interfaced and lining has been put in.
Cut carefully interfacing between double buttonholes and finish.
Sew on buttons.

WHITE SHELL STOLE (Fig. 110)
18" x 55" (without fringe)

5 - 2 oz. White Pompadour
1 pair No. 6 needles
Gauge: 6 sts = 1"
PATTERN: (Multiple of 6 sts plus 3)
Row 1 (wrong side): K 1, *YO, K 1, repeat between *'s, ending K 1.
Row 2: Knit, dropping all YO's of previous row off needle.
Row 3: K 1, K 3 tog., *YO 2 times, K 1, YO 2 times, Sl 2, K 3 tog., P2SSO; repeat between *'s, ending YO 2 times, K 1, YO 2 times, K 3 tog., K 1.
Row 4: K 1, *K 1, knit into front and back of double YO; repeat between *'s, ending K 2.
Rows 5 and 6: Repeat Rows 1 and 2.
Row 7: K 1, *K 1, YO 2 times, Sl 2, K 3 tog., P2SSO, YO 2 times, repeat between *'s, ending K 2.
Row 8: Repeat Row 4.
Repeat Rows 1 through 8 for pattern.

DIRECTIONS: Cast on 105 sts.
Work in pattern until 55" or desired length.
Bind off.
To trim with fringe: Cut 9" lengths, fold and tie in every 2nd stitch along ends.

DEWDROP BABY BLANKET (Fig. 117)
30" x 32"

3 - 4 oz. Knitting Worsted
1 pair No. 9 needles
GAUGE: 13 sts = 4"

NOTE: SSK is a decrease of one stitch worked as follows: Slip the first stitch KNITWISE; slip the next stitch KNITWISE; insert the tip of left-hand needle into the FRONTS of these two stitches from the left and knit together.

PATTERN: (Multiple of 6 sts plus 1)
Rows 1 and 3 (wrong side): K 2, *P 3, K 3, repeat between *'s, ending P 3, K 2.
Row 2: P 2, *K 3, P 3, repeat between *'s, ending K 3, P 2.
Row 4: K 2, *YO, Sl 1, K 2 tog., PSSO, YO, K 3, repeat between *'s, ending YO, Sl 1, K 2 tog., PSSO, YO, K2.
Rows 5 and 7: P 2, *K 3, P 3, repeat between *'s, ending K 3, P 2.
Row 6: K 2, *P 3, K 3, repeat between *'s, ending P 3, K 2.
Row 8: K 2 tog., *YO, K 3, YO, Sl 1, K 2 tog., PSSO, repeat between *'s, ending YO, K 3, YO, SSK.
Repeat Rows 1 through 8 for pattern.

DIRECTIONS: Cast on 131 sts.
Knit 7 rows (Garter stitch).
Row 1: K 5, work Row 1 of pattern, K 5.
Row 2: K 5, work Row 2 of pattern, K 5.
Continue in this manner, working 5 knit stitches on each side of consecutive Rows 3 through 8 and repeating this 8-row pattern until blanket measures 31".
K 7 rows.
Bind off. Block.

RIBBED CHEVRON SCARF (Fig. 115)
11" x 42"

2 - 4 oz. skeins Knitting Worsted
1 pair No. 8 needles
Gauge: 5 sts = 1"
PATTERN: (Multiple of 18 sts plus 1)
Rows 1 and 3: P 1 * (K 2, P 2) 2 times, K 1, (P 2, K 2) 2 times, P 1, repeat between *'s.
Rows 2 and 4: K 1, * (P 2, K 2) 2 times, P 1, (K 2, P 2) 2 times, K 1, repeat between *'s.

Rows 5 and 7: P 1, *P 1, K 2, P 2, K 2, P 3, (K 2, P 2) 2 times, repeat between *'s.
Rows 6 and 8: K 1, *K 1, P 2, K 2, P 2, K 3, (P 2, K 2) 2 times, repeat between*'s.
Rows 9 and 11: Repeat Rows 2 and 4.
Rows 10 and 12: Repeat Rows 1 and 3.
Rows 13 and 15: Repeat Rows 6 and 8.
Rows 14 and 16: Repeat Rows 5 and 7.
Repeat Rows 1 through 16 for pattern.
DIRECTIONS: Cast on 55 sts IN PATTERN AS PER ROW 1.
Rows 2 through 16: Work in pattern.
Continue to repeat 16-row pattern until piece measures 42", ending with Row 15.
Row 16: Bind off IN PATTERN AS PER ROW 16.
No blocking necessary.

MOSS DIAMOND SCARF (Fig. 115)
10" x 40"

2 - 4 oz. skeins Knitting Worsted
1 pair No. 8 needles
Gauge: 5 sts = 1"
PATTERN: (Multiple of 22 sts plus 1)
Row 1: P 1, *P 4, (K 1, P 1) 2 times, K 5, (P 1, K 1) 2 times, P 5, repeat between *'s.
Row 2 and all even rows: Knit knits and purl purls.
Row 3: K 1, *K 5, (K 1, P 1) 2 times, K 3, (P 1, K 1) 2 times, P 5, K 1, repeat between *'s.
Row 5: P 1, *K 1, P 5, (K 1, P 1) 5 times, P 4, K 1, P 1, repeat between *'s.
Row 7: K 1, *P 1, K 1, P 5 (K 1, P 1) 4 times, P 4, K 1, P 1, K 1, repeat between *'s.
Row 9: P 1, * (K 1, P 1) 2 times, P 4, (K 1, P 1) 3 times, P 4, (K 1, P 1) 2 times, repeat between *'s.
Row 11: K 1, * (P 1, K 1) 2 times, P 5, (K 1, P 1) 2 times, P 4, (K 1, P 1) 2 times, K 1, repeat between *'s.
Row 13: K 1, * (K 1, P 1) 3 times, P 4, K 1, P 5, (K 1, P 1) 2 times, K 2, repeat between *'s.
Row 15: K 1, *K 2, (P 1, K 1) 2 times, P 9, (K 1, P 1) 2 times, K 3, repeat between *'s.
Row 17: K 1, *K 3, (P 1, K 1) 2 times, P 7, (K 1, P 1) 2 times, K 4; repeat between *'s.
Rows 19, 21, 23, 25, 27, 29, 31, and 33: Repeat Rows 15, 13, 11, 9, 7, 5, 3, and 1.
Row 35: P 1, *P 3, (K 1, P 1) 2 times, K 7, (K 1, P 1) 2 times, P 4, repeat between *'s.
Row 36: Repeat Row 2.
Repeat Rows 1 through 36 for pattern.

DIRECTIONS:
Cast on 51 sts.
K 4 rows.
K 3, work Row 1 of pattern, K 3.
K 3, work Row 2 of Pattern, K 3.
Continue in this manner through 36 rows. Repeat this 36-row pattern until scarf measures approximately 40", ending with Row 36.
K 4 rows. Bind off. Block.

SNOWFLAKE CAP (Adult) (Fig. 111)

1 - 2 oz. Knitting Worsted - Main Color
1 - 2 oz. Knitting Worsted - Contrast Color
1 - button
6 - bobbins
1 pair each No. 6 and No. 9 needles
GAUGE: 4-½ sts = 1", 6 rows = 1"
CAP:
Wrap six bobbins to be used at numbered sections as indicated in chart (Fig. 178).
With Main Color and No. 9 needles, cast on 72 sts.
Work in ribbing of K 1, P 1 for 5 rows.
Working in Stockinette stitch, follow chart for 22 rows, ending with a P row.
Bind off 7 sts at the beginning of the next 4 rows; 6 sts at the beginning of the next 4 rows, ending with a purl row.
On the remaining 20 sts, work in K 1, P 1 ribbing until same length as a bound-off edge, ending on right side. Put these 20 sts on a stitch holder. Cut yarn leaving 15" end.
Sew edges of ribbing to bound-off edges using a back stitch.
NECKBAND: Change to No. 6 needles.
Row 1: With a No. 6 needle, cast on 20 sts knitwise (Method No. 1). Beginning at left front corner of cap and with right side of cap facing you, with same needle, pick up and knit 5 sts on side of ribbing border, 15 sts on left edge of cap, work 20 sts from stitch holder in ribbing, pick up and knit 15 sts on right side of cap, 5 st on side of ribbing border, and cast on 20 sts knitwise (Method No. 1).
Row 2: P 25, rib 50, P 25.
Row 3: K 25, rib 50, K 25.
Row 4: P 25, rib 50, P 25.
Row 5: (Double buttonhole row) K 8, bind off next 2 sts, knit until 6 sts on needle from first bound-off stitches, bind off next 2 sts, knit until 7 sts on needle from second bound-off stitches, rib 50, K 25.
Row 6: P 25, rib 50, P 7, cast on 2 sts, P 6, cast on 2 sts, P 8.
Row 7: Repeat Row 3.
Row 8: Repeat Row 2.
Row 9: Repeat Row 3.
Bind off in established pattern stitches.

FINISHING: Fold back buttonhole section of Stockinette part of band to edge of neck ribbing and line up buttonholes.

Overcast edges and buttonhole.
Fold other tab and overcast edges. Sew on button.

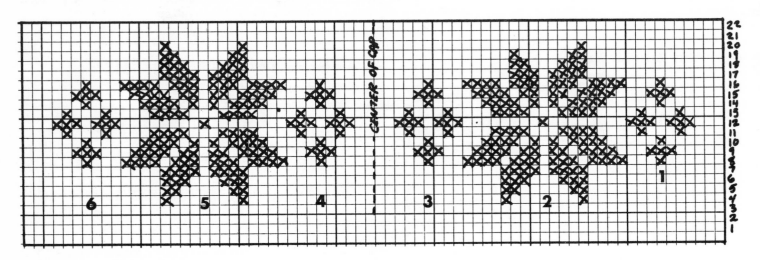

Fig. 178

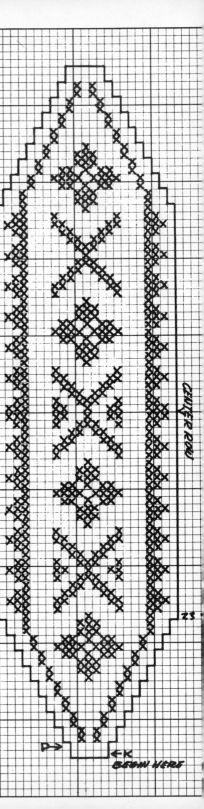

Fig. 179

HEADBAND (Fig. 111)

Knitting Worsted
1 - 2 oz. Main Color
1 - 2 oz. Contrast Color
1 pair No. 8 needles
1 Size 6 crochet hook
Gauge: 5 sts = 1"

HEADBAND
Work in Stockinette stitch and follow design in Chart (Fig. 179).
Row 1: Cast on 5 sts knitwise.
Row 2: P 5.
Row 3: Inc. 1 st in first stitch; knit across row to last stitch; inc. 1 st in last stitch.
Row 4: Purl.
Repeat these 2 rows until 23 sts on needle.

Work even for 54 rows.
Row 1 (Decrease): K 2 tog.; K to last 2 sts; K 2 tog.
Row 2: Purl.
Repeat these 2 rows until 5 sts remain.
Purl one row.
Bind off last row of chart in pattern.
FINISHING: With No. 6 crochet hook, ch 60 sts (first tie). Work one sc in each ch. Sl st to center st at end of headband and sc along one side. Ch 60 (second tie). Sc in each ch and sc along other side of headband. Fasten off. Weave in ends and block.

SKI CAPS (Fig. 111)

Knitting Worsted

1 - 2 oz. Color A
1 - 2 oz. Color B
1 - 2 oz. Color C
6 markers
1 each No. 5 and No. 8 - 16″ circular needles
1 set No. 8 d. p. needles
GAUGE: 5 sts = 1″
KNITNOTE: Ski cap is knitted on circular needles until too few

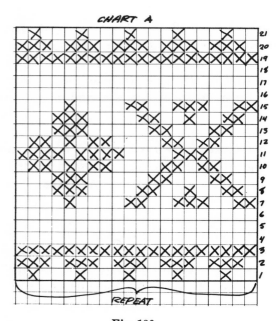

Fig. 180

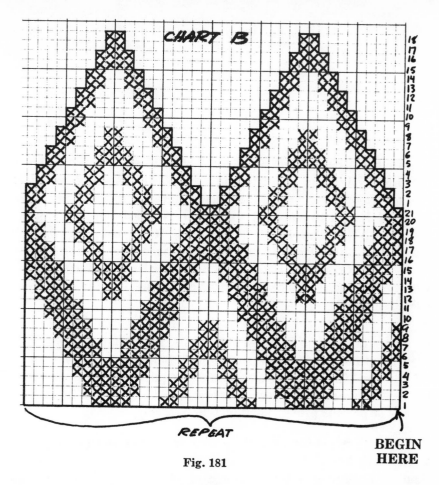

Fig. 181

stitches to work easily on needle. Transfer stitches then to double pointed needles for balance of pattern.

SKI CAP: With No. 5 circular needle, cast on 120 sts. Place a marker on needle. Join and work around and around in K 1, P 1 ribbing for 3″. Working from Chart A (Fig. 180) or Chart B (Fig. 181) and using No. 8 circular needle, work for 20 rounds. On round 21, place a marker every 20 sts (6 markers).

SHAPING TOP: Dec. 1 st before and after every marker EVERY OTHER ROW until 12 sts remain. Cut yarn, leaving a 10″ end. Thread yarn into yarn needle and pull end through each remaining stitch. Fasten and weave in ends.

If desired, trim top with pom pon, tassel or button.

TO ALL KNITTERS

In the writing and publishing of the RIGHT WAY TO KNIT BOOKS, I have had the help and cooperation of many, many people. Acknowledgements are rather inadequate to express my thankfulness but I wish to sincerely extend my appreciation to veteran knitters, Ruth Snyder, Patricia Kirtland, Ruth King, Evelyn Smith, Carole and Charlotte Stewart, for their excellence in knitting, to Edward G. Tracy, artist, for his guidance, patience and art supervision, and to the many knitters and other people for their interest and encouragement.

Knitting can do so much for people, not only for the individual's enjoyment but to help others enjoy this handicraft. Often I am asked, "What qualifications does a person require to teach knitting?" I usually assume this refers to persons who wish to teach knitting classes or become professional instructresses.

For these persons, I believe they must (1) like people; (2) have a thorough knowledge and experience in all grades of knitting difficulty—beginning, intermediate, and advanced; (3) have the ability to teach step-by-step meticulously detailed work; (4) have the ability to communicate and instill confidence; (5) have great patience; and (6) secure work experience in a yarn shop or art needlework department, if possible.

Of course, few knitters become or wish to become professional teachers but don't let that stop YOU, as an individual, from helping others. We all need and have a knitting friend, neighbor or acquaintance that we feel knows a little bit more than we do and whom we like to depend upon for help when needed. I am sure that you can help someone. Be willing to help to the best of your ability even if it's only to show someone how to bind off stitches. It's great fun to help others and a rewarding experience.

Knitting has also joined the fine arts. With the great interest in art and home decoration today, knit your own pictures, cushions, table mats, rugs, wall-hangings, etc. Try a silhouette using only knit and purl stitches. Knit a wall-hanging using your favorite stitches in wool, linen, straw or any material or mixture of materials you wish.

Fascinating pictures have been done in embroidery and crochet. Try painting in knitting by working a simple picture using various knit stitches; tie in new yarns; work by sections and sew them together. Make a knit sculpture.

KNITTERS CAN BE ARTISTS TOO! Enter your knitted artwork in the local fairs and arts and crafts shows. There are no limits to such artistic endeavors and there is no other feeling quite like the tremendous satisfaction of creating and working your own designs. Do start today to make your life and home more beautiful with knitting!

HAPPY KNITTING!